Idea Rights

Idea Rights

A Guide to Intellectual Property

Howard C. Anawalt

CAROLINA ACADEMIC PRESS
Durham, North Carolina

Library of Congress Cataloging-in-Publication Data

Anawalt, H. Clarke.
  Idea rights : a guide to intellectual property / Howard C. Anawalt.
     p. cm.
  Includes bibliographical references and index.
  ISBN 978-1-59460-313-6 (alk. paper)
  1. Intellectual property--United States. I. Title.

  KF2979.A745 2011
  346.04'8--dc22

                              2011005400

CAROLINA ACADEMIC PRESS
700 Kent Street
Durham, North Carolina 27701
Telephone (919) 489-7486
Fax (919) 493-5668
www.cap-press.com

Printed in the United States of America

For S, B, & P

Contents

List of Tables and Figures

Tables

Figures

Table of Principal Legal Authorities

Note: The authorities listed below are *legal* authorities, the Constitution, statutes, and cases that bind judges and parties. Many of these sources are available online at little or no cost. One such database is the Legal Information Institute at Cornell University.

Patents

Constitution

U.S. Const. art. I §8, cl. 8 (Patent and copyright clause)

Statutes

35 United States Code (U.S.C.) §§ 33, 100–103, 111, 112, 116, 131, 151, 154–156 161, 271–287

Cases

Copyrights

Constitution

U.S. Const. art. I § 8, cl. 8 (Patent and copyright clause)

Statutes

17 United States Code (U.S.C.) §§ 102–107, 201, 302–305, 180–182, 201, 302, 401, 408–412, 501–513

Cases

Community for Creative Non-Violence v. Reid, 490 U.S. 730 (1989), 64
Computer Assoc. Int'l, Inc. v. Altai, Inc., 982 F.2d 693 (2d Cir.1992), 82
Davidson & Assocs. v. Jung, 422 F.3d 630 (8th Cir.2005), 88
Effects Associates, Inc. v. Cohen, 908 F.2d 555 (9th Cir.1990), *cert. denied*, 498 U.S. 1103 (1991)178, 179
Feist Publications, Inc. v. Rural Tel. Serv. Co., 499 U.S. 340 (1991), 67, 78, 79
Gener-Villar v. Adcom Group, Inc., 560 F. Supp. 2d 112 (D.P.R. 2008), 77
Horgan v. Macmillan, Inc., 789 F.2d 157 (2d Cir. 1986), 77
Lexmark Int'l, Inc. v. Static Control Components, Inc., 387 F.3d 522 (6th Cir.2004), 82
Lotus Development Corp. v. Borland Intern., Inc., 49 F.3d 807, (1st Cir.1995), judgment aff'd by an equally divided court without opinion, 516 U.S. 233 (1996), 82
MAI Sys. Corp. v. Peak Computer, Inc., 991 F.2d 511 (9th Cir.1995), 67, 93, 248
New York Times Co. v. Tasini, 533 U.S. 483, 495–96 (2001), 63
Nichols v. Universal Pictures Corp., 45 F.2d 119 (2d Cir.1930), 62
Perfect 10, Inc. v. Amazon.com, Inc., 508 F.3d 1146 (9th Cir.2007), 93, 244
Reed Elsevier, Inc. v. Muchnick, 130 S.Ct. 1237 (2010), 68
Sega Enters. Ltd. v. Accolade, Inc., 977 F.2d 1510 (9th Cir.1992), 86
Sony BMG Music Entertainment v. Tenenbaum, 2010 WL 2705499, 93 U.S.P.Q.2d 1867 (D.Mass.2010), 85
Suntrust Bank v. Houghton Mifflin Co., 268 F.3d 1257 (11th Cir.2001), Re-hearing and Rehearing *en Banc* denied 275 F.3d 58 (2001), 91
Time, Inc. v. Bernard Geis Associates, 293 F. Supp. 130, 143 (S.D.N.Y. 1968), 77
Wheaton v. Peters, 8 Pet [33 U.S.] 591 (1834), 73
Williams Electronics, Inc. v. Artic International, Inc., 685 F.2d 870 (3d Cir.1982), 81
Zella v. E.W. Scripps Co., 529 F. Supp. 2d 1124 (C.D.Cal.2007), 78

Trademarks

Constitution

U.S. Const. art. I §8, cl. 3 (Commerce clause regarding federal rules)

Statutes

15 United States Code (U.S.C.) §1125 (The Lanham Act), 15 U.S.C. §1052, 15 U.S.C. §1111, Cal. Bus. & Prof. Code §14245 (2009)

Note: Trademark law originates with state rather than federal regulation. Federal regulation of trademarks is based on the commerce clause, not the patent and copyright clause.

Cases

Trade Secrets

Constitution

U.S. Const. art. I § 8, cl. 3 (Commerce clause regarding federal rules)

Statutes

18 United States Code (U.S.C.) § 1832, the Uniform Trade Secrets Act (USTA) in the forty two states that have adopted it, Cal. Lab. Code 2860, 2870–2872

Cases

Coca-Cola Bottling Co. of Shreveport, Inc. v. Coca-Cola Co., 107 F.R.D. 288 (D. Del.1985) 157

Desny v. Wilder, 46 Cal.2d 715 (1956), 8, 150

E .I. du Pont deNemours & Co. v. Christopher, 431 F.2d 1012 (5th Cir.1970), 161

Jostens, Inc. v. National Computer Systems, Inc., 318 N.W.2d 691 (Minn.1982), 157

Kewanee Oil Co. v. Bicron Corp., 416 U.S. 470 (1974), 155, 160

Ruckelshaus v. Monsanto Co., 467 U.S. 986 (1984), 153

U.S. v. Dubilier Condenser Corporation, 289 U.S. 178 (1933), 153

Influential Secondary Sources

Restatement (Third) of Unfair Competition § 43 (1995) and the earlier Restatement of Torts (First) § 757. Professor William Prosser described the latter as one of the most influential pieces of non-authoritative legal discussion in the United States.

Other Legal Theories and Remedies

Constitution

U.S. Const. art. I § 8, cl. 3 (Commerce clause regarding federal rules)

Statutes

15 United States Code (U.S.C.) § 1 15 U.S.C. § 1064, 17 U.S.C. § 512, 17 U.S.C.
    § 503–505, 17 U.S.C. § 901 *et seq.* (1984), 17 U.S.C. § 1201 *et seq.* Cal. Civ.
    Code § 1670.5, Cal. Bus. and Prof. Code § 16600, Cal. Lab. Code
    §§ 2870–2872

Cases

Altera Corp. v. Clear Logic, Inc., 424 F.3d 1079 (9th Cir.2005), 174
Beghin-Say Intern. Inc. v. Ole-Bendy Rasmussen, 733 F. 2d 1568 (Fed.Cir.1984),
    180
Bonito Boats, Inc. v. Thunder Craft Boats, Inc., 489 U.S. 141 (1989), 175
eBay, Inc., v. MercExchange, LLC, 547 U.S. 388 (2006), 122, 186, 243
Effects Associates, Inc. v. Cohen, 908 F.2d 555 (9th Cir.1990), *cert.* denied, 498
    U.S. 1103 (1991), 178, 179
Goodyear Tire & Rubber Co. v. Releasomers, Inc., 824 F.2d 953 (Fed.Cir.1987), 186
Hadley v. Baxendale, 9 Exch. 341, 156 Eng. Rep. 145 (1854), 185
Jacobsen v. Katzer, 535 F.3d 1373 (Fed.Cir.2008), 182
Midler v. Ford Motor Co., 849 F.2d 460 (9 Cir. 1988), 173
Robertson v. Rochester Folding Box Company, 171 N. Y. 442 (1902), 173
Tuttle v. Buck, 107 Minn. 145, 119 N.W. 946 (Minn.1909), 171, 182
United States v. Microsoft, 253 F.3d 34, 63 (D.C.Cir.2001), 182, 183
Zacchini v. Scripps-Howard Broadcasting Co., 351 N.E.2d 454 (1976), reversed
    by *Zacchini v. Scripps-Howard Broadcasting Co.,* 433 U.S. 562, 578 (1977), 172

Influential Secondary Source

Samuel D. Warren & Louis D. Brandeis, *The Right to Privacy,* 4 HARV. L. REV.
    193 (1890)

Policy

Note: The authorities listed above are *legal* authorities, that is, they state law
that will bind judges and parties. The inquiry dealing with policy asks: *what are
good laws?* Thus, no references can bind our judgment. That judgment depends
on history, human needs, desires, capacities, etc. The legal references below
point directions for consideration. See the "References" at the end of Chapter Seven.

Statutes and Constitution

Magna Carta Paras. 25 and 30
The Statute on Monopolies (21, James I Ch. 3, 1623)
The Statute of Anne (8 Anne Ch. 19, 1710)
U.S. Const. Art. I §8, cl 8 (the patent and copyright clause)

Cases

A & M Records, Inc. v. Napster, Inc., 239 F.3d 1004 (9th Cir.2001)
Capitol Records v. Thomas-Rasset, 93 U.S.P.Q.2d 1989 (D.Minn.2010)
Citizens United v. Federal Election Commission, 130 S.Ct. 876, 899–900 (2010)
Dred Scott v. Sandford, 19 How. 393, 15 L.Ed. 691 (1857)
Graham v. John Deere Co. of Kansas City, 383 U.S. 1 (1966)
Santa Clara County v. Southern Pac. R. Co., 118 U.S. 394 (1886)
Warner Bros. Entm't v. RDR Books, 575 F. Supp. 2d 513, 539–40 (S.D.N.Y. 2008)
White v. Samsung Elecs. Am., Inc., 989 F.2d 1512 (9th Cir.1993) (Kozinski, J., dissenting)

Preface

I hope this short book on intellectual property is helpful for each reader, including students, attorneys, judges, scholars, and the interested general reader. I want to thank Liz Hanellin for editing and the editors and staff at Carolina Academic Press. I also wish to thank the many colleagues, attorneys, judges, students, tech workers, and friends who have shared their understanding of this field with me.

Idea Rights

Chapter One

Intellectual Property

Introduction: Iowa Tech

Suppose a small company, Iowa Technologies (Iowa Tech), located in Des Moines, Iowa, develops and patents a new type of dye that is washable and non-toxic. It also obtains a federally registered trademark for the mark "Exotic Plum," which it uses to market a whole range of color products. This combination of features proves extremely powerful in the marketplace, because these dyes work well in crayons, watercolors, pens—all the types of things that children use. The patent and the trademark add value to the business, as well. They give Iowa Tech aspects of control over their product and its marketing. Overnight these dyes and the name propel little Iowa Tech into a financial success.

After a while Iowa Tech has difficulty supplying the demand for its products. At first it solves that problem by increasing its access to suppliers of necessary ingredients. However, it soon appears that the best choice will be to have others manufacture products for it. Iowa Tech licenses other manufacturers to use its patented technologies to manufacture products, which it will then market under its trademarks.

As Iowa Tech continues with its research, it develops new processes for making the dye. It also develops software and hardware that improve the way that printing is done, especially on home or business based computer printers. Because of its success, it faces prospects of morphing from a small dye company into something completely different.

As it grows, Iowa Tech will face many decisions concerning what to do with its intellectual property. To make sound decisions it will need to understand the limits and functions of intellectual property law. It will also need to tailor its choices in the light of what it seeks to accomplish. Seeking the maximum legal protection does not necessarily serve a business interest. In many instances sound reasons exist for choosing some course other than maximum protection.

The public has interests in the scope of intellectual property protection granted to Iowa Tech or any other business entity. Each one of the legal doctrines which we will review was intended to serve a public interest. The whole of the fabric of intellectual property is justified to the extent that it serves broad public needs and

interests, including a healthy environment, public resources, innovation, and ef-
ficient commercial and industrial practices.

What Is Intellectual Property?

It is possible to acquire legal rights to control innovations and other idea products. Reciprocally, one may be obliged to observe certain duties with respect to them. "Intellectual property" refers generally to the range of those legal doctrines. The term is of recent origin, having appeared only occasionally in United States legal decisions in the nineteenth century. In recent decades it has gained currency. A Google search for the phrase "intellectual property" in 2011 produced more that fifty million hits. In business discussion, the term often refers to "proprietary" matters, which may or may not be protected by law. In law, it is reserved for only those matters which are protected by law. Our inquiry into the field will show that "idea rights" or "idea duties" more accurately describes the field, but "intellectual property" is now firmly established.

A Sketch of Legal Doctrines

Patents, copyrights, trademarks and trade secrets form the core of intellectual property. These doctrines arose out of a social and historical context that valued freedom to engage in commerce. Since approximately the twelfth century, the Anglo-American legal tradition has increasingly favored a policy that permits everyone to pursue a lawful business or profession. Monopolies have been resented, and legal rules have been enacted to free society from their yoke. Intellectual property rules, are intended to be limited exceptions to this liberty. In addition, the United States legal system values liberty to use ideas.

Patents

A patent is a government issued document that describes a new and useful invention. It gives the patent owner a property right to practice an invention as it is described. Property rights are incorporated in a "thing." For example in the case of real estate, one receives a deed which describes the property one owns—a plot of land. In the case of a patent, the property is abstract—a right to exclude others from using a certain process or producing a certain product. Like owning a share of stock, one does not own some specific identifiable thing.

Property rights of all kinds give the owner powerful remedies against anyone who interferes with them. For example, Iowa Tech could obtain an injunction against a company that used its formula without permission, and could do so in many cases before a full trial in the case.

Chapter Two examines patent law. Patents traditionally have covered industrial inventions, and they still do. They are what European law refers to as "industrial property." As commerce and industry have changed, so too, has the application of patent law. In the twentieth century patents were extended to cover such things as software and a whole variety of practical applications that reach far beyond the original understanding of industrial processes and products.

Patent law requires one to file an application in which the inventor states in clear terms exactly what the invention does. If the Patent Office agrees that the claimed invention is new, useful, and not obvious, a patent will issue.[1] Ownership of patents can be transferred to others.

Copyrights

Copyright law also covers inventive works and is examined in Chapter Three. While patent law gives rights to an underlying method or system, copyright protects only the particular elaborations, the "expressions," of an idea. Iowa Tech has copyright protection of its software as soon it is recorded in any way, whether in the form of source code or object code. The automatic nature of a copyright is a major feature of copyright. That marks a big difference from patent law. Patents require examination and government issue. Copyrights belong to the author (in some instances the employer) once a work is written down or in anyway "fixed" in some medium of expression. A copyright is classified as property, and its ownership can be transferred to others. The term of copyright control lasts much longer than the term of a patent.

Originally, copyrights covered softer-edged cultural contributions. Rights were intended to be granted to creators of songs, plays, music, maps, and the like. That is still true, but more functional types of works, such as computer software, have now been added to the list.

In some areas, patent law and copyright law overlap. The primary example of this is software. Software can be patented and copyrighted. This overlap

---

1. Patent law and practice often uses words in a specialized way. For instance, "a patent will issue" means a patent will be granted.

presents difficult theoretical problems. In a nutshell the problem is this: Patents are supposed to cover systems and functional products. On the other hand, the copyright law specifically provides that copyrights cannot "extend to any idea, procedure, process, system, method of operation, concept, principle, or discovery."

Figure 1-1. Exotic Plum

Trademarks

Trademarks and service marks serve to identify the source of goods and services. Iowa Tech has gained name recognition for its dye. The trademark "Exotic Plum" identifies the source of a product. Rights to that trademark can be enforced under all state laws. The trademark rights are also protected by federal law, as the dye products are sold beyond Iowa and are part of interstate commerce. Federal registration of the mark offers advantages, including a presumption that it is valid.

Chapter Four covers trademarks. This is the oldest form of intellectual property in Anglo-American legal culture. Also, it is the area of law where the non-lawyer is likely to feel most comfortable. We see trademarks every day. We are deluged by them. It is also a field of law where the non-lawyer's expectation of what the law is will be closest to the target. As noted, trademarks and service marks are intended to identify the source of stuff we buy or services we employ. This traditional role continues today. But trademarks also have changed in their application. They now allow trademark owners to make legal claims in situations where there is in fact no confusion as to the source of goods or services. Some marks are granted special protection because they are "famous." The Internet has also altered trademark practices. One of the hottest areas of dispute is ownership of Internet domain names.

Figure 1-2. Property, Torts, and Contracts

Trade Secrets

During the process of development, Iowa Tech may wish to keep certain inventions, plans or other valuable information to itself. Trade secret law allows one to protect such secrets. A business or individual can choose to keep important information closely guarded within its own entity. It may also choose to reveal it to others on reasonably clear conditions of confidentiality. To the extent that the revelations to other parties are articulated clearly enough, the law will require that these third parties respect the secrecy. This obligation, however, only extends to those who have either agreed to confidentiality or have some kind of status relationship, such as employment, that might impose such a duty.

The three prior doctrines, patents, copyrights and trademarks, all establish property rights. Trade secret laws establish general civil duties (or torts) rather than property rights. The distinction between a property right and a general civil obligation (or "tort") carries important practical consequences. The practical difference is illustrated by a simple comparison. One may recover for personal injuries and property damage caused by a negligent driver. However, to do so you will have to prove the other driver was negligent. On the other hand, a patent or copyright owner can usually obtain damages and injunctions without demonstrating some negligence or other fault on the part of an infringer. The remedies may include punitive damages and injunctions. For example, copyright infringement can be established without a showing of any negligence or other form of fault.

Trade secret law is examined in Chapter Five. Trade secrets comprise information which is best kept private. The information can be of virtually any kind so long as it gives commercial or industrial value. It could be an invention, a supply source, or the idea for a play. This is the one area where it is tempting to say that law protects an idea in itself. That, however, is plainly not true. As the California Supreme Court stated years ago, "The idea man who blurts out his idea without having first made his bargain has no one but himself to blame for the loss of his bargaining power."[2] What is protected is reasonable efforts to keep a secret or maintain confidentiality.

Contracts

Contracts are used to control idea products. A contract is an enforceable agreement between parties. Typically one party promises to do something in exchange for the other party agreeing to do something else. In the Iowa Tech situation, Iowa Tech entered contracts that gave others permission to use its dye patent. A contract allows parties to create rules that govern their relations with each other. With few exceptions, IP contracts follow the same rules

---

2. Desny v. Wilder, 46 Cal.2d 715, 739 (1956).

as other contracts. Chapters Five and Six explore the uses of contracts in the intellectual property field.

Table 1-1. Table of IP Doctrines

Doctrine	Core Concept	Legal Formalities	Term
Patent Chapter 2	Exclude others from use	Obtain patent from Patent Office	20 years
Copyright Chapter 3	Exclusive right to make copies, displays, etc.	None. Exists from moment of fixing an expression	Lifetime + 75 years; 95 years for corporations
Trademark Chapter 4	Identify Source	Use of the mark	None
Trade Secret Chapter 5	Protect efforts to keep secrets	None. Identify and safeguard secrets	None
Contract Chapters 5, 6	A "this for that" promise; nothing special about IP	None, unless some particular rule requires a writing	None; limitations on time to sue for breach

Other Kinds of Protection

In addition to the four main doctrines of intellectual property, other legal theories give one party control over idea related activities. These include the right to privacy, the right to publicity, plant patent, special protection for boat hull molds, special protection for semiconductor masks, and "digital locks." There are also legal theories which counter intellectual property claims, for example, antitrust. Chapter Six examines these additional legal theories. That chapter also covers the general subject of remedies in civil cases—damages, injunctions, attorney fees and court costs. In general, each of these is available in an appropriate case brought under any applicable legal theory.

Freedom of Activity

As to each and every claim of intellectual property rights, there is a countervailing legal argument that the law should favor free flow of information and freedom to engage in commerce. These arguments will appear throughout the coverage of the doctrines.

Policy

Chapter Seven addresses policy questions: Why should we have intellectual property laws? What are good intellectual property rules? What should be the relation of the United States to the rest of the world on these matters? Chapter Seven examines the history of intellectual property policy and several examples of current concern.

Policy questions also have practical effects. When Iowa Tech makes its intellectual property choices, it will be wise for it to consider how the public will react to what it does. Also, the company will often be well served if it takes into account the intellectual property interests of others, especially its business partners. Taking a broad view is also useful when dealing with competitors, even ones with which one has a current legal conflict.

What is at stake in IP is *control*. Each side to an intellectual property controversy usually has a defensible legal position. Each party has a right to present its position in court. Unfortunately, the time and expense of litigation may turn out to be the trump card in litigation. A party with a weak claim may triumph over one with a strong claim if it has more time and money to put into the case.

Natural History of Innovation

The Santa Clara Valley lies about fifty miles south of San Francisco. About thirty five years ago, the region picked up the nickname "Silicon Valley." The name was based on the phenomenal emergence of semiconductor technology, most of which was and is based on the special properties of the element silicon. The name is now synonymous with rapid advance in all aspects computer and related technologies. Innovative companies of Silicon Valley have often followed a similar pattern of development: A small group of people will get together and form a "start up" company. The company will try to exploit an invention or an application of an existing technology in a new way. To do this the company may need to confine information to itself and trusted others during its early phases. It may also need to get financial backing and organize production, distribution and marketing facilities. It will often require access to existing technologies in order to complete its project. Even the fortunate company that starts out with a stunning and sweeping patent usually needs access to others' technology in order to get its products out the door. Some of these technologies may be protected by patents or copyrights. At the outset, the start-up wants access to technologies.

As it grows, it will usually seek to establish control rights of its own. To do this, a company will need to gain an understanding of intellectual property doctrines and make choices. The decisions are not automatic. Simply because a means of protection is available does not mean one should use it. For example, sometimes a patent is more useful, while at other times maintaining secrecy is. Thus, when a company starts out, it is often "pro-access," but after it succeeds it becomes "pro-property rights."

Some companies may determine that the better course is to rely less on exclusive intellectual property and more on a healthy or cooperative relation with the broader public. The Open Source movement in software, for example, relinquishes tight control over copyrighted expressions in favor of cooperative development.

Concluding Thoughts

Changing social conditions and technologies present new intellectual property issues. For example, computer and Internet technologies have presented new questions in each of the major fields of intellectual property. Most often existing law is interpreted and applied to resolve the questions. We will see that to have been the case with regard to software patents and copyrights. On other occasions, the legislature adopts new legislation, as was the case with the Semiconductor Chip Protection Act and the "Digital Millennium Copyright Act" (DMCA). While these changes make intellectual property a volatile field, many basic principles have tended to stay in place and continue to govern outcomes.

As we move ahead with this study it will be useful to keep a few questions in mind. What appear to be general legal principles that guide the different areas of law? For example, with regard to patent law, one such principle is that an innovator must disclose an invention that is new, useful, and not obvious in order to receive a patent. Are there any common threads that run among the patents, copyrights and other intellectual property doctrines? One such thread is the need to contribute to the public interest in order to justify the control which one receives from intellectual property rights. For example, with regard to trademarks, such an interest is the value of identifying the source of goods and services so that the public may rely on certain suppliers for consistent quality. Also, it is important to think about practicalities, such as what remedies may be available if one prevails in an intellectual property case.

One might also ask whether there are general principles that unite the field of intellectual property and make it more than an umbrella that covers disparate types of interests. If there is a general theme, it appears to be a struggle between liberty to engage in productive activity and efforts by other parties to control that activity. Put another way, there is a spectrum: freedom to act at one end and control at the other. Anglo-American social history has favored commercial freedom and resisted monopoly. In recent decades, prominent economic entities have shifted public emphasis toward the control side of that spectrum.

Chapter Two

Patents

Introduction

Patent law is the classic area of invention protection law. It is intended to provide a reward for the true inventor, the creator of the proverbial "better mousetrap." The core idea is to reward innovation by granting a limited monopoly over its use. Under United States law, a patent is a description of exactly what an invention does together with an explanation of the "best mode" of doing it. Once a patent is granted by the United States Patent and Trademark Office (USPTO or Patent Office), the owner of a patent gains the right to exclude others from practicing his or her invention for a period of twenty years. The requirements for getting a patent are straightforward. The inventor files an application disclosing the invention with the Patent Office. The Patent Office examines the proposed patent, and if it concludes that the claimed invention is "new, useful, and not obvious," a patent issues upon payment of the required fees. One must maintain the patent by continuing to pay fees to the Patent Office.

A patent is a document that embodies a property right. Like a deed to land or a "pink slip" for an automobile, it represents the legal title to property. Unlike land or a car, though, the property that is covered by a patent is an abstract thing: a new process or thing. The patentee and the public know exactly what property rights are covered by examining what is called the "claims" section of the patent. Those claims spell out the description of the process or thing that the patentee owns.

As with other documents, a patent is subject to interpretation, and its validity can be challenged in court. In the event of litigation, the scope of a patent's ownership rights is a question of law which is determined by a judge. A jury can come into play on other questions, such as whether claims in a patent have actually been violated by someone else's product or process.

At the end of the patent term the patentee owns nothing. The patented process enters the public domain.

Patents and Invention

The wheel appears first in history among the Sumerians in about 3500 BC. It was speedily adopted by all cultures having any contact with the originators. Progress can be slow. Even with the advantage of using wheels daily, it took Europeans a long time to figure out that a wheel could turn free of its axle! Free turning wheels offer big advantages, especially with horse drawn carts and chariots. A wheel free of the axle easily negotiates ruts. That profound, yet simple, innovation appears to have been introduced by the Celts millennia after the first use of the wheel.

Because useful innovations are so quickly adopted by others, it is rare that they will be invented independently in more than one place. The cross-fertilization of cultures prevents that. Yet there are examples. For instance, remnants of the earliest man-made permanent shelters may be those found in Chichibu, Japan. They appear to date from 500,000 BC. It seems unlikely that shelters dating 100,000 years or so later in Terra Amata, France were derived from the Chichibu shelters thousands of miles east.[1]

Let us speculate a minute on the origins of the wheel. By 3500 BC, the Sumerian civilization had been developing for about twenty centuries. During all that time, people had been moving things to build shelters, then cities. From the beginning, they must have rolled or dragged heavy objects along the ground. We all do that instinctively whether working in an attic or a garden. People noticed that smooth roundish objects moved more easily. People throughout a community would notice the ease of movement and prefer that to difficulty. Knowledge of rolling is not an individual thing. Rolling can be seen anywhere by many people. At some point knowledge of rolling took the step of attaching a rounded object, a wheel, to a platform or container to make a cart.

Technology development derives from a number of factors. One element is discovery. We do not create forces or tools, so much as we discover them. Rolling is a fact of the natural world that we observe, then harness. Another element is community knowledge. The building of a language or writing system is an example. Finally, there is the individual contribution. Someone says, "Hey, let's try this!"

---

1. Our species, *homo sapiens,* traces back 200,000 years. These shelter remains are controversial in age and structure. There appears to be credible evidence that some such structures existed in both places, and if so, would likely have been erected by a species other that our own. A very nice reconstruction of Terra Amata can be viewed at Terra Amata Shelter | The Smithsonian Institution's Human Origins Program, http://humanorigins.si.edu/evidence/behavior/terra-amata-shelter.

Figure 2-1. Railroad Wheels

Technology is built on knowledge, insight, and practice. None of these thrives in isolation. The social climate definitely influences the speed and direction of technology development. For example, much technology has been developed and improved to wage war more successfully. Today in economically advanced nations much technology is driven by convenience and marketing. Most of us do not need ever faster computers, fully featured cellphones, or wrinkle reducing surgeries. Humans desire convenience and pleasure, but most will forsake both to serve genuine needs.

"Patent" comes from the French phrase "*lettres patentes*," which literally means open letters. A patent grants a limited monopoly, the right to exclude others from using the application of the idea (or method or system), for a period of years. The reward for disclosing a new applied idea to the public is the monopoly which is granted. The patent openly "teaches" both the innovation and the best way to do it. The dissemination of knowledge is called "disclosure." The patent system seeks to speed up the process of innovation by rewarding inventors who disclose their new processes openly to the public. Patent law is governed by federal laws permitted by a specific constitutional provision which allows for creation of patent and copyright laws. The constitutional purpose of these laws is to serve a public, not a private interest.[2] The Patent Act

---

2. U.S. Const. art. I §8, cl. 8., Graham v. John Deere Co. of Kansas City, 383 U.S. 1, 5–6 (1966).

specifies that patents are property rights.[3] To maintain the patent, the owner must pay the annual patent fees.

A serviceable definition of a patent is: An exclusive right to prevent others from using an application of knowledge for a period of time. That right is defined solely by the current Patent Act, which at present is the "Patent Act of 1952." 35 U.S.C. §1 et seq. Patents are tied to the search for useful knowledge, problem solving, economy of effort, and achievement of results that can improve conditions of life. Because it grants a monopoly over discovery and applied knowledge, it raises serious and deep problems of monopoly control. A monopoly over a particularly popular or useful invention, of course, produces great income, and its value can be capitalized. Even rather trivial patents, when added up, can grant significant power of control. Add to this the cost of maintaining a lawsuit, and one readily sees that patents function as part of a package that can give certain players great advantages in an economy. As a result, patents are often pursued greedily.

The United States Patent Act provides for a grant of a patent to one who is the first to invent a new, useful, and not obvious way of doing something. To obtain the patent one must fully disclose the invention to the United States Patent and Trademark Office, including disclosing the "best mode" of carrying out the invention. The description, called a "specification" in the Act, "shall contain a written description of the invention, and of the manner and process of making and using it, in such full, clear, concise, and exact terms as to enable any person skilled in the art to which it pertains, or with which it is most nearly connected, to make and use the same, and shall set forth the best mode contemplated by the inventor of carrying out his invention."[4]

The patent code also contains a specific provision whereby an inventor may fully disclose the patent, yet waive the rights. This offers a worthwhile choice for someone pursuing an open source strategy in software or who is otherwise committed to actions that involve less private control of inventive works. 35 U.S.C. §157.

Xerography is a fairly recent invention. It is the plain paper method of copying documents, first successfully marketed by the Xerox Corporation in the early 1960s. Like photography, it captures an image. Like mimeographing, dittoing, and making carbon copies it reproduces multiple copies on plain paper. Xerography combines these two features—a photographic image (rather than

---

3. "Subject to the provisions of this title, patents shall have the attributes of personal property." 35 U.S.C. §261.

4. 35 U.S.C. §112. Patent law and practice has unusual word usages or jargon: "prosecute" means to apply for a patent; "specification" means a description, the verb "the patent issued" means it was granted, "claims" refers to the legally enforceable rights, etc.

Figure 2-2. Carlson Xerox Patent, Document

Patented Oct. 6, 1942 | **2,297,691**

UNITED STATES PATENT OFFICE

2,297,691

ELECTROPHOTOGRAPHY

Chester F. Carlson, Jackson Heights, N. Y.

Application April 4, 1939, Serial No. 265,925

27 Claims.   (Cl. 95—5)

This invention relates to photography.

An object of the invention is to improve methods of photography and to provide improved means and devices for use in photography.

Other objects of the invention will be apparent from the following description and accompanying drawing taken in connection with the appended claims.

The invention comprises the features of construction, combination of elements, arrangement of parts, and methods of manufacture and operation referred to above or which will be brought out and exemplified in the disclosure hereinafter set forth, including the illustration in the drawing.

In the drawing:

Figure 1 is a section through a photographic plate according to my invention and illustrates a preferred method of applying an electric charge to it preparatory to photographic exposure;

Figures 2, 2a and 2b illustrate three methods of photographically exposing the plate;

Figures 3 and 4 show a method of developing the electrostatic latent image produced on the plate by the preceding steps;

Figure 5 shows a method of transferring the image to a sheet of suitable material such as paper;

Figures 6 and 7 illustrate methods of fixing the image onto the sheet;

Figure 8 illustrates a modified means for charging and exposing the photographic plate;

Figure 9 shows another method of developing the image; and

Figure 10 is an enlargement of a half-tone produced by the process.

A feature of the present invention resides in the use of photoelectric or photoconductive materials for photographic purposes. In its preferred form the invention involves the use of materials which are insulators in the dark but which become partial conductors when illuminated. These materials respond to light, being slightly conductive whenever they are illuminated and again becoming insulating when the light is cut off. They can be called photoconductive insulating materials.

In carrying out the invention the photoconductive insulating material is used to control electric charges in such a way as to produce an electrostatic latent image (so named by its analogy to the ordinary photographic latent image). The electrostatic latent image is then developed to make a visible picture as will be more fully described in the following detailed specification.

While a preferred embodiment of the invention is described herein, it is contemplated that considerable variation may be made in the method of procedure and the construction of parts without departing from the spirit of the invention. In the following description and in the claims, parts will be identified by specific names for convenience, but they are intended to be as generic in their application to similar parts as the art will permit.

Referring to the drawing Figure 1 shows a cross-section of a photographic plate 20 according to the invention comprising a thin layer 21 of photoconductive insulating material bonded to a metal plate 22.

Any one of a variety of photoconductive insulating materials may be used for layer 21. Following are a few of the materials which I have found suitable: (1) sulfur, (2) anthracene, (3) anthraquinone, (4) melted mixtures of sulfur and selenium with the sulfur predominating, (5) melted mixtures of sulfur with up to a few percent of anthracene, (6) the compound formed by heating and melting together sulfur and anthracene in proportions of about 1 part sulfur to three parts anthracene by weight, the heating being continued until reaction is complete, (7) linseed oil boiled with sulfur and dried in a thin layer.

Other photoconductive materials having insulating characteristics in the dark may also be used.

The plate 22 may be of almost any suitable metal which does not deleteriously react with the photoconductor used. Zinc or aluminum plates are suitable for sulfur and anthracene layers. Brass may also be used. The surface of the metal may be etched to improve the adherence of the photoconductive layer.

Sulfur coated plates may be prepared by placing a few crystals of pure sulfur onto the etched surface of the metal plate and heating the plate until the sulfur melts, then flowing the sulfur uniformly over the surface of the plate and allowing any excess to run off, and cooling the plate to solidify the layer. If desired the layer can be made thinner and smoothed with fine emery paper after it has solidified, finishing with a polishing powder such as chalk.

Anthracene and anthraquinone coated plates may be made by melting the material onto an etched metal plate and quickly cooling the plate in cold water, whereby a thin glossy layer is obtained on the plate. However, due to the strong tendency of these materials to sublime or evapo-

Source: U.S. Patent Office, patent number 2,297,691.

a typed one) and instant reproduction. Xerography takes advantage of a property of selenium to capture an image. Selenium is an electrical insulator in the dark, but becomes a conductor when light shines on it. When you project an image of a document on an electrically charged selenium surface in a dark chamber, a mirror image appears on the surface. That image can be captured by inky resin and transferred to piece of plain paper.

The inventor, Chester F. Carlson, disclosed his invention in his patent entitled, Electrophotography, U.S. Pat. 2,297,691. The patent stated: "A feature of the present invention resides in the use of photoelectric or photoconductive materials for photographic purposes. In its preferred form the invention involves the use of materials which are insulators in the dark but which become partial conductors when illuminated." Carlson's 1942 patent apparently did not produce royalties for him, because it had expired before his copying machines were successfully marketed in 1960 by the Haloid Corporation, which later on became Xerox. The original patent disseminated the ideas behind the basic process. Subsequent related patents helped produce a dominant position for Xerox.[5]

* * *

A Pause

Patents are the strongest form of intellectual property—the Queen on the chessboard. The "claims" stated in a patent clearly define the property. Those who wish to use a patented process must obtain permission from the patent owner, and there is no privilege such as "fair use," which we will see applies in copyright. The reward of a patent is a short-lived monopoly to the inventor for his or her contribution to the public good. The monopoly granted is an exception to the prevalent public policy which firmly decries monopolies.

The Patent Office and the Federal Circuit

Patents protect new methods of controlling or altering the physical world. When an inventor gets a new idea of how to accomplish something, he or she may get a patent on the resulting process once it is "reduced to practice."

> But the right of property which a patentee has in his invention, and his right to its exclusive use, is derived altogether from these statutory

---

5. *See* SCM Corporation v. Xerox Corporation, 645 F.2d 1195 (2d Cir. 1980).

Figure 2-3. Carlson Xerox Patent, Drawing

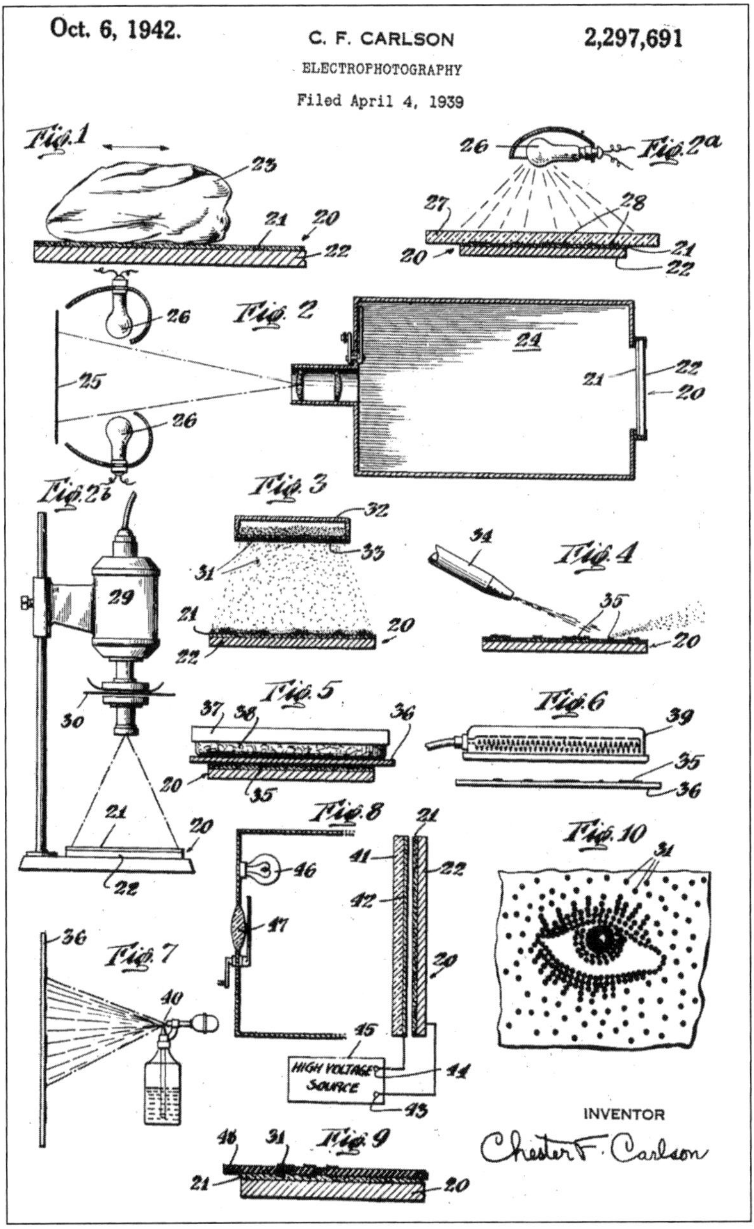

Source: U.S. Patent Office, patent number 2,297,691.

Table 2-1. Patent Law Basic Concepts

A property right
Reward innovation by control of *process*
Sharply defined right
Application is examined before patent is issued
Short term (relatively)
Clear notice to others *(Claims!)*
One may litigate scope of claims; validity
Hard edged control over process
Now includes software that physically changes matter or directs a machine
Encourages innovators
Not intended as a form of capital (e.g., from which one derives rent)
Litigation in patent cases is very expensive
Originates in 1628 as an *exception* to a law banning monopolies

provisions; and this court (has) always held that an inventor has no right of property in his invention, upon which he can maintain a suit, unless he obtains a patent for it, according to the acts of Congress; and that his rights are to be regulated and measured by these laws, and cannot go beyond them.[6]

The patent grants rights to the resulting process but not to the underlying ideas. Ideas cannot be owned by patent.[7]

The type of patent discussed so far is called a utility patent. It is the type we commonly think of when we hear the word "patent."[8] There are two other

---

6. Brown v. Duchesne, 60 U.S. (19 How.) 183 (1856).

7. The core concept is a right to exclude others from using a practical application of an idea, rather than to an idea in itself. Thus the word "process" captures the general idea of a patent, even though the statute actually lists a "process" as one of five categories of utility patents. Often such a power to exclude others is called a "monopoly" in a common, not legalistic sense of the term. "Monopoly |məˈnäpəlē| — 1 the exclusive possession or control of the supply or trade in a commodity or service: *his likely motive was to protect his regional monopoly on furs.*" Apple Dictionary. See Joyce v. General Motors Corp., 49 Ohio St.3d 93, 551 N.E.2d 172, 176 (1990).

8. Utility patent applications are technically called nonprovisional utility patent applications. The statute permits the filing of a "provisional application," which is one which lacks the critical element of the claims which create the enforceable core of the utility patent. 35 U.S.C. § 111 (b). "Design patents" are granted for purely ornamental designs. 35 U.S.C.

Figure 2-4. A Design Patent

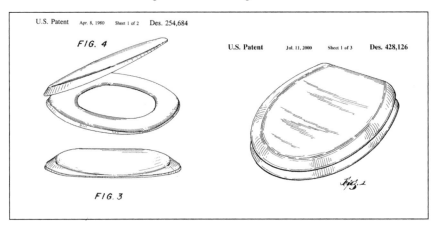

Source: U.S. Patent Office, patent numbers Des. 254,684 and Des. 428,126.

kinds of patents under United States law. The second is the "design patent," which is issued strictly for decorative designs which have no utilitarian function. 35 U.S.C. §171. In a design patent, the entire claim is in the drawings. The third type of patent is a plant patent granted to "whoever invents or discovers and asexually reproduces any distinct and new variety of plant."[9] In 2007, the Patent Office estimated that it receives approximately 350,000 patent applications each year, and that the vast majority of these are for utility patents.

The basic standard for a utility patent is: "Whoever invents or discovers any new and useful process, machine, manufacture, or composition of matter, or any new and useful improvement thereof, may obtain a patent therefor, subject to the conditions and requirements of this title." 35 U.S.C. §101. Thus,

---

§171. The terminology can be confusing, because the utility patent is concerned above all with underlying processes or "design."

9. Plant patents are granted pursuant to the Plant Patent Act of 1930 (PPA), 35 U.S.C. §161. Protection is limited to asexual reproduction, not sexual reproduction by producing seeds. "Before passage of the Plant Patent Act in 1930, it was the common perception that plants and other living organisms were not eligible for patent protection because living organisms were products of nature." Nicholas J. Seay, *Protecting the Seeds of Innovation: Patenting Plants*, 16 AIPLA Q.J. 418, 419 (1989). One may also be issued a utility patent for a plant under 35 U.S.C. §101. J.E.M. AG Supply, Inc. v. Pioneer Hi-Bred Int'l, Inc., 534 U.S. 124, 606 (2001). A third way to obtain legal rights over plant reproduction to obtain a Certificate of Plant Variety Protection for a "novel variety" of plant pursuant to the Plant Variety Protection Act of 1970 (PVPA), 7 U.S.C. §2481 (1982).

there are five categories of utility patents—process, machine, manufacture, composition of matter, plus improvements of any of these. All five are the product of an inventive aspect contributed by a human. Patent law protects innovation when it has become a workable process or a thing. The Supreme Court observed that the intention of Congress was for patent law to "include anything under the sun that is made by man."[10] In most respects, the phrase "new process" captures the essence of what is protected by a patent.

Government creates the rights which are protected by all intellectual property doctrines. Patent rights are created exclusively by the federal government. There is no patent right until the Patent Office has examined the claims and agrees that they represent something which is in fact new, useful, and not obvious.[11] The language of the patent document, in particular the language of the "claims," determines exactly what rights are granted to the patentee.

Patent Office rules determine content and form of applications: All applications and patents must cover certain items. The core requirements are:

- A complete description of the claimed invention, including the manner in which it differs from prior art. This is called the "specification."
- A statement of the claims which will end up defining what is really covered by the patent.
- Drawings, when necessary or useful.
- An oath or declaration as to who is the inventor.
- The prescribed filing, search, and examination fees.[12]

The organization of the application will vary according to the habits and preferences of the attorney or inventor who writes the application.

A 2007 patent for a "Multi-Layered Hanging Cleaning Sponge," U.S. Pat. 7,124,465, provides an example of a simple invention. The Abstract summarizes the invention: "The cleaning sponge contains a cavity that is cut radially inward through one of the sides of the sponge.... the sponge has two holding arms that are formed when the cavity is cut and form a channel, allowing the sponge to be placed on a faucet or any other hanging member.... and may be cut in any decorative shape desired." The fish shape would also be the subject matter for a separate decorative "design patent." 35 U.S.C. § 171. Apart from

---

10. Diamond v. Chakrabarty, 447 U.S. 303 (1980).
11. 35 U.S.C. § 131 and §§ 151–154.
12. Rules of Practice in Patent Cases, 37 C.F. R. § 1.51; 35 U.S.C. 112; Manual of Patent Examining Procedure (MPEP) § 601, http://www.uspto.gov/web/offices/pac/mpep/documents/ 0600_601.htm#sect601.

Table 2-2. General Layout of Patent Application

Captions (Name, number, classifications, etc.)
Abstract
References Cited
Claims (the heart of a patent)
Background of the Invention
Summary of the Invention
Brief Description of the Drawings
Detailed Description of the Invention
Inventor's oath

the cavity, the shape has no function. The cavity in the sponge performs the central function of the invention, which is to hang on a faucet.

An examiner in the Patent Office examines the application. "The Director shall cause an examination to be made of the application and the alleged new invention; and if on such examination it appears that the applicant is entitled to a patent under the law, the Director shall issue a patent therefor." 35 U.S.C. § 131. The examination is a matter of exercising judgment about the facts. The examiner asks: Is the invention new? Is it useful? Is it obvious? Does the application sufficiently define a field of use?

Review by a patent examiner can not assure accuracy. The sheer volume of applications and the mass of knowledge and prior art (earlier inventions or knowledge) in any given field make the weeding out process rife with potential for error. Nevertheless, to accomplish its job, the Patent Office must have the operative facts before it, so it can make a decision. Thus, Patent Office practice places a supreme emphasis on honesty in all dealings with it. The patent applicant must take an oath that she is the "true inventor." The applicant and her attorney are required to disclose all they know about the prior art that relates to the claimed invention. Deception or fraud in the patent application process can result in the patent being held invalid. One may also be subject to criminal prosecution for false statements. 18 U.S.C. § 1001.

The Patent Office Manual describes the patent application process:

> On taking up an application for examination or a patent in a reexamination proceeding, the examiner shall make a thorough study thereof and shall make a thorough investigation of the available prior art relating to the subject matter of the claimed invention.... In rejecting

Figure 2-5. Hanging Sponge Patent

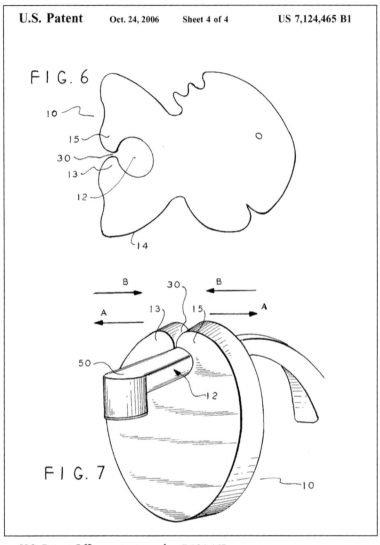

Source: U.S. Patent Office, patent number 7,124,465.

claims for want of novelty or for obviousness, the examiner must cite the best references at his or her command. When a reference is complex or shows or describes inventions other than that claimed by the applicant, the particular part relied on must be designated as nearly

Figure 2-6. Patent Application Process

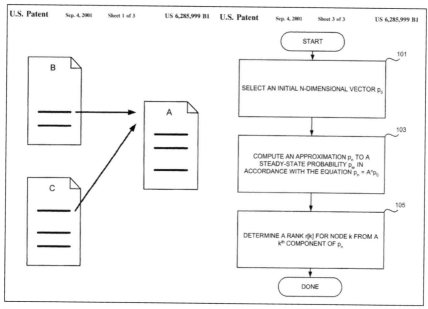

Source: U.S. Patent Office, patent number 6,285,999.

as practicable. The pertinence of each reference, if not apparent, must be clearly explained and each rejected claim specified.[13]

In addition, the *Manual of Patent Examining Procedure (MPEP)* provides that "all business with the Patent and Trademark Office should be transacted in writing. The personal attendance of applicants or their attorneys or agents at the Patent and Trademark Office is unnecessary." MPEP § 1.2. The patent application process ("prosecution," as it is called in patent practice) is a quiet affair to be conducted "with decorum and courtesy."[14]

A patentee can bring an infringement case in a Federal District Court in any appropriate place in the nation. A defendant can argue both that its actions did not violate the patent and that the patent is not valid. After trial, either party can appeal to a higher court when it believes that the trial court has made an error. Since 1982 only one of the thirteen Courts of Appeal in the United

---

13. MANUAL OF PATENT EXAMINING PROCEDURE (MPEP), § 1.104.
14. MPEP § 1.3.

States, the Federal Circuit, has authority to rule on appeals involving patents. 28 U.S.C. §1295.

While both the patentee and an alleged infringer can obtain a review of the Patent Office process in court, that review is limited. First of all, most of the decisions made in the granting process concern what courts term "questions of fact." A call made by an umpire in a baseball game provides an example of the way we handle questions of fact in daily life. There is not much room to argue with the umpire's call. He is watching the strike zone from behind the plate and can see the ball. In a similar fashion, courts usually give lots of leeway to the original decision maker on questions of fact. In a patent case, the original decision maker is the patent examiner. A Federal District Court will review the facts determined by the Patent Office, but the patent once issued will be presumed valid. 35 U.S.C. §282. In addition to reviewing the factual determinations, the Federal District Court and the Federal Circuit review the meaning of the law as applied to the case. The Supreme Court does that, too, but only on rare occasions.

To summarize this process: Decisions about what is obvious, useful, or new, are made mainly by a Patent Office examiner looking into the facts. A legal standard is also involved in each of these inquiries. The examiner makes three kinds of judgments: 1) Fact: "What happened?" 2) Law: "What does the rule tell me to do?" 3) Mixed: "How does the rule apply?" The first question should be determined strictly by facts. The second strictly by law. The third should be determined by sound judgment, but never by bias or departure from law.

The Patent Office prosecution process is streamlined and relatively predictable. When one goes to court, an entirely different atmosphere prevails. Motions and trials in court are contentious. They involve witnesses, depositions, cross examination and often much procedural delay. The time, effort, and cost of patent lawsuits has allowed them to displace polo as the sport of kings.

New, Useful, Non-Obvious

35 U.S.C. §101 requires that to be patentable an invention must be "new and useful." 35 U.S.C. §103 adds the requirement that the application must not claim a method which would be obvious to those skilled in the art or methods of the industry. The process must be "non-obvious" to become the subject of a patent. Thus, a claimed invention must be new, useful, and non-obvious.

The three requirements spring from one concept: Patents should be granted only for practical new things or methods for getting things done. Allowing patents for an obvious process would interfere with progress, not advance it, because the patent would interfere with employing common skill. Both the patent statute and the Constitution forbid monopolies for matters of existing public knowledge: "Congress may not authorize the issuance of patents whose effects are to remove existent knowledge from the public domain, or to restrict free access to materials already available."[15]

Suppose that one day while you are mopping the floor you think up a way of drying the floor as you mop. You tell your idea to some friends. One friend says, "That's great! Why don't you patent that!" Another says, "Oh, you can't patent stuff like that. Mopping has been around since we moved from dirt floors." Each friend has given you a piece of advice which is on track. A new mopping method may be patentable, but your method may not be new given the existing "state of the art" in mopping. Many patents have issued for mops and other cleaning methods. One patent granted in 2007 for a "combined cleaning pad and cleaning implement" is eighty-three pages long and refers to more than a hundred U.S. patents as prior art. (U.S. Pat. 7,163,349). If you consult a skilled attorney about your proposal, the bottom line of her advice could resemble the reaction of either of your friends. However, there is one more practical first step. Ask yourself, "what is the value of patenting a method of mopping?" If there is little value to the new mopping method, then it is not likely to be worth seeking a patent in the first place.

The Patent Act states the general requirement of newness in section 101. In addition it spells out a list of known processes or "prior art" which prevent one from receiving a patent.[16] Prior art that will prevent issuance of a patent includes matters which have already been patented or which are the subject of a prior pending application. This means that one may need to search the existing patents to see whether one's device or system is already covered by a patent or application.

One need not come up with a big new step like inventing the wheel or xerography. A modest change is enough. The invention only needs to differ in some appreciably "new" way from what was done in the past. No "flash of creative genius," is required.[17] Most patents are granted for small changes or improve-

---

15. Graham v. John Deere Co. of Kansas City, 383 U.S. 1, 6 (1966).
16. The list includes matters "1) known by others, 2) used by others or the public, 3) already patented, 4) sold, 5) described in a printed publication, 6) abandoned or 7) invented by someone other than the applicant." 35 U.S.C. § 102. United States law allows one to use an invention experimentally for a one year grace period without losing the capacity to obtain a patent. Atlanta Attachment Co. v. Leggett & Platt, Inc., 516 F.3d 1361 (Fed.Cir.2008).
17. Graham v. John Deere Co. of Kansas City, 383 U.S. 1, 12 (1966).

ments. A big inventive step, like the plain paper copier is recognized as a "pi-oneer patent." "Pioneers enjoy the benefits of their contribution to the art in the form of broader claims. Without extensive prior art to confine and cabin their claims, pioneers acquire broader claims than non-pioneers who must craft narrow claims to evade the strictures of a crowded art field. Thus, claim scope itself generally supplies broader exclusive entitlements to the pioneer."[18]

Search and Prior Art

Patents concern granting a limited monopoly to exclude others from using a new technique—some application of newly acquired knowledge. Thus, it focusses attention on what has been done before, or "prior art." Since one needs to show the technique is new, one must show it is not old, that it has not been done before. Patent law obliges you not to use another's patented process. Thus, the patent system encourages searches in two instances: if you want a patent, you must search; if you want to avoid consequences of infringement, you may have to search.

Since the problem of search will be with us throughout, here are some initial observations:

Need to Search

The need to find prior art varies. If one works in a field which is old and well developed, it is often easy to keep up with prior art and patents. Much is known, even well settled. If a new thing comes along, the collegial grapevine passes it along. The ancient art of glassblowing provides a good example. In such a field the basics are likely well known. If some invention comes along and is patented, the news will likely travel fast. However, while apparently stable and old fashioned, glassblowing might be greatly changed by an innovation that allows better or cheaper products.

On the other hand, some industries require much searching to keep track of what is new. Development of pharmaceuticals, for example, often involves expensive research and incremental changes. Semiconductor composition, design, and manufacturing techniques are another example. Both of these fields are replete with patents. Thus, a predictably higher burden likely exists when searching these fields for prior art.

---

18. Augustine Medical, Inc. v. Gaymar Industries, Inc., 181 F.3d 1291, 1301 (Fed. Cir. 1999).

Application versus Potential Infringement

When applying for a patent, the applicant is obliged to call prior art to the attention of the USPTO. The legal obligation is consistent and high.

On the other hand, one need not necessarily search for patents that may cover a process or device one wishes to employ. If faced with a potential infringement claim, one may choose to wait for a demand by the patentee. The choice of whether to search or not is economic. A potential infringer has an incentive to search, if the actual damages or costs of infringement are high. For example, if a whole line of products may need to be recalled due to infringement, one may be more inclined to search. The reasons for reticence to search include the cost and delay of conducting a search.[19] Often a company will choose to ignore doing a search and wait for a demand letter. Then the company can modify its behavior and avoid liability for treble damages.

Prior art often makes it difficult to show that an invention is new. However, it is almost always easy to establish usefulness. If the applicant can point to any use, that will usually suffice. The applicant does not have to produce a working model, but preposterous claims, like a perpetual motion machine will be denied.[20]

An invention may be judged useful even if its purpose is to fool people. In the *Juicy Whip* case, the patent claims covered a beverage dispenser which displayed a pleasing looking liquid which was never dispensed. Instead, the machine pumped out a freshly mixed water and syrup concoction. The purpose of the display was to look appealing; the purpose of the on-demand mixing was to prevent bacteria growth. The patent owner sued competitors who used the invention without permission.

The defendants responded that the invention was designed to trick the public, thus was not useful. The Federal District Court agreed. The Federal Cir-

---

19. "To a surprising degree, inventors simply ignore patents. The sheer volume of outstanding patents, coupled with the lack of specificity in many claims and complications arising from the doctrine of equivalents, makes an exhaustive search of the prior art expensive. For some entities, the price of such an inquiry may be prohibitive, in that the search costs likely will outweigh the potential gains. In addition, the ever-looming danger of treble damages resulting from a finding of willful infringement creates perverse incentives to remain ignorant of patented technology." Alan Devlin, *The Misunderstood Function of Disclosure in Patent Law*, 23 Harv. J.L. & Tech. 401, 404 (2010). See, also, In re Seagate Technologies, LLC, 497 F.3d 1360 (Fed. Cir. 2007), regarding the standard of proof for willful damages.
20. Newman v. Quigg, 877 F.2d 1575 (Fed. Cir. 1989).

cuit, the appeals court which decides all patent appeals, disagreed. It stated that "it is not at all unusual for a product to be designed to appear to viewers to be something it is not." The Court referred to examples such as cubic zirconium "diamonds" and imitation leather. "Much of the value of these products resides in the fact that they appear to be something they are not."[21]

The Supreme Court examined the usefulness requirement in *Brenner v. Manson*, 383 U.S. 519 (1966). Manson had applied for a patent for a process of making certain known steroids. The Patent Office denied his claim because Manson did not disclose a particular way the resulting compound could be used. The Supreme Court agreed with the Patent Office and affirmed the rejection of Manson's claim. The crux of the matter was that Manson had claimed a process with possible but unknown value.

In explaining the rejection of the patent, the Court emphasized that if some specific demonstrated usefulness were not shown, then a patent might discourage, rather than encourage progress:

> Until the process claim has been reduced to production of a product shown to be useful, the metes and bounds of that monopoly are not capable of precise delineation. It may engross a vast, unknown, and perhaps unknowable area.... Unless and until a process is refined and developed to this point—where specific benefit exists in currently available form—there is insufficient justification for permitting an applicant to engross what may prove to be a broad field.[22]

The Court viewed Manson's process as creating only an ingredient that might aid investigation, rather than offering a practice which would do so. A better research method, such as a better microscope, would qualify as useful, because its use as an improved tool would have been evident.

Once the examiner finds that an invention is new and useful, she must proceed to determine whether it is obvious—whether a skilled person in that field would easily come up with such a device or process. As noted, the logic is that a monopoly covering what is obvious retards science and technology. In *Graham v. John Deere Co. of Kansas City*, 383 U.S. 1 (1966) the Supreme Court

---

21. Juicy Whip, Inc. v. Orange Bang, Inc., 185 F. 3d 1364 (Fed. Cir. 1999). In the 19th century the courts did interpose some value judgment on the use of the invention. Patents for gambling machines were denied. Today, United States patent law does not make a judgment on the purposes for which the invention may be used. An exception is 2 U.S.C. §2181(a), which forbids patents "for any invention or discovery which is useful solely in the utilization of special nuclear material or atomic energy in an atomic weapon."

22. Brenner v. Manson, 383 U.S. 519, 533–37 (1966).

Figure 2-7. Juicy Whip Patent

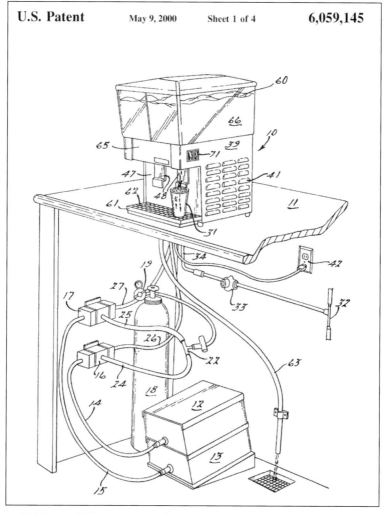

Source: U.S. Patent Office, patent number 6,059,145.

stated that this concept has been embedded in United States patent law from the beginning. The *Graham* case involved an old technology, plows. Even earlier than the wheel, some form of plow figured in all cultures to make it possible to break the earth and plant ever larger fields of crops. Improvements on plows have been consistently made over time, and some of those have been patented under the United States or other patent systems.

A plow is essentially a hoe or spade which is dragged through the earth to create a ditch and heave dirt to the side so that seeds or seedlings can be planted in the ditch. As it travels through the earth both the plow blade and the thinner metal part, the shank, are vulnerable to damage by hitting rocks. The shank, being the skinniest part, is vulnerable to snapping. Graham, the inventor, equipped a plow with a spring shock absorber, and he was awarded a patent for it. The spring allows the plow head and shank to give way to a rock, then snap back into plowing mode after it passes it. Later he improved on his design and applied for a patent on the improvement.

Graham's new design simply changed the placement of the face plate or hinge plate. The new placement would focus less stress at the fulcrum of the plate that engaged the spring. Given the state of the art—all of the available knowledge, including Grahams's prior patent—the Court held that the improvement was obvious to those with skill in designing such mechanisms. "Certainly a person having ordinary skill in the prior art, given the fact that the flex in the shank could be utilized more effectively if allowed to run the entire length of the shank, would immediately see that the thing to do was what Graham did, i.e., invert the shank and the hinge plate."

The patent code sets forth the rule on obviousness: "A patent may not be obtained ... if the differences between the subject matter sought to be patented and the prior art are such that the subject matter as a whole would have been obvious at the time the invention was made to a person having ordinary skill in the art to which said subject matter pertains."[23] In the *Graham* case, the Supreme Court applied that rule to the facts at hand. "Under § 103, the scope and content of the prior art are to be determined; differences between the prior art and the claims at issue are to be ascertained; and the level of ordinary skill in the pertinent art resolved."[24]

In 2005, the Federal Circuit reviewed a decision of a Federal District Court which had found a patent for an electronic throttle assembly invalid because it was obvious in light of prior art.[25] When one drives a car one controls the speed of the car by the pressure of one's foot on an accelerator pedal on the floor. Originally that foot pressure was transmitted by levers to open or close the valves of the carburetor. Most cars today use electronic sensors to determine foot position. A signal from the sensors causes small motors to open and close the valves. The District Court found that the patent claimed an improvement

---

23. 35 U.S.C. § 103.
24. 383 U.S. 1, 17.
25. Teleflex, Inc. v. KSR Intern. Co., 119 Fed.Appx. 282 (Fed.Cir.(Mich.) 2005) *reversed*, KSR International Co. v. Teleflex Inc. 550 U.S. 398 (2007).

Figure 2-8. Graham Plow Patent, Original

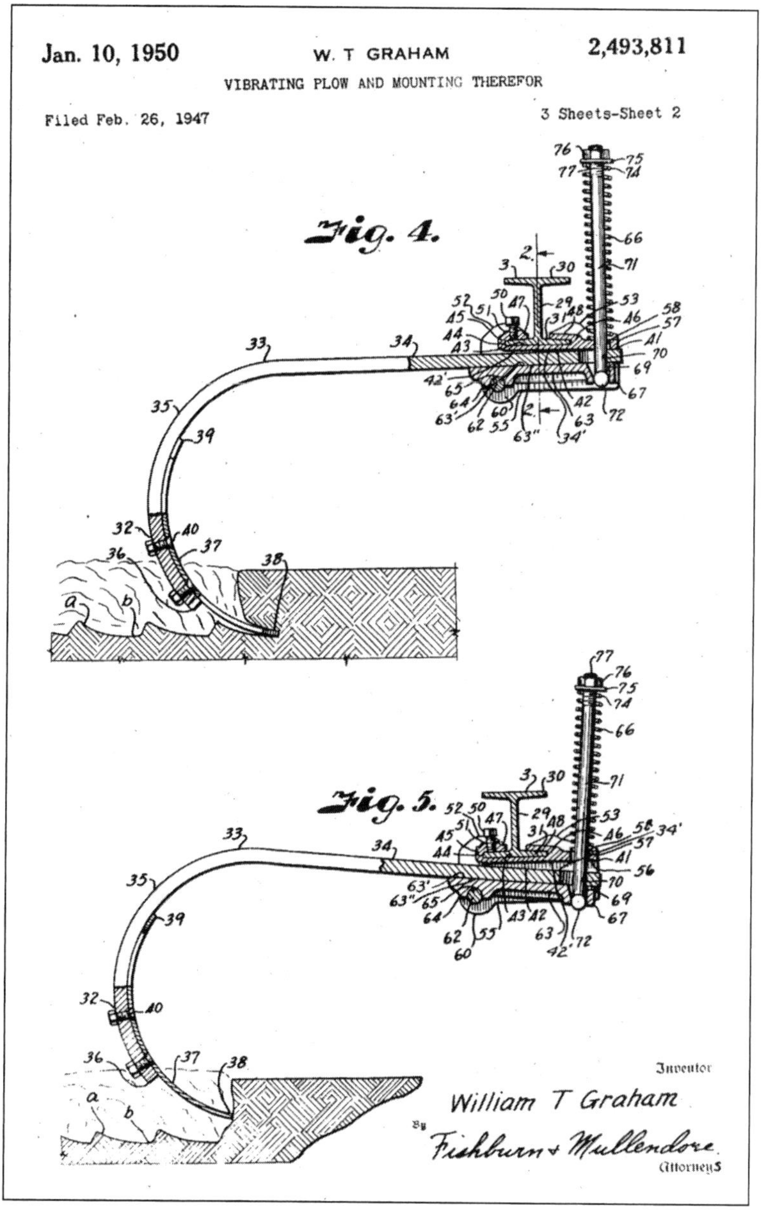

Source: U.S. Patent Office, patent number 2,493,811.

Figure 2-9. Graham Plow Patent, Improved

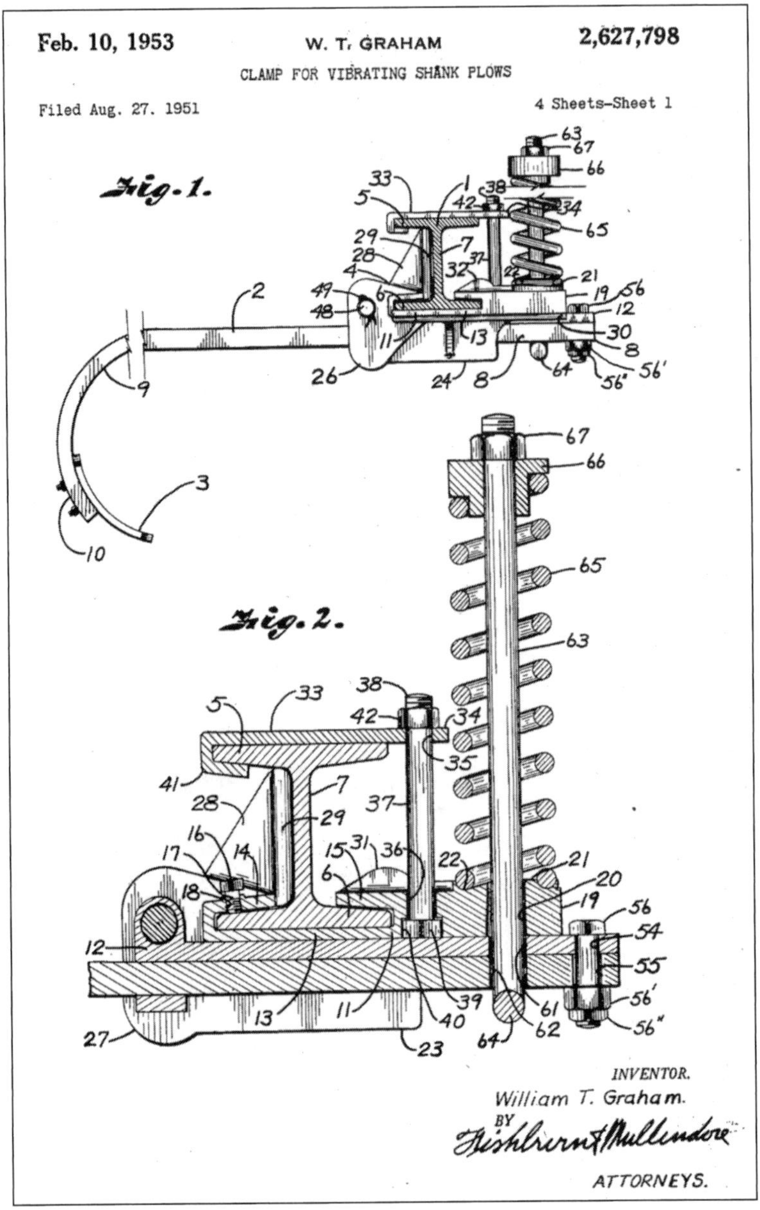

Source: U.S. Patent Office, patent number 2,627,798.

that was obvious in light of the existing electronic throttle controls. However, the Federal Circuit found that the District Court was in error to find the patent claim obvious and therefore invalid.

In reaching its conclusion, the Federal Circuit stated that to show obviousness, an alleged infringer must show that existing prior art contained "some 'suggestion, teaching, or motivation' that would have led a person of ordinary skill in the art to combine the relevant prior art teachings in the manner claimed." In other words, one would show that prior art guided one to the particular solution. The Supreme Court reversed, rejecting this approach to obviousness as far too limited:

> The obviousness analysis cannot be confined by a formalistic conception of the words teaching, suggestion, and motivation, or by overemphasis on the importance of published articles and the explicit content of issued patents. The diversity of inventive pursuits and of modern technology counsels against limiting the analysis in this way. In many fields it may be that there is little discussion of obvious techniques or combinations, and it often may be the case that market demand, rather than scientific literature, will drive design trends. Granting patent protection to advances that would occur in the ordinary course without real innovation retards progress and may, in the case of patents combining previously known elements, deprive prior inventions of their value or utility.[26]

In short, obviousness may exist because general knowledge has advanced. Requiring one to point to some specific suggestion in the literature undermines the whole concept: an approach may be so obvious that a patent or professional article never mentions it. This kind of obviousness occurs in daily life. One can hold a door open with one's hand—or free the hand and use one's foot! Those who are skilled build up an analogous understanding of their particular art.

Let us recap three things: 1) Whether an invention is new, useful, and nonobvious is primarily a matter of fact. 2) Once a patent is issued, the patent holder has the big advantage of having a court presume that the patent is valid. 35 U.S.C. § 282. 3) The scope of patents is determined by the patent code. That is, Congress determines what may be patented. The courts neither contract nor expand on the statutory provisions, but are bound to follow the limits established by Congress.

---

26. KSR International Co. v. Teleflex Inc. 550 U.S. 398, 419 (2007).

Figure 2-10. KSR Accelerator

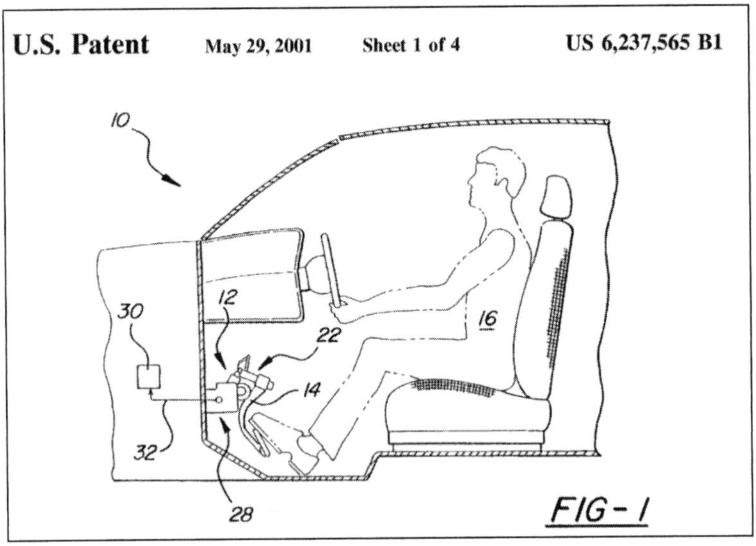

Source: U.S. Patent Office, patent number 6,237,565.

Software and the Limits of Patentability

At the core of much of today's technology lies software in some form. Software involves the transmission of data by electronic means. Software also functions to control physical objects much as do mechanical devices like wheels and gears. The nature of software has raised questions about the limits of what can be patented. Starting in the 1970s, the courts began to wrestle with these questions. Four Supreme Court cases have been decided that give relatively clear guidance as to what those limits are. The most recent of the four cases is *Bilski v. Kappos*, 130 S.Ct. 3218 (2010). These cases drew on earlier decisions that also had to deal with how much one may claim ownership of the realm of applied ideas.

Clocks, switches, thermostats, TVs, and many other devices can be controlled by software. A car manufactured today will likely have dozens of such software controlled processes. Software directly controls machines. The electronic automobile accelerator in the *KSR* case discussed above provides an example. In an old fashioned car engine, the pressure of one's foot pulls a cable which opens and closes a valve, thus, regulating the mixture of gasoline and air the goes into an engine. In a computerized assembly, like the one in *KSR*, the foot position no longer directly pulls a cable. Instead, the foot position is sensed, and a computer directs a motor to open and close the valve. The sensing of foot position in effect replaces the muscle power that previously opened and closed the valve. The Supreme Court described the process in KSR: "In newer cars, computer-controlled throttles do not operate through force transferred from the pedal by a mechanical link, but open and close valves in response to electronic signals." A computer controls the intake of gasoline, and it depends completely on software to direct it.

Software consists of instructions which are translated into electronic charges. Algorithms *govern* the operations of a device. The word "algorithm" means a step by step process.[27] Software falls readily into the requirements for what is patentable in that it is a process that implements action. The patent code provides: "The term 'process' means process, art, or method, and includes a new use of a known process, machine, manufacture, composition of matter, or material."[28]

Software is like a recipe for baking a cake, except that it goes further and functions as the baker, too. A cake recipe states a process of combining and heating ingredients, often accompanied with details that elaborate the process. One follows the process to produce the cake. Software operates in a similar way, except that it directly controls a machine. The software provides the "recipe," and that recipe directly controls the computer. A program has a basic structure, and the operations of that structure are set forth in detail and in a set of instructions which can be directly applied by a machine. The big difference between software and a cake recipe is that software directly controls a machine or some part of it. There is no intervening decision maker between the software and the machine or its output.

Software patents cover all sorts of useful processes. For instance, a patent was issued in 1983 granting a patent for software that enabled a computer to screen for dangerous heart rhythms. In *Arrhythmia Research Technology v. Corazonix Corp.*, 958 F. 2d 1053 (Fed. Cir. 1992) that patent was challenged, and its validity affirmed. The issue was whether the patent claimed ownership of a broad set of abstract ideas, e.g., a mathematical algorithm or formula. If so, the patent

---

27. An algorithm is simply a step by step means of doing something. A recipe for a chocolate cake is an algorithm. "Algorithm (as in 'rule') *n.* : a precise rule (or set of rules) specifying how to solve some problem." Nisus Thesaurus.

28. 35 U.S.C. § 100 (b). The potential breadth of the term "process" in the code has caused interpretive problems. Justice Stevens (speaking for three other Justices) devotes a long concurring opinion essentially to the term "process" in *Bilski v. Kappos*, discussed below. It is for this reason that the word "process" captures the essence of patentable subject matter.

would have been invalid. The Court of Appeals held that the patent made a narrower claim than that: "The computer-performed operations transform a particular input signal to a different output signal, in accordance with the internal structure of the computer as configured by electronic instructions."[29]

Cases like *Arrhythmia* and its heart monitoring software raise a general question: What are the outer limits of patentability? Do some claims reach too far, because they claim ownership to basic knowledge or law of nature? Are there others that are so broad that they interfere with basic activities? These questions have been present in United States patent law from the beginning. Much as we admire inventors and benefit from their advances, society would not allow a monopoly of such basic concepts as the use of zero, long division, or applications of the effects of gravity for any period of time. Furthermore, *all* human knowledge is cumulative. As creatures we scarcely ever "invent" something new. We discover how things work and apply that knowledge to solving problems.

One of the early cases to probe the limits of patent law involved the discovery of long distance communication by electric impulse—telegraphy. Samuel F. B. Morse was an accomplished American painter. In 1829, when he was nearing forty, he travelled to Europe to paint. On his return trip three years later he got acquainted with a group of "gentlemen of extensive reading and intelligence" with whom he discussed recent "experiments and discoveries in relation to electro-magnetism, and the affinity of electricity to magnetism.... Before he landed in the United States, he had conceived and drawn out in his sketch book, the form of an instrument for an electro-magnetic telegraph."[30] The heart of the invention was the capacity to get magnets to open and close at great distance by transmitting a current of electricity.

It took Morse several years to master the problem of getting electricity to travel a sufficient distance and to gather financial resources. Starting in 1838, he was issued a series of patents. Some of his patent claims were contested, and this litigation yielded what attorneys call a "leading case" regarding the limits of patentability. One of his claims was so broad that it reserved for him "the use of the motive power of the electric or galvanic current, which I call electro-magnetism, however developed for marking or printing intelligible characters, signs, or letters, at any distances." The Court stated: "It is impossible to misunderstand the extent of this claim. He claims the exclusive right to every improvement where the motive power is the electric or galvanic current, and the result is the marking or printing intelligible characters, signs, or letters at a

29. Arrhythmia Research Technology, Inc. v. Corazonix Corp., 958 F.2d 1053, 1060 (Fed.Cir.1992).

30. O'Reilly v. Morse, 56 U.S. 62, 69–70 (1854).

distance."[31] The Court found that the claim swept too far, and limited his monopoly to the applications of electricity described in his patent.[32]

Today, the Patent Act allows one to obtain a patent for a discovery of "any new and useful process, machine, manufacture, or composition of matter." The law provided a similar broad scope when the *Telegraph* case was decided. Morse's discovery was certainly useful and new at the time, and it was not obvious. Congress had not specified limits to this wide scope, yet it appeared wrong to the Court to let anyone own pure knowledge or processes of nature. It has been difficult for the courts and commentators to state and agree on general principles which would resolve issues like those in the *Telegraph* case. Also, to this day, Congress has not stated limiting principles regarding the discoveries one may patent.

Over time, the Supreme Court began to articulate a principle that one cannot patent a phenomenon of nature, nor an abstract general rule, such as a mathematical method. In *Bilski v. Kappos*, 130 S.Ct. 3218 (2010), the Supreme Court restated that limiting principle: "The Court's precedents provide three specific exceptions to § 101's broad patent-eligibility principles: 'laws of nature, physical phenomena, and abstract ideas.'"[33]

Prior to the decision of the Federal Circuit in the *Arrhythmia* case, the Supreme Court had considered three cases dealing with the limits of patenting software. When synthesized, they provide reasonably clear guidelines. Nevertheless, turmoil remained for decades. The meaning of the three cases was debated, and some

---

31. The Court also commented on the inhibiting effects on innovation: "Nor is this all, while he shuts the door against inventions of other persons, the patentee would be able to avail himself of new discoveries in the properties and powers of electro-magnetism which scientific men might bring to light. For he says he does not confine his claim to the machinery or parts of machinery, which he specifies; but claims for himself a monopoly in its use, however developed, for the purpose of printing at a distance." O'Reilly v. Morse, 56 U.S. 62, 112–113 (1854).

32. The decision implies a limiting principle of patent scope: One ought not to be able to own basic functions of nature or general abstractions, such as mathematical equations. Instead, one ought to be limited to ownership of relatively discrete applications of ideas and phenomena. That limitation is the subject of cases that have followed the *Telegraph* case, including those discussed.

33. The phrase "laws of nature, physical phenomena, and abstract ideas" is quoted from Diamond v. Chakrabarty, 447 U.S. 303 (1980), a case which emphasizes the broad scope of the Patent Act. In the Chakrabarty case, the Court had stated that Congress' intention was that one be able to patent "anything under the sun that is made by man." In that case, the Court approved a patent for a new bacterium which had been engineered in a laboratory. In general, what can be patented under this broad rule is the application of a principle to solve a problem.

Figure 2-11. Morse Telegraph Patent

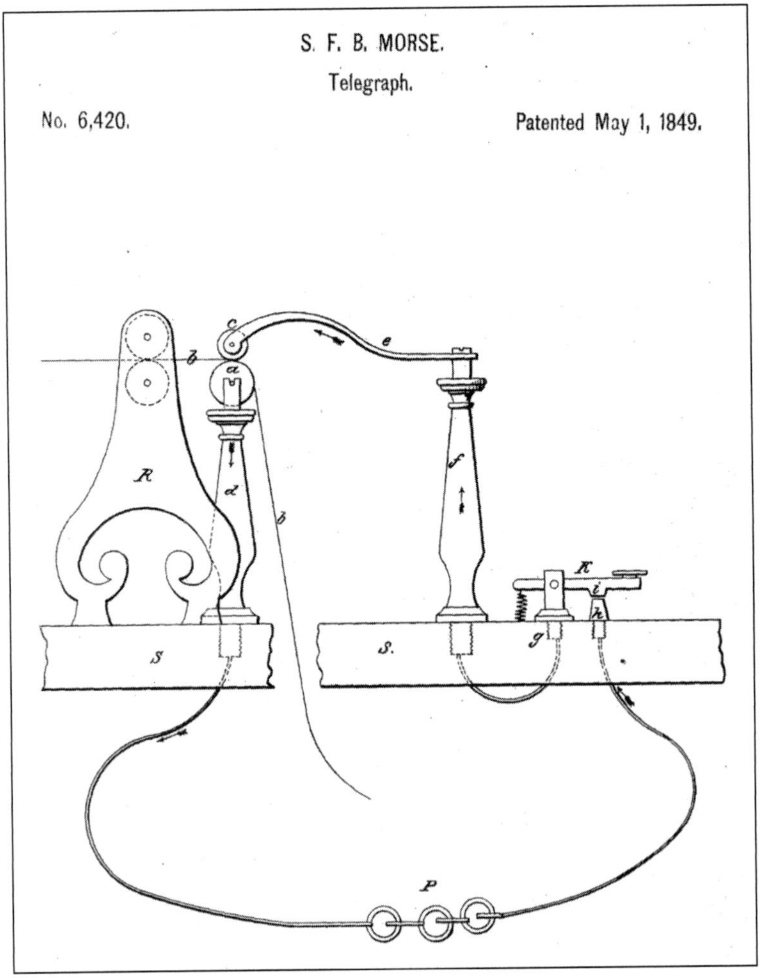

Source: U.S. Patent Office, patent number 6,420.

commentators challenged the validity of the Courts' analyses.[34] The Supreme Court has now spoken again on the matter in the *Bilski* case. To understand the state of the law one needs to understand the four cases as a whole.

_____

34. For example Professor Donald Chisum concluded that the result in *Gottschalk v. Benson* was "not supported by any of the authorities upon which it relied, that the Court misunderstood the nature of the subject matter before it, and that the Court failed to offer any viable

In the first of the four cases, *Gottschalk v. Benson*, 409 U.S. 63 (1972), the Court considered a patent which claimed a method for programming a computer to convert binary numbers into their decimal equivalents. Binary numbers are base two, that is, composed only of zeros and ones. For example, the decimal number 667 is 1010011011 in pure binary. Binary numbers are difficult for humans to read. Transposing such numbers from one form to the other is laborious to say the least. Benson's method employed an intermediate step which first converted binary numbers into smaller chunks, called "binary coded decimals (BCDs)." Each binary number from 1 to 9 is converted into a BCD. Once this is done, one can string those BCDs together as one does numbers 1 through 10. BCDs are easier for humans to handle.[35]

The Court stated: "The method sought to be patented varies the ordinary arithmetic steps a human would use by changing the order of the steps, changing the symbolism for writing the multiplier used in some steps, and by taking subtotals after each successive operation. The mathematical procedures can be carried out in existing computers long in use, no new machinery being necessary. And, as noted, they can also be performed without a computer." The Court rejected the patent. It explained:

> The patent sought is on a method of programming a general-purpose digital computer to convert signals from binary-coded decimal form into pure binary form. A procedure for solving a given type of mathematical problem is known as an 'algorithm.' The procedures set forth in the present claims are of that kind; that is to say, they are a generalized formulation for programs to solve mathematical problems of converting one form of numerical representation to another. From the generic formulation, programs may be developed as specific applications.

The patent claimed too much. It either claimed a broad principle in which a conversion method is akin to a law of nature or failed to tie an otherwise patentable process closely enough to a specific application.

The *Benson* case did not forbid the patenting of software. It established some benchmarks for determining whether a software claim reaches too far:

- To the extent that the claim is stated in a purely symbolic or mathematical format one cannot own it.

---

policy justification for excluding by judicial fiat mathematical algorithms from the patent system." Donald Chisum, *The Patentability of Algorithms*, 47 U. Pitt. L. Rev. 959, 1020 (1986).

35. One can see how the BCDs work by visiting the Wikipedia entry, "Binary-coded decimal," http://en.wikipedia.org/w/index.php?title=Binary-coded_decimal&oldid=387456954 (last visited Sept. 29, 2010).

- Patent claims which include a basic algorithm must be limited to applications which control some identified task.
- Since an algorithm (step by step process) might be performed by either a human or a machine, claims will more likely be permissible if they control a physical process, rather than direct human activities.[36]

Figure 2-12. BCD Clock

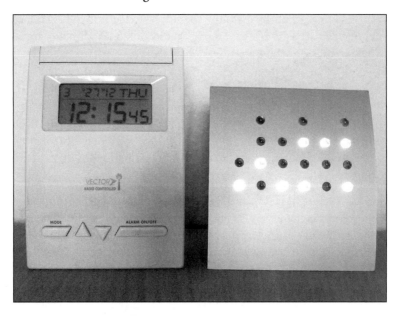

In 1972, when *Benson* was decided, software controlled processes were just beginning to burst into daily life. Mainframe computing had been around for quite some time, but the development of the integrated circuit in the 1960s revolutionized micro-control processes. It became possible to pack potent electronic components into everything from watches to desktop computers. Today the average laptop contains more computing power than could have been mustered anywhere in the 1960s. The number of patent grants for software surged along with this development. One study shows an increase in software patents granted from 765 in 1976 to 24,891 in 2002.

---

36. As we shall see, these three principles have been reaffirmed in the *Bilski* case. Thus, *Bilski* restates a core understanding that has governed patent law for more than 150 years and has guided the scope of software patents for nearly forty years.

In the second case, *Parker v. Flook*, 437 U.S. 584 (1978), the court considered a computerized process for continually monitoring processes in catalytic conversion. Dangerous conditions or alarm limits could thereby be identified. The Court summarized the process:

> In essence, the method consists of three steps: an initial step which merely measures the present value of the process variable (*e.g.*, the temperature); an intermediate step which uses an algorithm to calculate an updated alarm-limit value; and a final step in which the actual alarm limit is adjusted to the updated value. The only difference between the conventional methods of changing alarm limits and that described in respondent's application rests *in the second step—the mathematical algorithm or formula.*[37]

The Court concluded, "Respondent's application simply provides a new and presumably better method for calculating alarm limit values." Calculation standing alone did not provide a sufficient basis for a patent.

The last case of this original trio closely tracked the facts of *Flook*. In *Diamond v. Diehr*, 450 U.S. 175 (1981), the inventor claimed a method of calculation and updating a data point, just as Flook's did. However, Diehr's claimed invention integrated the calculation into a process which directly triggered a physical action. The Diehr invention calculated the time and temperature variables involved in curing and caused the rubber mold to pop open. The Court summarized the claimed invention:

> "Respondents characterize their contribution to the art to reside in the process of constantly measuring the actual temperature inside the mold. These temperature measurements are then automatically fed into a computer which repeatedly recalculates the cure time by use of the Arrhenius equation. When the recalculated time equals the actual time that has elapsed since the press was closed, *the computer signals a device to open the press.*"[38]

This application of software integrated to a physical process sufficed for patentability. What was the difference? A physical result, it seems. The press pops open. This result lends great force to the proposition noted in *Benson* that "transformation and reduction of an article 'to a different state or thing' is the clue to the patentability of a process claim."

---

37. 437 U.S. 584, 585 (italics added).
38. Diamond v. Diehr, 450 U.S. 175, 197 (1981) (italics added).

In 1998, during the interim between the decisions in *Benson, Flook,* and *Diehr,* and the decision in *Bilski,* the Federal Circuit approved a patent that stretched the limits of patentability. The patent claimed a method of using computers in business transactions. (U.S. Pat. 5,193,056.) The Federal Circuit described the patent as follows: "The '056 patent is generally directed to a data processing system ... for implementing an investment structure.... In essence, the system ... facilitates a structure whereby mutual funds (Spokes) pool their assets in an investment portfolio (Hub) organized as a partnership."[39] The process described was not tied to any particular machine or configuration of software. State Street Bank wanted to use the system or one similar to it, so it entered negotiations with Signature Financial Group, Inc., the owner (assignee) of this patent, to try to get a license. Negotiations broke down, so the bank sued Signature to get the patent declared invalid. The bank won in the District Court, then Signature appealed to the Federal Circuit.

The Federal Circuit reversed the trial court decision and declared the patent to be valid. The Federal Circuit decision reviewed its prior precedents on software and the three Supreme Court decisions, *Benson, Flook, and Diehr.* The Court concluded: "Today, we hold that the transformation of data, representing discrete dollar amounts, by a machine through a series of mathematical calculations into a final share price, constitutes a practical application of a mathematical algorithm, formula, or calculation, because it produces 'a useful, concrete and tangible result'—a final share price momentarily fixed for recording and reporting purposes and even accepted and relied upon by regulatory authorities and in subsequent trades." The bank sought review by the Supreme Court, but the Court declined to take the case.

The logic of the Federal Circuit in the *State Street* was widely followed. It authorized two things: A broad construction of what is permissible, and a general approval of patents for business methods. It also represented approval of patents whose end result is to instruct human decision makers, rather than physically control processes.

In 2008 a similar type of patent was reviewed by the Federal Circuit in the *Bilski* case.[40] This time the Federal Circuit denied the applicant's claims. It also repudiated the analysis it had applied in the *State Street* case.[41] The disappointed

39. State Street Bank and Trust v. Signature Financial Group, Inc., 149 F. 3d 1368, 1370 (Fed. Cir. 1998), *cert. denied,* 525 U.S. 1093 (1999). The *State Street* holding was disapproved in the *Bilski* decision discussed below.

40. In re Bilski, 545 F.3d 943, 949–50 (Fed.Cir.2008) (en banc).

41. In the *Bilski* decision discussed below, the Federal Circuit stated that "those portions of our opinions in *State Street* ... relying solely on a 'useful, concrete and tangible result' analysis should no longer be relied on." In re Bilski, 545 F.3d 943, 960. The Supreme

Figure 2-13. The State Street Hub and Spoke Patent

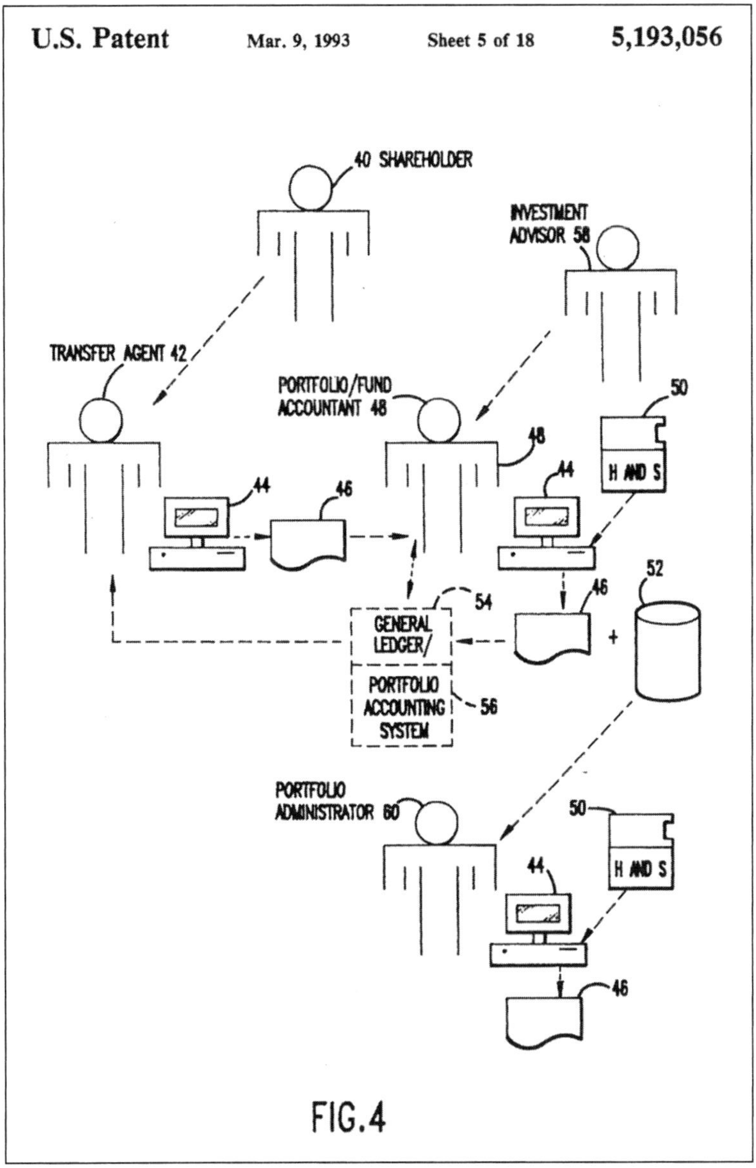

Source: U.S. Patent Office, patent number 5,193,056.

applicants sought review by the Supreme Court. The Court accepted review in the *Bilski* case, returning to the limits of software patentability for the first time in thirty years.

The *Bilski* Case

In the early 2000s, Bernard L. Bilski and Rand A. Warsaw applied for a patent on a method for predicting risk parameters in financial transactions, such as hedge funds. Claim 1 claimed "a method for managing the consumption risk costs of a commodity sold by a commodity provider at a fixed price." The claim further described steps that initiated two sets of commodity purchases. The first set of purchases would be based on historical pricing. The second set of purchases would be based on trends that ran against that historical data. Thus, the second set of purchases would "hedge" the risk created by the first set of purchases.[42] The Federal Circuit described the program: "In essence, the claim is for a method of hedging risk in the field of commodities trading. For example, coal power plants (i.e., the "consumers") purchase coal to produce electricity and are averse to the risk of a spike in demand … Importantly, however, the claim is not limited to transactions involving actual commodities, and the application discloses that the recited transactions may simply involve options, i.e., rights to purchase or sell the commodity at a particular price within a particular timeframe."[43]

The Federal Circuit affirmed the Patent Office decision rejecting the claims of the patent. It drew a precise line as to what is required to obtain a software patent: "[A]n applicant may show that a process claim satisfies § 101 either by showing that his claim is tied to a particular machine, or by showing that his claim transforms an article."[44]

The patent applicants admitted that their software was not tied to a particular machine. "As to machine implementation, Applicants themselves admit that

---

Court granted review. It affirmed the Federal Circuit decision, but did neither approved, nor disapproved the specific comments on State Street. Thus, the disapproval of *State Street* is firm law, though not because the Supreme Court said so. A District Court wondered, "whether the end has arrived for business method patents, … without expressly overruling State Street, the [Federal Circuit] *Bilski* majority struck down its underpinnings." Cyber-Source Corp. v. Retail Decisions, Inc., 620 F.Supp.2d 1068, 1081 (N.D.Cal.2009).

42. "Hedge (as in 'security') *n.* : taking two positions that will offset each other if prices change and so limiting financial risk." Nisus Thesaurus.

43. In re Bilski, 545 F.3d 943, 949–50 (Fed.Cir.2008) (en banc); cert. granted *sub nom.* Bilski v. Doll, 129 S.Ct. 2735 (2009).

44. In re Bilski, 545 F.3d 943, 961–62.

the language of claim 1 does not limit any process step to any specific machine or apparatus."[45] The Court then examined the question of whether the software transformed a material condition:

> We hold that the Applicants' process as claimed does not transform any article to a different state or thing. Purported transformations or manipulations simply of public or private legal obligations or relationships, business risks, or other such abstractions cannot meet the test because they are not physical objects or substances, and they are not representative of physical objects or substances. Applicants' process at most incorporates only such ineligible transformations. [T]he process as claimed encompasses the exchange of only options, which are simply legal rights to purchase some commodity at a given price in a given time period.... The claim only refers to "transactions" involving the exchange of these legal rights at a "fixed rate corresponding to a risk position." *See* '892 application cl. 1. Thus, claim 1 does not involve the transformation of any physical object or substance, or an electronic signal representative of any physical object or substance.[46]

The program failed to claim a machine-like process or an integral step in a transformation of matter. According to the Federal Circuit, such a transformation would be necessary for patentability.

Bilski petitioned the Supreme Court to review the case. This time, unlike the petition in the *State Street* case, the Court exercised its discretion in favor of review and granted *certiorari*.[47] The Supreme Court decision affirmed the Federal Circuit ruling, but did so with its own reasoning. We now examine the Supreme Court's decision in this important case.

Oral Argument

In November 2009, the Court heard oral arguments in the case. The Justices showed great interest in the basic issue raised by the Federal Circuit: Does

---

45. 545 F.3d 943, 962.

46. 545 F.3d 943, 963–64.

47. Bilski v. Doll, 129 S.Ct. 2735 (2009), *cert. granted.* That ruling states (in full): "Petition for writ of certiorari to the United States Court of Appeals for the Federal Circuit granted." Bilski v. Kappos, 130 S.Ct. 3218 (2010) (No. 08-964), announced the decision on the merits of the case. The name changed because in 2010 David Kappos became the new Director of the USPTO. *Certiorari* is a Latin term. The modern usage of this term denotes a process by which the Supreme Court has nearly infinite discretion to grant or deny review of the case.

patent protection extend to processes that are not embodied in a machine or do not alter the state of matter? Another way of putting the question is: Does the invention simply instruct a human being to do something? A colloquy between Justice Breyer and attorney J. Michael Jakes illustrated the matter:

> JUSTICE BREYER: You know, I have a great, wonderful, really original method of teaching antitrust law, and it kept 80 percent of the students awake. They learned things.
> (Laughter.).... It was fabulous. And I could probably have reduced it to a set of steps and other teachers could have followed it. That you are going to say is patentable, too?
> MR. JAKES: Potentially.[48]

Questions by some Justices indicated that the case might be decided without ruling on that broad question. For example, they might determine that "business methods" are not patentable, and leave aside the general issue of the role of machines. Justice Sotomayor pursued that line of inquiry:

> JUSTICE SOTOMAYOR: How about if we say something as simple as patent law doesn't cover business matters instead of what the Federal Circuit has begun to say, which is technology is tied to a machine or a transformation of the substance, but I have no idea what the limits of that ruling will impose in the computer world, in the biomedical world, all of the *amici* who are talking about how it will destroy industries? If we are unsure about that, wouldn't the safer practice be simply to say it doesn't involve business methods?[49]

The question also shows a traditional methodology of a court in the Anglo-American system. A court's primary role is to decide the particular case before it, rather than pass on abstract or policy questions. Naturally, appellate courts implicitly decide larger issues, and to some extent they frankly establish broad rules in their decisions. This is especially true with regard to the Supreme Court. Yet the theory of limited decision still holds an important role today. An appellate court is always at liberty to pull back its broad language by referring to its narrow ruling or "holding" in a prior precedent.

---

48. Transcript of argument in Bilski v. Doll, 129 S.Ct. 2735 (U.S.).
49. *Id.*

The Supreme Court Decision

The Supreme Court affirmed the Federal Circuit's decision that Bilski's process was not patentable. The ruling was narrow: 1) The Court declined to state a general rule regarding patent scope. Instead it restated general principles from the Patent Act and prior precedents. 2) It determined that the claims in this particular application failed to achieve patentability. "Rather than adopting categorical rules that might have wide-ranging and unforeseen impacts, the Court resolves this case narrowly on the basis of this Court's decisions in *Benson, Flook,* and *Diehr,* which show that petitioners' claims are not patentable processes because they are attempts to patent abstract ideas. Indeed, all members of the Court agree that the patent application at issue here falls outside of §101 because it claims an abstract idea."[50]

The decision is about fifty pages long. Justice Kennedy wrote the opinion for the majority, portions of which are quoted above. Justice Stevens concurred in a lengthy opinion. Justices Ginsburg, Breyer, and Sotomayor joined. Justice Breyer wrote a short additional concurring opinion which stressed the Court's unanimity on fundamental issues.

A total of twenty-one appellate judges had reviewed this case — nine Supreme Court Justices, plus twelve members of the Federal Circuit. Of that group all but one, Judge Newman of the Federal Circuit, agreed that the patent claimed matters that are beyond the permissible scope of 35 U.S.C. §101. At the start of the majority opinion, Justice Kennedy endorsed the careful patent analyses conducted by five separate opinions in the Federal Circuit. He stated, "Students of patent law would be well advised to study these scholarly opinions."

Justice Stevens and his three colleagues would have had the Court take a firmer stand against what many perceive as "patents run wild." They wanted the Court to be clearer in restoring "patent law to its historical and constitutional moorings."

> The Court correctly holds that the machine-or-transformation test is not the sole test for what constitutes a patentable process; rather, it is a critical clue. But the Court is quite wrong, in my view, to suggest that any series of steps that is not itself an abstract idea or law of nature may

---

50. Bilski v. Kappos, 130 S.Ct. 3218, 3230 (2010), Part III opinion of Justice Kennedy for the majority. Thus, the Supreme Court strongly reaffirmed the teaching of the original trio of precedents.

Table 2-3. Software Patent Guidelines after *Bilski*

A patent cannot claim an algorithm in the abstract.
Software is far more likely patentable when it changes in matter or governs a machine.
Software which merely "crunches" data ought not be patentable.
A patent application needs to identify a clear problem that is addressed.
Applicants should take special care to assure software is new and not obvious.

constitute a "process" within the meaning of § 101. The language in the Court's opinion to this effect can only cause mischief.[51]

Specifically these Justices would reject "business method" patents categorically. They would have the Court state "methods of doing business are not, in themselves, covered by the statute."[52]

The decision in the *Bilski* case is decisive in its rejection of overly expansive claims for software patents. Nevertheless, it will not end debate on the validity of the boundaries it has drawn, nor will it eliminate divergence of interpretations of its result. Nevertheless one can state firm guidelines based on a quartet of Supreme Court cases: *Benson, Flook, Diehr,* and *Bilski*.

These guidelines will work for most cases. However, there are some notes of caution. First, Congress can change the current statute with a stroke of a pen. Congress is especially attentive to lobbying. Second, the decision does not rule on any specific patent, other than Bilski's. The case holds only that Bilski could not obtain a patent for his business process. Third, patents are issued by examiners who struggle to apply the rules in the context of mighty caseloads. This load is bound to cause variation in results. Finally, enterprises and individual with lots of money can pursue, obtain and seek to enforce patents. On the other hand, most people and companies are of modest means, and it is overwhelmingly expensive for them to defend themselves in a patent lawsuit.

A Patented Golf Swing

Let us consider one additional issued patent. The patent is of a type that concerned many of the Justices in the *Bilski* case, that, is a patent on the way

---

51. *Id.* J. Stevens, concurring, Bilski v. Kappos, 130 S.Ct. 3218, 3232.

52. *Id.* J. Stevens, Part IV, 130 S.Ct. 3218, 3258. Justice Breyer wrote a brief concurrence "in order to highlight the substantial *agreement* among many Members of the Court on many of the fundamental issues of patent law raised by this case."

a human being might perform a given action. This patent claims a monopoly to a simple human gesture or posture—a method of executing a putt in golf. As summarized in the patent, "the invention is a putting method in which the golfer controls the speed of the putt and the direction of the putt primarily with the golfer's dominant throwing hand, yet uses the golfer's non-dominant hand to maintain the blade of the putter stable."[53] The patent augmented by "a schematic drawing illustrating a golfer using a putting grip in accordance with the invention." The patent does not appear to have been either challenged or enforced, and it seems unlikely that it would be. Sports patents might be a nuisance, but similar patents covering medical and surgical techniques could pose a real interference with the actions of skilled professionals. To deal with one aspect of this problem, Congress amended the patent code to absolve practitioners of patent infringement liability for "performance of a medical or surgical procedure on a body.[54]

Justice Stevens commented on this type of extension of patent law in his *Bilski* concurrence. If the word "process" is allowed its fullest broad meaning, it can include all manner of things. Doing anything is accomplished by a process, which in turn can be described. Justice Stevens concluded that such a breadth of patentable activities "would render § 101 almost comical. A process for training a dog, a series of dance steps, a method of shooting a basketball, maybe even words, stories, or songs if framed as the steps of typing letters or uttering sounds—all would be patent-eligible. I am confident that the term 'process' in § 101 is not nearly so capacious."[55]

---

53. "Method of Putting," U.S. Pat. 5,616,089. In June 2009, after the Federal Circuit decision but before the Supreme Court ruling in *Bilski*, Deborah Dunagan and others filled for an intellectual property management system. Its first claim claims: "A computerized system for an intellectual property (IP) framework, including: a strategic planning computer module for formulating business strategies [and a] computer module for managing creation of said inventions based on said business strategies." United States Patent Application Code Dunagan; Deborah et al. 20100332285. The assignee is IBM Corporation.

54. 35 U.S.C. § 287(c) (2001).

55. Bilski v. Kappos, 130 S.Ct. 3218, 3238. A 2009 study indicated that a 25.5 billions dollar loss is caused annually by the "deadweight" of "substandard patents. "Achieving an adequate balance of rights to compensate true innovators and fostering the use of patented technology is the goal of a well-functioning patent system. A patent regime that makes it too easy to obtain and enforce a patent could create too many of these monopoly "embarrassments" that would reduce economic welfare by virtue of their monopoly status yet not promote economic welfare because they do not reward true innovations." T. Randolph Beard, George S. Ford, Ph.D., Thomas M. Koutsky, and Lawrence J. Spiwak, *Quantifying the Cost of Substandard Patents: Some Preliminary Evidence*, 12 YALE J. L. & TECH. 240 (2010).

Figure 2-14. Patented Golf Swing

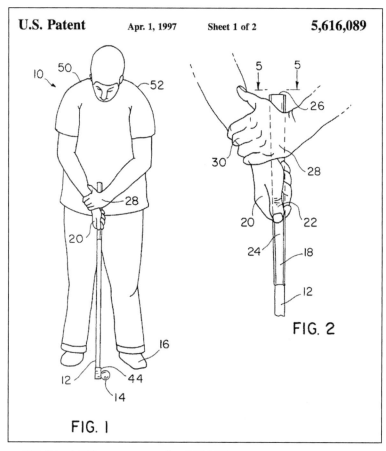

Source: U.S. Patent Office, patent number 5,616,089.

The Internet

The range of patentable subject matter includes such modern technologies as biotechnology, computer processes, chemicals, drugs, and Internet applications and enabling technologies. The infrastructure and application of the Internet is replete with patentable technologies. One example is U.S. Patent 7,487,447 entitled "Web page zoom feature" issued February 3, 2009 to John J. Jerger and assigned to Google, Inc. The abstract of the patent describes the invention as follows:

Methods and apparatus, including computer program products, related to a cross-browser compliant web page zoom feature. A method includes receiving a web page with machine-readable instructions and a zoom factor for the web page; processing a document object model representation of the web page in accordance with the machine-readable instructions; and displaying the web page in a web browser according to the document object model representation.

In essence, the patent claims a method for allowing users to change the size of the display of images and words from an Internet connection or computer. The patent lists prior art (patents) dating back to 1998. Provided the claims are not faulty or the invention is not precluded by obviousness or undisclosed prior art, the patent appears to cover classic patentable subject matter, in the sense that the process clearly governs the effects of physical inputs and outputs. It determines the flow of electronic information resulting in a visible "zoomed" display.

Figure 2-15. Web Zoom Patent

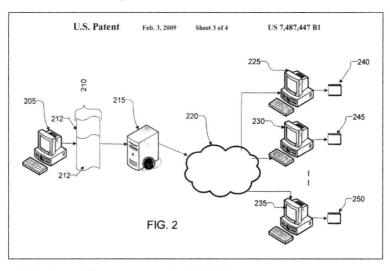

Source: U.S. Patent Office, patent number 7,487,447.

Enforcement

The patent code provides that with few exceptions "whoever without authority makes, uses, offers to sell, or sells any patented invention, within the United States or imports into the United States any patented invention during the term of the patent therefor, infringes the patent." 35 U.S.C. §271. Actively inducing an infringement also creates liability.

An action for enforcement can be brought in Federal District Court anywhere in the United States. Since the claims in a patent describe what is owned, a patent infringement case is more accurately described as a claims infringement case. The patent owner has a right to exclude others from practicing the claimed process. Under the "doctrine of equivalents" the patent owner may also prevent others from using a similar equivalent process. Control of the invention may not extend beyond the claims as approved by the USTPO, but the patentee's right of control does extend to applications which can be judged to be, in effect, equivalent to the patented claim.

In a 1997 case, the Supreme Court unanimously reaffirmed the "doctrine of equivalents" according to which "a product or process that does not literally infringe upon the express terms of a patent claim may nonetheless be found to infringe if there is 'equivalence' between the elements of the accused product or process and the claimed elements of the patented invention."[56] Hilton Davis had patented an improved process (ultrafiltration) for filtering out impurities in dye. Warner-Jenkinson came up with a similar process which it put into production. Only after it had started to use the process did Warner-Jenkinson discover the Hilton Davis patent. Hilton Davis then sued for infringement of its claimed process. One who infringes a patent innocently or by accident is nonetheless liable. During the litigation, Hilton Davis conceded that while the filtration processes were similar, they were not identical. The trial court allowed a jury to decide whether Warner-Jenkinson had infringed the process by using an equivalent. Warner-Jenkinson appealed, claiming that patent liability could not extend to an equivalent, but must be based on infringing the claims as stated. It asked that the "doctrine of equivalents" be overturned. In a unanimous opinion, the Supreme Court reaffirmed that doctrine, stating, "a product or process that does not literally infringe upon the express terms of a patent claim may nonetheless be found to infringe if there is 'equivalence' between the elements of the accused product or process and the claimed elements of the patented invention."[57]

---

56. Warner-Jenkinson Co. Inc. v. Hilton Davis Chem. Co., 520 U.S. 17, 21 (1997).
57. 520 U.S. 17, 21 (1997).

The doctrine of equivalents addresses a difficulty: The Patent Act restricts the scope of a patent to that which is actually approved in the claims. On the other hand, a patentee ought to receive the full scope of an approved grant. Is it fair to avoid being too literal in interpreting the language of the claim? The Court concluded that allowing the extension to equivalent items was permitted by the statute so long as each necessary element of the claim was met. It stated that the essential question must be: "Does the accused product or process contain elements identical or equivalent to each claimed element of the patented invention?" Only if this is the case, will the doctrine of equivalents be met.

Patent infringement trials can be heard and decided by either a judge and jury or by a judge sitting without a jury. Whether a jury is involved depends on whether a party demands one and whether a jury is permissible on the issues at hand. When a jury is used in an infringement case, the jury is allowed to decide what the facts are and whether there has been an infringement. For example, in the *Warner-Jenkinson* case, a jury had been allowed to apply the doctrine of equivalents to the facts at hand. The jury found that the patent was valid, and that it had been infringed. The Federal Circuit determined that was proper procedure, and the Supreme Court did not disagree. It simply commented that there "was ample support in our prior cases for that holding."[58]

However, in a jury trial, the judge must still interpret that law. Judges decide legal questions; juries must stick to facts or application of law to facts. In a patent case, one of the crucial issues is the meaning of the patent and its claims. In *Markman v. Westview Instruments, Inc.*, 517 U.S. 370 (1996), the Supreme Court decided that the trial judge must make that decision. "The construction of written instruments is one of those things that judges often do and are likely to do better than jurors unburdened by training in exegesis. Patent construction in particular 'is a special occupation, requiring, like all others, special training and practice.' "[59] The decision means that interpretation of the patent document is essentially like interpreting the meaning of a case or statute. As a result of this decision, the meaning of the patent document is determined in a special hearing before a judge called a "Markman hearing."

An infringer is subject to liability for compensatory damages and may be enjoined from further infringement. Attorney fees may also be awarded to either party in exceptional cases. Also, an infringer may be held liable for up to

---

58. 520 U.S. 17, 38–39.
59. 517 U.S. 370, 388.

three times the amount of actual damages for willful infringement. The Federal Circuit summed up the matter: "Because patent infringement is a strict liability offense, the nature of the offense is only relevant in determining whether enhanced damages are warranted. Although a trial court's discretion in awarding enhanced damages has a long lineage in patent law, the current statute, similar to its predecessors, is devoid of any standard for awarding them. Absent a statutory guide, we have held that an award of enhanced damages requires a showing of willful infringement."[60]

An alleged infringer can present a variety of defenses. One is to show that the patent does not cover the allegedly infringing activity. Another is to show that the patent is invalid. A patent may be held invalid because it lacks novelty, is obvious, or because the applicant did not make adequate disclosures to the Patent Office. A patent may also be held invalid or unenforceable due to "inequitable conduct" on the part of the patentee. Patent law does not include a privilege of fair use, as does copyright. Also, as noted above, a successful defendant may receive an award of attorney fees.

Three matters require a party to show that the opponents engaged in some sort of "extra bad" conduct in order for certain remedies to apply. To obtain enhanced or treble damages the defendant must be shown to have acted willfully in the sense that it engaged in bad faith or some deliberate attempt to violate the patentee's rights. "Inequitable conduct" on the part of a patentee will bar enforcement of the patent. For example this may occur when the patentee or his attorney has failed to act with candor and good toward the Patent Office. Finally, a prevailing party to a lawsuit may gain an award of damages only when it shows that the case is "exceptional." Determining whether some act is in bad faith, lacks candor, or is exceptional all grant a court a large range of discretion. These criteria also overlap. For example, to obtain attorney fees one must show "inequitable conduct before the PTO; litigation misconduct; vexatious, unjustified, and otherwise bad faith litigation; a frivolous suit or willful infringement."[61]

Practical Guidelines

Those engaged in inventive activities need guidance in dealing with patent issues. Here are some useful guidelines:

---

60. In re Seagate, 497 F.3d 1360, 1368 (Fed.Cir.2007). The "strict liability" aspect of patent and copyright law is discussed further in Chapter Seven.

61. Epcon Gas Systems, Inc. v. Bauer Compressors, Inc. 279 F.3d 1022, 1034 C.A.Fed. (Mich. 2002).

1. If one can know a field of work well, it will usually demand relatively little attention to patent issues.[62] For example, those who work in an old technology such as glassblowing are likely to hear of advances in their fields. If one conceives a very useful innovation, the value of a patent ought to be considered. If another party holds a patent that one has not heard of, it is usually reasonably safe to react after receiving notice from the patentee.

2. Other fields, such as pharmaceuticals and semiconductors, are replete with patent patents and patent applications. Also, large corporate enterprises often use patents aggressively. When factors such as these arise, one needs to heighten the attention given to patents.

3. Applying for and maintaining patents is time consuming and expensive. It is best to explore the value of a patent before getting too far along the application process. A good approach is to work with an attorney to devise guidelines that will help assess potential patents and defenses to potential infringements on a regular basis. One ought to be able to obtain such counsel at reasonable cost. Attorneys that fail to provide such services rule themselves out of certain opportunities.

4. The decision of whether to grant a patent depends on assessing "prior art" and obviousness. Litigation may raise the same questions. When one considers a patent application or faces a serious claim of infringement, one may need to conduct patent searches and study what is obvious in the field. In either case, one needs prompt assistance of an attorney.

Concluding Comments

Patents are the strongest form of invention protection. A patent allows control of an underlying or general process. However, general principles and laws of nature cannot be patented. The right granted is "the right to exclude others from making, using, offering for sale, or selling the invention throughout the United States or importing the invention into the United States."[63] The patent owner can use the process during its patent term and prevent others from using it. The owner can license the use to others or put the patent on the shelf and make no use of it at all.

Patents can be enforced by powerful remedies, including damages, injunctions, and often attorney fees. Unlike a trade secret, the patent holder need not protect the secrecy of his or her invention. Once a trade secret is disclosed,

---

62. It is worthwhile to review the discussion of searches early in this chapter.
63. 35 U.S.C. § 154.

the trade secret holder simply loses control. The trade secret holder may get remedies against those who disclose his secret, but the genie is out of the bottle and cannot be put back in. Unlike a copyright holder, the patentee can control a system or a method. The copyright holder controls particular expressions only. During the term of twenty years, the patentee holds sway over the entire field covered by the claims set forth in the patent.

Table 2-4. Patent Guidelines

General Rule	Comment	Source
Subject matter. Any process which is new, useful, and not obvious to the practitioner in the field.	Four broad categories: process, machine, manufacture, or composition of matter or any improvement of them.	35 U.S.C. §§ 100–103
Government grant. Inventor must apply for a patent and fully *disclose* the technology and best method. USPTO decides whether to grant.	The key is full disclosure. A government created monopoly is given in return for teaching the public exactly how to practice a useful invention.	35 U.S.C. §§ 111, 112, 116, 151
What rights? Exclusive right to practice the invention.	It is more accurately a right to *exclude others* from using the claimed invention or equivalent.	35 U.S.C. § 271
How long? A limited time. 20 years.	A short term, subject to some adjustments. Compare copyright.	35 U.S.C. §§ 154–156
Reduce to practice. The invention must be "reduced to practice."	Ideas cannot be owned. What is protected is the resulting application. One cannot own mathematical formulas, etc.	35 U.S.C. § 101, 112, *Benson* case, 409 U.S. 63
How do you know what is covered? Study the *claims* of the patent. These describe the invention and its scope.	The patent specifically points out and describes the invention in the claims section so the public can follow it.	35 U.S.C. §§ 112, 154 (a) (1)
Interpretation of claims. The final interpretation of claims is by a judge, not a jury.	This means that interpretation of what is covered is "legalistic," subject to heavy lawyering on the meaning of language.	*Markman* case, 517 U.S. 370
Who owns? The inventor or assignee owns the patent as personal property.	The inventor remains owner, unless he or she assigns expressly or by clear implication.	35 U.S.C. § 261; *Dubilier*, 289 U.S. 178
Novelty. The invention must be new. This is determined by comparing with what is known, i.e., "prior art."	Pressure placed on innovators to review existing art, including patents. A small patent claim may block a big innovation.	35 U.S.C. §§ 101, 102
Useful. Virtually any innovation that can serve a purpose will do.	U.S. patent law does not judge the social desirability of the resulting process.	35 U.S.C. § 101

Table 2-4. Patent Guidelines, *continued*

General Rule	Comment	Source
Not obvious. A patent should not be granted for things that would be obvious to skilled persons in the field.	Intended to prevent patents from stopping normal practices simply because a party has run to the Patent Office.	35 U.S.C. §103
Presumed valid. Once granted, a patent is presumed valid.	Major defenses are to show claim does not cover defendant's item or patent is invalid.	35 U.S.C. §§281–285
Infringement. Any non-permitted use of a claim infringes. Also, use of a substantial equivalent infringes. Strict liability.	Remedies include damages, injunctions, attorney fees. There is no general privilege like "fair use" in copyright.	35 U.S.C. §§271–287
Application process. Procedure before Patent Office is the key.	Clear specific rights (claims) are defined by an expensive administrative process.	35 U.S.C. §§33, 131
Major purpose. Rewards "the better mouse trap."	Emphasis is on useful things that command power in the marketplace.	U.S. Const. art. I, §8

Chapter Three

Copyrights

Introduction

Copyright law evolves from the premise: Don't copy another's work without his or her permission. The basic norms of copyright follow a pattern of expectations which is widely understood in our culture. They have often been taught in early years of school. For example, suppose a seventh grade teacher has asked each class member to write a report on a Latin American country. One student has put off the report, perhaps due to laziness or rebellion. A couple of days before it is due, she borrows another's paper "to get some ideas." Instead, she basically copies it, changing a word here and there. She then traces a map from a book, adds it to the paper as an illustration, and submits the combination to her teacher as her own paper. Both the text of the paper and the tracing amount to copying under the law, as well as under our ordinary expectations. That is because she looked at others' pieces of work and replicated the essence of that work. She copied what is expressed in the paper and the map. The map and the paper contained someone else's expressions, not her own. In general, copyright law forbids copying someone else's expressions of ideas, unless one has a permissible reason for it. This last sentence sets forth much of what United States copyright law sets forth: Do not copy without a good enough reason.

The Latin American paper example also illustrates the concept of the "good enough reason" for copying. This is called "fair use" in copyright law. It is easy to understand that copying the text of another's paper is wrong in the school context. It is cheating. The girl didn't do her own work, and the teacher should discipline her for that. On the other hand, if she had written her own paper and illustrated it with a map (traced, scanned, downloaded, or machine copied) that would usually be fine in the school context. She should acknowledge the source. This would likely satisfy the present statutory requirements of fair use under the Copyright Act, as well as standards of academic honesty.

While these basic concepts are carried forward in the Copyright Act, they have become complicated and to some degree obscured by such things as extremely long terms of copyright ownership, transfers of copyrights to parties who are not authors, and the extension of copyright to software.

Basic Concepts and Rules

Copyright protects original *expression,* but not ideas that form the basis for the expression. An author of a story, poem, or song uses language, expressions, and concepts that are part of the social fabric. These common elements do not originate with the author, but are products of his or her culture. Copyright law protects only what an author or composer contributes: the way she tells the story, phases the music, etc. A useful working definition for copyright is: A grant of an exclusive right over copies of expressions, but not the component ideas.

Thus, one will have to show more than a general similarity of plot to prevail in a copyright case. Judge Learned Hand examined this limitation in a 1930 case decided under the 1909 Copyright Act. where an author claimed another had infringed her play. The play was driven by a story line in which a boy and girl fall in love. The two were from different religious backgrounds, Jewish and Irish Catholic, and their respective fathers vehemently opposed the marriage. Judge Hand explained:

> We assume that the plaintiff's play is altogether original, even to an extent that in fact it is hard to believe. We assume further that, so far as it has been anticipated by earlier plays of which she knew nothing, that fact is immaterial. Still, as we have already said, her copyright did not cover everything that might be drawn from her play; its content went to some extent into the public domain. We have to decide how much, and while we are as aware as anyone that the line, wherever it is drawn, will seem arbitrary, that is no excuse for not drawing it; it is a question such as courts must answer in nearly all cases. Whatever may be the difficulties a priori, we have no question on which side of the line this case falls. A comedy based upon conflicts between Irish and Jews, into which the marriage of their children enters, is no more susceptible of copyright than the outline of Romeo and Juliet.[1]

The rule remains the same under the 1976 Copyright Act which applies to all works created after 1978:

> "Copyright protection subsists ... in original works of authorship fixed in any tangible medium of expression ... *In no case does copyright protection for an original work of authorship extend to any idea,* proce-

---

1. Nichols v. Universal Pictures Corp., 45 F.2d 119, 122 (2d Cir. 1930).

dure, process, system, method of operation, concept, principle, or discovery, regardless of the form in which it is described, explained, illustrated, or embodied in such work."[2]

In many respects copyright law begins and ends with this simple statement of principle. If you think about it, play with it, and apply it to some examples around you, you will be able to anticipate many, if not most, of the issues that end up in court!

It a nutshell, the fundamental concept in the statute is that copyright gives ownership of the expressive aspects of fixed works. In general terms, only the copyright owner is authorized to make copies of the work. That said, the current copyright law establishes many details that govern the protection of these works of authorship. It sets up eight categories of works that are protected and specifies six rights that accrue to the author of a protected work. The Copyright Act fully defines the copyright owners rights.[3]

Statutory details concerning ownership:
Works protected. The statute lists eight different categories of protected:
   (1) literary works;
   (2) musical works, including any accompanying words;
   (3) dramatic works, including any accompanying music;
   (4) pantomimes and choreographic works;
   (5) pictorial, graphic, and sculptural works;
   (6) motion pictures and other audiovisual works;
   (7) sound recordings; and
   (8) architectural works.

In addition, copyright protects compilations, including collections of data, so long as those present some originality of arrangement.[4]

Authors and Works Made for Hire

Ownership of a copyright "vests initially in the author or authors of the work," except for works "made for hire." Most works for hire are created by

---

2. 17 U.S.C. § 102 (italics added).

3. "The 1976 Act rejected the doctrine of indivisibility, recasting the copyright as a bundle of discrete 'exclusive rights,' 17 U.S.C. § 106 creates six separate each of which 'may be transferred … and owned separately.' § 201(d)(2)." New York Times Co. v. Tasini, 533 U.S. 483, 495–96 (2001). The "bundle of rights" is a form of private property.

4. 17 U.S.C. § 103.

employees whose scope of employment includes creating copyrightable works.[5] In addition, a work made for hire may include certain kind of works done by an independent contractor who is bound by contract to produce such a work. An independent contractor's work is a work for hire only when if falls into one of nine statutory categories, including part of a movie, a translation, or an atlas.[6]

Corporations own many of the commercially important copyrighted works in the United States. Companies and corporations own works "prepared by an employee within the scope of his or her employment" or assigned to the company.[7]

Six Separate Rights

The core concept is the right to prevent others *copying*, rather than to control use. Copyright allows a book author to prevent copying of chapters of a book, but does not control use of the book or any system explained in the book. Patent law, on the other hand, lets the patentee control uses of a patented process. Activities which equate to copying give rise to infringement claims.

The 1976 Copyright Act divides the core concept of an exclusive right to copy into the six separate rights: to copy, derive, distribute, perform (performable works), display, and perform digital sound recordings.[8] The six different rights attempt to protect the variety of expressions covered by the statute. Choreographic works, for example, are "copied" in different ways than a book

---

5. 17 U.S.C. §201.

6. 17 U.S.C. §101 defines a work made for hire as 1) "a work prepared by an employee within the scope of his or her employment" or 2) a specially commissioned ;or one of the following nine categories: a contribution to a collective work, part of a motion picture or other audiovisual work, a translation, a supplementary work, a compilation, an instructional text, a test, answer material for a test, or an atlas. To qualify as a specially commissioned work for hire, the parties must agree "in a written instrument signed by them that the work shall be considered a work made for hire." Community for Creative Non-Violence v. Reid, 490 U.S. 730 (1989) explicitly the work for hire doctrine.

7. Corporations acquire ownership in one of two ways: 1) A work for hire can arise when the scope of employment includes producing a work of the kind created *or* when an independent contractor creates one of nine types of works specifically mentioned in 17 U.S.C. §101. 2) Corporations acquire many of their copyrights by employment contracts whereby the employee agrees to assign the copyright to the corporation. "The reality today is that more and more works are produced as works of corporate authorship." Laura N. Gasaway, *Libraries, Users, and the Problems of Authorship in the Digital Age*, 52 DePaul L. Rev. 1193, 1202–3 (2003).

8. 17 U.S.C. §106.

is.[9] Usually the copy would be in the form of a performance that imitates aspects of the choreographed dance. However, a federal appellate court has ruled that a book of photographs of a dance may infringe the copyright of the underlying choreography. It commented "A snapshot of a single moment in a dance sequence may communicate a great deal. It may, for example, capture a gesture, the composition of dancers' bodies or the placement of dancers on the stage."[10]

The copyright owner does not have the right to control what one does with a legally acquired copy of a book or other item. One who buys a book owns that copy. The owner may loan it to others, although the may be restricted from such things as displaying or reading them for a fee. This is called the "doctrine of first sale."[11] Thus, one who buys a copyrighted book can lend it to friends. If a friend writes you a letter, you "own" the letter, but she owns the copyright to the letter. This doctrine points out a fundamental concept. The physical embodiment—book, painting, sheet of music—and the copyrighted expression are separate things in law. However, the doctrine of first sale does not apply to most software which one acquires, because software is usually distributed under a license to use the software, rather than by sale of a copy of the software. When you "buy" new software, whether on a disk or by download, you have actually purchased a contractual permission to use the software, not a copy which you own.[12]

A key concept of what is protected is the term "work." The Copyright Act itself contains more than fifty special definitions of terms. These are intended to give firm guidance to courts when interpreting the Act. The term "work" is used hundreds of times in the Act, and it appears more than ninety times in the definitions section alone (17 U.S.C. § 101), yet it is not specifically defined itself. However, it is clear in the many specific definitions of types of works that the noun "work" is intended to refer to an expression, but not the ideas that drive it, nor the bits and pieces that are stitched together to create it.

---

9. 17 U.S.C. § 102. The procedures and scope of protection vary among these categories. A performed song presents the most significant difference. The performed song often comprises two copyrights. The songwriter owns the copyright of the song, while the performer owns the "performance right," which controls copies of the performance. Recordings are marked with a ℗ symbol, rather than a ©.

10. Horgan v. Macmillan, Inc., 789 F.2d 157, 163 (2d Cir. 1986).

11. 17 U.S.C. § 109.

12. "The first sale doctrine does not apply to a person who possesses a copy of the copyrighted work without owning it, such as a licensee." Vernor v. Autodesk, Inc., 621 F.3d 1102 (9th Cir. 2010). A handy way to check this is to browse the "documents" (hardcopy of electronic) that you agree to when you "purchase" software.

Let us take one example of a defined work. Architectural works are a recent addition to the list of copyrightable works. Including architectural works under copyright presents devilish problems for they are primarily functional, yet have expressive qualities. In 1959 a congressional committee observed:

> It should also be borne in mind that architectural works (in the form of either plans or structures) embody functional ideas and mechanical processes or methods of construction. It is axiomatic that copyright does not protect the ideas or methods expounded in a work, but protects only the author's "expression" or form of ex-position of the ideas or methods.[13]

The Act defines this type of work: "An 'architectural work' is the design of a building as embodied in any tangible medium of expression, including a building, architectural plans, or drawings. The work includes the overall form as well as the arrangement and composition of spaces and elements in the design, but does not include individual standard features."[14] The definition emphasizes that what is copyrightable is the design as represented (embodied) in the entire thing—the particular building design or its plans. An idea may drive the particular set of plans, but cannot itself be copyrighted. For example, an architect may conceive of a work as one giant flying buttress. The concept of such a buttress building cannot be copyrighted, but the expression of it in the plans or their execution can be. It is always the expression that gains protection, not the concepts utilized in the expression. The arena of architectural copyright can present real difficulty for attorneys whose practice may involve architecture and buildings. A pair of attorneys whose practice focuses on building construction issues note the concerns of architects themselves: "Permitting architects to place limitations on their brethren as to which designs they may utilize in the performance of their duties would simply complicate the practice of architecture and ultimately lessen creativity within the profession."[15]

---

13. Copyright Law Revision Studies, prepared for the Subcommittee on Patents, Trademarks, and Copyrights of the Committee on the Judiciary of the United States Senate (Study 27, "Copyright in Architectural Works," p. 67), 86th Congress, 2nd Session (1959). Available at http://www.copyright.gov. Protection was added in 1990. Architectural Works Copyright Protection Act, Pub. L. No. 101-650, §702(a), 104 Stat. 5133 (1990) (amending 17 U.S.C.A. §101). See, PHILIP L. BRUNER AND PATRICK J. O'CONNOR, JR., BRUNER AND O'CONNOR ON CONSTRUCTION LAW, §17:87 (2010).

14. 17 U.S.C. §101.

15. PHILIP L. BRUNER AND PATRICK J. O'CONNOR, JR., BRUNER AND O'CONNOR ON CONSTRUCTION LAW, §17:87 (2010).

To qualify for protection, the work needs to express some *originality*, but not much. The act requires that the protected item be "an original work of authorship." This follows the constitutional provision enabling Congress to grant authors exclusive rights to their writings, rather than what is common to other writings. U.S. Const. art. I §#8, cl. 8. The Supreme Court has held that alphabetical listings in a telephone book do not present enough originality to claim copyright protection.[16] On the other hand, compilations of facts may be copyrighted, so long as the creator has employed some degree of arrangement beyond the obvious. It is the arrangement, not the information, which receives copyright protection. Compilations of the wholesale prices of coins have been held to be sufficiently original, for example.[17] By contrast, a patent requires a higher degree of innovation. The applicant must demonstrate to the patent examiner that the claimed invention is novel, useful, and not an obvious solution to problem solvers in the field of invention.

A copyright is *automatic*—one does not have to file anything with a government agency to have a copyright.[18] Once an expression is written down, sketched, or typed into a computer memory the copyright exists. It comes into being instantaneously when "fixed" in any sort of a medium that can capture the expression, even one which can be instantly erased such as volatile memory of a computer.[19] Thus, a common expression, such as, "I'm going to file for a copyright," is wrong. One does not have to file anywhere to obtain the copyright.

The automatic nature of protection is an important feature of copyright law. Compare this aspect with patents. A patent must be applied for and granted. A copyright exists as soon as the work is placed (or "fixed") in some tangible medium. Notes jotted down or a letter written to a friend enjoy exactly the same copyright as a blockbuster movie released two weeks ago. Giving notice

---

16. Feist Publications, Inc. v. Rural Tel. Serv. Co., 499 U.S. 340, 350–53 (1991).

17. CDN Inc. v. Kapes, 197 F. 3d 1256 (9th Cir. 1999).

18. No formalities are required to secure the copyright under the current 1976 Act. This is in accord with a long standing approach taken by other nations. Notice of copyright is not required under the 1976 act, except for certain works published before 1989. 17 U.S.C. §401 (c). By contrast, the prior 1909 act, required notice of the copyright be placed on published items.

19. A copyright comes into being as soon as it is fixed in any tangible medium of expression, now known or later developed 17 U.S.C. §102 (a). If you write something on your computer the work is instantly fixed in the RAM. You realize how fleeting this "fixing" is when you lose your work because you shut down your computer without saving the work to the hard drive. See MAI Sys. Corp. v. Peak Computer, Inc., 991 F.2d 511, 518 (9th Cir.1995), which is discussed later in this chapter.

of copyright, for example, using the © symbol, is not required, but providing such notice is useful as it informs others that they should respect one's rights.

While a copyright occurs as soon as a work is fixed, the copyright owner must register that copyright with the Copyright Office in order to able to enforce the copyright. Registering a copyright is accomplished by completing the form, paying a modest registration fee and depositing two copies of the work.[20] Registration can be done online. In most cases one can proceed with an infringement action, as long as the work has been registered before going to court.[21] Also, registration within five years of first publication provides prima facie evidence of the validity of the copyright.[22]

In general, the copyright vests in the author of the work, subject to the limitations of the work for hire doctrine discussed above. There can be more that one author, and when that is the case, they share the ownership.[23] Both published and unpublished works are protected by copyright.[24] One's private diary or a letter to a friend enjoy the same copyright protection as any other expression. For example, a letter written by Stephen King, will have the same basic protection as any of his published novels.

An author cannot strictly control even admitted direct copying of his work, because the public enjoys a broad privilege to use the author's expressions, so long as the use is "fair." As in the case of "copyrightable work," "expression," and "copy," the concept of *"fair use"* is intended to be broad in scope. The concept is stated in 17 U.S.C. § 107: "the fair use of a copyrighted work is not an infringement of copyright." The Act refines fair use in specific instances in fifteen additional sections.[25] The public's privilege of fair use contrasts sharply with patent law which, with few exceptions, gives an owner the legal right to prevent any use of a patented invention without permission. Patents control the use of underlying methods and do not permit fair use.

Copyrights last for a very long time. In most instances, the term is measured from the date of creation. The term is the lifetime of the author plus sev-

---

20. An excellent summary of the law and procedure is available from the Copyright Office. Copyright Office Basics — http://www.copyright.gov/circs/circ1.html#cr. Registration can be done online. U.S. Copyright Office — Online Services (eCO: Electronic Copyright Office) — http://www.copyright.gov/eco. See Reed Elsevier, Inc. v. Muchnick, 130 S.Ct. 1237 (2010).

21. 17 U.S.C. §§ 401 and 411.

22. 17 U.S.C. § 410 (c).

23. 17 U.S.C. § 201.

24. 17 U.S.C. § 104.

25. 17 U.S.C. § 108 through § 122. Some of these provisions go into excruciating detail. In 2006, these sections took up more than seventy pages in the printed code.

enty years. For works owned by a corporation the period is ninety five years.[26] Once again, compare this with patents. A patent is granted a much shorter life-span—generally twenty years.

While copyright is broad and automatic, when one compares it with a patent, a copyright is relatively weak. Copyright protects only particular expressions, and protects those only against copying. It does not grant one the right to prevent others from using an underlying idea, system, or method. The rights established are also counterbalanced by the public's privilege to copy the works, when the copying is "fair use." These limitations on the strength of copyright are counterbalanced by its long term, the power of licensing, and the ability of a well heeled copyright owner to bring lengthy and expensive legal actions. Also, as we shall discuss, the ability of a copyright owner to obtain "statutory damages" can inhibit many from taking full advantage of the fair use privilege.

Copyright originally concerned works that made cultural contributions or presented information and knowledge—songs, novels, history books, paintings, maps and the like. These add to the fullness of life and knowledge, but they do not directly accomplish practical tasks or change material conditions. Thus, until relatively recently, such works were unlikely to command the strong monetary return that a patented machine would. A farmer might have a need to purchase a threshing machine, but he could do his farming without buying a novel or a piece of sheet music. One might explain this long term as a means to allow the creator more time to gain a financial benefit. This might have been true in the past, but today popular entertainment and software can generate create large returns for copyright owners, even over a short period.[27]

We conclude this examination of basic concepts with a short example from Shakespeare. Much of his appeal is that his poems, story lines, and characters are so recognizably common! What sets him apart is his deft choice of words,

26. See 17 U.S.C. § 302 and also § 101. Corporate and anonymous works have terms which are the shorter of 120 years from date of creation or ninety five years from first publication. 17 U.S.C. § 302. United States copyright law is governed today by two sets of statutes. The Copyright Act of 1976 governs all works created after January 1, 1978. The 1909 Copyright Act governs older works, many of which, surprisingly, enjoy enforceable copyrights today. It allows copyrights for a twenty-eight year period starting on publication, renewable for a second twenty eight years period. Copyright Act of 1909, § 24 and 17 U.S.C. § 104A. For the most part the discussion of copyright in this book will be directed to the 1976 Act. Cases decided under the 1909 Act often have great authority under today's 1976 Act. That is because *concepts* have continued forward from the prior Act. 17 U.S.C. § 302 provides a separate term for a "work for hire," and 17 U.S.C. § 201 (b) provides that the employer "for whom the work was prepared" is the owner.

27. The historical purposes of copyright and patent law are explored in Chapter Seven.

mood, incidents—in a word, his expression. A look at a few lines from his Sonnet 18 helps one to understand limiting protection to expressive aspects. The first lines begin:

Shall I compare thee to a summer's day?
Thou art more lovely and more temperate:
Rough winds do shake the darling buds of May,
And summer's lease hath all too short a date:

These four lines evoke the loveliness of a loved one, the transience of the season, the fact that life is short. Such words and images enrich our lives. If Shakespeare were a contemporary poet, he would own a copyright of these lines as soon as he penned them. Yet he would not own the idea of comparing a beautiful person to a summer day or any of the other images and suggestions that he combines. Also, though he would own the copyright of those four lines, they could be copied word for word without infringing the copyright, so long as the use could be considered "fair."

Copyright would allow Shakespeare to protect the particular way he expressed a driving idea—lovely as a summer's day. The combination of the lines of his poem are Shakespeare's *expression* of the beauty of his love. The motivating idea—a beauty more fragile yet complete than a summer's day—is something that Shakespeare could never own by copyright. The concept is wonderful. Yet the concept itself cannot be owned. Any book you pick up in a bookstore will present the same basic kinds of copyright questions as do Shakespeare's Sonnet and a phrase like "lovely as spring." Copyright does not allow ownership of ideas, commonplaces, and systems of organization. The language of 17 U.S.C. §102 makes this distinction: expressions are protected, ideas and the like are not.

Copyright cases usually present three questions: 1) What does the plaintiff's work *express?* 2) Does the defendant's work *copy* (or display, etc.) that expression in some substantial way? 3) If so, is the defendant's copying nevertheless a *fair use?*

Deciding these matters involves stating what the law is, then applying it to the facts. Only a judge can determine what the law is, while a jury is entitled to decide the facts. Separating the two questions is not easy in a copyright. For example, drawing the line between concept and the expressions of it is hard to do in Shakespeare's sonnet. In a jury trial a judge would instruct the jury to decide what were the protected expressions in the Sonnet and what would be fair use of it. The Court would tell the jury to follow the law with "instructions" such as these:

- The right to exclude others from copying extends only to how the author expressed the ideas in the copyrighted work. The copyright is not violated when someone uses an idea from a copyrighted work, as long as the particular way of expressing that idea in the work is not copied.

- The defendant contends that there is no copyright infringement. There is no copyright infringement where the defendant made fair use of a copyrighted work by reproducing copies for criticism, comment, news reporting, teaching, scholarship, or research.[28]

The jury should go over the facts and come to a fair conclusion on these questions.

The boundaries of a given copyright—what is owned—are never drawn precisely until a case goes to court. The exact scope of what is protected is not determined until after the court decides what is expressed. In addition, the court must decide that the alleged copy actually used some substantial part of the expression. Attorneys can advise clients on what is likely be viewed as an infringement, but with far less certainty than is the case with a potential patent claim infringement. As noted above, while the cost is not great, one must register a copyright with Copyright Office before being able to pursue a case in court.

The fluidity of copyright makes it advantageous for parties to a copyright controversy to discuss reasonably, decide what use is permitted, and avoid going to court. On the other hand, the fluidity gives hold-up power to a party with lots of money to spend on litigation. A party with a weak case can pursue or defend a case which it would likely lose if it were to proceed all the way to judgment. The need to discuss is valuable in a legal system. However, use of money power to dominate a case distorts the goals of the law.

* * *

A Pause

Copyright coverage has burgeoned from printing books and maps to include software and Internet distribution of works. Before we examine that development, let us compare copyright with its federal cousin, patent law.[29] Copyright resembles patent law in that both have central provisions that guide the whole—e.g., 35 U.S.C. §§ 101–103, 112; 17 U.S.C. §§ 102, 106. Each creates a property right, and each is premised on rewarding a creator for contribution to the public. U.S. Const. art. I § #8, cl. 8. Each branch of law is also completely controlled by an act of Congress.

---

28. Ninth Circuit Model Civil Jury Instructions, online at http://www.ce9.uscourts.gov.
29. The origins of Anglo-American copyright laws are discussed in Chapter Seven.

On the other hand there are marked differences. Patents are hard to obtain but grant more powerful rights—control of use and no privilege of fair use. Patents are established to compensate an inventor for having invented some physical thing or method. Patents protect things like the "better mouse trap," or the method of producing a plain paper copy. The reward for doing this is tight control over the method for a short period. A patent provides a definite statement of rights in the claims.

By contrast, copyrights are easy to obtain and last for a long time. The effective rights of a copyright are not determined until the scope of the "expression" and fair use are defined by litigation. Comparisons are summarized in the table below.

Table 3-1. Comparing Patents and Copyrights

Patents	Copyrights
Property right	Property right
Original purpose: Reward innovation by control of process	Original purpose: Reward creation of cultural works and knowledge by inhibiting copies
Sharply defined	Conceptual
Examined before issued	Automatic; self issue
Short term (relatively)	Long term (a very long time today)
Clear notice to others (Claims!)	Must judge for oneself (What is expressed?)
Litigate scope of claims; validity	Litigate to determine expression; existence of privilege to copy (fair use)
Hard edged control over process	Soft edged "control" over copies
Expanded protection. Now includes software and applied algorithms, etc.	Now includes software, including operating systems, microcode, etc.
Expense of litigation gives advantage to deep pockets owner	Expense of litigation gives advantage to deep pockets owner

Maps and Photographs

As with patent law, copyright law is established pursuant to a constitutional provision: "The Congress shall have Power. To promote the Progress of Science and useful Arts, by securing for limited Times to *Authors* and Inventors the exclusive Right to their respective *Writings* and Discoveries." U.S. Const. art. I § 8, cl. 8. (Italics added.) Only Congress can establish national copyright laws.[30]

The scope of the constitutional power depends on two questions: What is a writing? Who can be an author? Congress may act, but only to protect writings. Is a map a writing? Is a photo a writing? Who or what can qualify an author?

We commonly refer to writings and pictures as different sorts of things. The adage "a picture is worth a thousand words" emphasizes the difference. Also, we do not refer to a painter as an author. On the other hand, when taking down notes during a voyage one may choose to sketch a drawing of a situation rather than rely on words. At the time the Constitution was adopted, drawing accurate maps was one of the principal purposes of exploratory expeditions. The notes of George Vancouver's explorations of the Pacific Northwest in 1791–95 were filled with sketches and maps. Would these maps have been considered writings at that time? In its first session, Congress considered that question and granted copyright protection to maps. The second session added engravings.[31] Thus, contemporaneously with the framing of the Constitution, Congress expressed a view that "writings" was a broad category.

In 1865, the copyright law was amended to "include photographs and the negatives thereof which shall hereafter be made, and shall enure to the benefit of the authors of the same in the same manner, and to the same extent, and upon the same conditions as to the authors of prints and engravings." In the early nineteenth century creating maps and etchings involved human labor of sketching and engraving images, but a photograph gave protection to an image created immediately by a machine, a camera.

This change raised new issues: Could a machine be an author? Had Congress gone beyond its powers in this act? In 1884, a case involving this issue reached

---

30. There is, for example, no federal "common law copyright." The individual states were permitted to recognize a common law copyright until Congress abolished it by the 1976 Copyright Act. The Supreme Court rejected such a federal common law early United States history. "It is clear, there can be no common law of the United States. The federal government is composed of ... sovereign and independent states; each of which may have its local usages, customs and common law. There is no principle which pervades the union and has the authority of law, that is not embodied in the constitution or laws of the union. The common law could be made a part of our federal system, only by legislative adoption." Wheaton v. Peters, 8 Pet [33 U.S.] 591 at 659 (1834).

31. 1 Stat. 124 (1790) and 2 Stat 171 (1802).

Figure 3-1. Oscar Wilde, Sarony Photo

Source: Corbis Images, used with permission.

the Supreme Court. The decision and its reasoning marked the boundaries of copyright in ways that influence the law to this day.

In the 1880s, a celebrated American photographer, Napoleon Sarony, made a series of photographs of the English writer, Oscar Wilde. One of these photos was reproduced without Sarony's consent by Burrow-Giles Lithographic Company, which sold many thousands of copies.[32] Sarony sued Burrow-Giles. He won and was awarded a substantial sum in damages. Burrow-Giles obtained a review by the Supreme Court. The lithographer contended that the Copyright Act could not constitutionally extend to a photograph. Unlike maps and written documents of the time, the original of a photo was sketched by a piece of machinery. Burrows-Giles argued machine could not be an author, thus the photograph could not qualify for copyright.

The Supreme Court ruled in favor of Sarony, holding that a posed photograph could qualify for copyright protection. Here are some extracts from the Court's opinion.

> The constitutional question is not free from difficulty.... The argument here is that a photograph is not a writing nor the production of an author ...
>
> The first congress of the United States, sitting immediately after the formation of the constitution, enacted that the 'author or authors of any map, chart, book, or books, ... shall have the sole right and liberty of printing, reprinting, publishing, and vending the same for the period of fourteen years'....
>
> The construction placed upon the constitution by the first act of 1790 and the act of 1802, by the men who were contemporary with its formation, many of whom were members of the convention which framed it, is of itself entitled to very great weight, and when it is remembered that the rights thus established have not been disputed during a period of nearly a century, it is almost conclusive. Unless, therefore, photographs can be distinguished in the classification of this point from the maps, charts, designs, engravings, etchings, cuts, and other prints, it is difficult to see why congress cannot make them the subject of copyright as well as the others. These statutes certainly answer the objection that books only, or writing, in the limited sense of a book and its author, are within the constitutional provision. Both these words are susceptible of a more enlarged definition than this. An author in that sense is 'he to whom anything owes its origin; originator; maker; one who completes a work of science or literature.'....
>
> The only reason why photographs were not included in the extended

---

32. Burrow-Giles reproduced the photographs by a photolithographic process. Thus, its process combined the older notion of handmade lithography with the newfangled invention, photography.

list in the act of 1802 is, probably, that they did not exist, as photography, as an art, was then unknown, and the scientific principle on which it rests, and the chemicals and machinery by which it is operated, have all been discovered long since that statute was enacted.[33]

Having decided that a photo qualifies as a writing, the Court proceeded to examine who the "author" was. Was it the camera, a mechanical thing, or was it the photographer?

But it is said that an engraving, a painting, a print, does embody the intellectual conception of its author, in which there is novelty, invention, originality, and therefore comes within the purpose of the constitution in securing its exclusive use or sale to its author, while a photograph is the mere mechanical reproduction of the physical features or outlines of some object ...

The third finding of facts [by the trial court] says, in regard to the photograph in question, that it is a 'useful, new, harmonious, characteristic, and graceful picture, and that plaintiff made the same entirely from his own original mental conception, to which he gave visible form by posing the said Oscar Wilde in front of the camera, selecting and arranging the costume, draperies, and other various accessories in said photograph, arranging the subject so as to present graceful outlines, arranging and disposing the light and shade, suggesting and evoking the desired expression, and from such disposition, arrangement, or representation, made entirely by plaintiff, he produced the picture in suit.' These findings, we think, show this photograph to be an original work of art, the product of plaintiff's intellectual invention, of which plaintiff is the author.[34]

The Court concluded that Sarony, exercised his creativity by posing Wilde and choosing lighting effects. The factual determinations made by the trial court were crucial in coming to this conclusion. As a general rule, appellate courts, including the Supreme Court, accept what a trial judge or jury decides were the facts. This is because a trial court sees and hears the witnesses and looks over the other evidence as it is presented in court; an appellate court does not. A trial judge or jury is in a far better position to evaluate the evidence, thus, an appellate court accepts its decision as to what the facts of the case were. Findings of facts play an extremely important role in copyright law.

---

33. Burrow-Giles Lithographic Co. v. Sarony, 111 U.S. 53, 58 (1884) (italics added).
34. Burrow-Giles Lithographic Co. v. Sarony, 111 U.S. 53, 60–61 (italics added).

The extent to which an author's work is an "expression" as opposed to underlying ideas or a system is largely a question of fact. If someone else has made a similar work, that work only violates the first author's copyright if it has been copied. Independent creation of a similar work is not copying. Whether the second party copied the first work is also a question of fact. To copy one must have seen the first work. Having access to a prior work is some evidence that one might have seen it. Also, similarity to the first work is important evidence. Thus, access plus similarity provides a basis for deciding whether there has been copying.

The century and more since the *Sarony* case has seen huge advances in photography. Now one can buy a digital camera that automatically focuses and compensates for all sorts of photographer ineptitude. One can simply point and shoot. In addition, digital photography offers enhanced means for the photographer to manipulate, color, crop, or alter images after the shoot.

The current state of the law is to accept photography to the fullest extent — the camera pointed by the tourist to catch a candid shot will get full copyright protection.[35] Thus, authorship may come down to simply being on the scene and pointing a camera. One example, famous at the time, was the filming of the assassination of President John F. Kennedy by Abraham Zapruder, a Kennedy admirer who happened to be on the spot when the President was shot. His film was about thirty seconds long and was taken with a state of the art camera from a good vantage point. He sold his film rights to *Time* magazine. In a case which evolved from that sale, the trial judge had no difficulty finding that the film was copyrighted.[36]

---

35. For example, in Gener-Villar v. Adcom Group, Inc., 560 F. Supp. 2d 112 (D.P.R. 2008) a trial judge concluded that digital photos of products which had been cropped and manipulated by using a computer program (Photoshop) were copyrightable. The case is also a good example of how a trial judge states findings of fact.

36. The judge stated: "The Zapruder pictures in fact have many elements of creativity. Among other things, Zapruder selected the kind of camera (movies, not snapshots), the kind of film (color), the kind of lens (telephoto), the area in which the pictures were to be taken, the time they were to be taken, and (after testing several sites) the spot on which the camera would be operated." Time, Inc. v. Bernard Geis Associates, 293 F. Supp. 130, 143 (S.D.N.Y. 1968). The defendant's use of the film was found to be fair, therefore privileged.

Phonebooks and Originality

Infringement

As we have seen, 17 U.S.C. §106 grants six exclusive rights: copy, derive, distribute, perform (performable works), display, and perform digital sound recordings. Anyone who does any of those things without the permission of the copyright holder may be subject to suit for infringement. One who claims infringement must show the work has been registered, that he is the owner, and that one of those six rights has been violated.[37]

The core concept is copying. One has to peek at another's work and copy it. Thus, independent creation does not violate copyright, nor does using the underlying ideas. In *Sarony* it was quite clear that the defendant had copied Sarony's work. "A jury being waived, the court made a finding of facts on which a judgment in favor of the plaintiff was rendered for the sum of $600 for the plates and 85,000 copies sold and exposed to sale, and $10 for copies found in his possession." The copying was clear. The whole point of the defendant's activity had been to make good photolithographic copies of the Sarony photo and sell them, and it does not appear that the defendant contested the matter of copying.

In other cases, proof of copying is hotly contested. A work does not infringe simply because its expressions are similar. Expressions may be similar without being copied. Often there is no direct evidence of the copying, such as a witness to the process. Thus, a plaintiff often proves copying by creating an inference: The defendant saw or heard the work and the defendant's work is much the same as that of the plaintiff. Therefore, he probably copied it. The inference is like seeing the postman drive up, open up the mail box and reach in: One infers he or she dropped off mail—or picked some up.

Professor Alan Latman summed up proof of infringement: "Since direct evidence of copying is rarely, if ever, available, a plaintiff may prove copying by showing access and 'substantial similarity'... his kind of litany, laced with respectable authorities, is intoned fairly early in the legal analyses of many thoughtful judicial opinions addressing issues of copyright infringement."[38]

---

37. Feist Publications, Inc. v. Rural Tel. Serv. Co., 499 U.S. 340, 350–53 (1991).

38. Alan Latman, *"Probative Similarity" as Proof of Copying: Toward Dispelling Some Myths in Copyright Infringement,* 90 COLUM. L. REV. 1187, 1188 (1990). The article was published six years after Professor Latman's death. The editors noted that his incomplete manuscript "was already well formulated and near completion, bearing the hallmark of Professor Latman's eloquence, insight and erudition." Zella v. E.W. Scripps Co., 529 F. Supp. 2d 1124 (C.D.Cal. 2007) provides a good example of proof of "substantially similar."

Today, many works are created or stored by digital means. Copying of such works does often provide direct evidence of copying. For example, evidence of downloading or similar computer files may show copying.

What Is Original Work?

A photographer like Sarony qualifies as an originator or author, thus his work qualifies for protection. Sarony was the one who arranged the lighting, costume and pose of Oscar Wilde. Is there any minimum quantum of creativity that the author must contribute? Patent law requires that an inventor demonstrate novelty to the Patent Office to gain a patent, but copyright law requires no such demonstration. The copyright is automatic, and inspiration, whimsy, even being on the spot to catch a photo of a commonplace event provides sufficient creativity. Congress can supply any limits it wishes, but has not chosen to do so except to require "originality." In *Sarony* the Court accepted posing and artistic arrangement of a model as meeting the constitutional standard. How much judgment or creativity must one apply to be an author? A century later the Supreme Court returned to the question of the threshold of originality for copyright.

In *Feist Publications, Inc. v. Rural Tel. Serv. Co.*, 499 U.S. 340 (1991), Feist published regional telephone directories, which allowed telephone users to look at one directory rather than several local ones to find a number. Feist sought Rural's permission to copy its local white pages and include them in its directory. Rural refused, but Feist went ahead and copied them anyway. It edited them and included the copied material in its regional directory. Rural sued Feist for infringement and won its case at both trial and appellate levels. A long string of federal cases had held that telephone directories are copyrightable arrangements of data. The Supreme Court granted review of the case.

As in *Sarony*, it was clear that the defendant, Feist, had copied the plaintiff's work. However, the information in the directories was factual. The Court stated:

> The *sine qua non* of copyright is originality. To qualify for copyright protection, a work must be original to the author.... Original, as the term is used in copyright, means only that the work was independently created by the author (as opposed to copied from other works), and that it possesses at least some minimal degree of creativity.... To be sure, the requisite level of creativity is extremely low; even a slight amount will suffice.[39]

---

39. 499 U.S. 340, 345–6.

The Court held that the Constitution requires an author to contribute some minimum of originality, such as selection and arrangement. It stated that "there is nothing remotely creative about arranging names alphabetically in a white pages directory. It is an age-old practice, firmly rooted in tradition and so commonplace that it has come to be expected as a matter of course." The Court rejected the proposition that effort, such as gathering data, suffices to create a copyright. The Court stated, "In summary, the 1976 revisions to the Copyright Act leave no doubt that originality, not 'sweat of the brow,' is the touchstone of copyright protection in directories and other fact-based works."[40] Thus, the Court concluded, "copyright in a factual compilation is thin."

Software

As with photography, it was not originally clear that copyright extends to software. In 1978 Congress established the National Commission on New Technological Uses of Copyrighted Works (CONTU) to look into the matter. CONTU concluded that the 1976 Act needed clarification to assure software was covered. The commission recommended that the 1976 copyright law "should be amended ... to make it explicit that computer programs, to the extent that they embody an author's original creation, are proper subject matter of copyright." Commissioner and author John Hersey dissented from part of the recommendation. He agreed that copyright is appropriate for the human readable renditions of programs, but is "an inappropriate, as well as unnecessary, way of protecting the usable forms of computer programs." He explained:

> [A] program, once it enters a computer and is activated, does not communicate information of its own, intelligible to a human being. It utters work. Work is its only utterance and its only purpose. So far as the mode of expression of the original writing is concerned, the matter ends there; it has indeed become irrelevant even before that point. The mature program is purely and simply a mechanical substitute for human labor.[41]

---

40. 499 U.S. 340, 359–60.

41. 1978 Nat'l Commission of New Tech. Uses of Copyrighted Works, Hersey dissent, online at CONTU Final Report, http://digital-law-online.info/CONTU/PDF. John Hersey was the author of *A Bell for Adano* (1945) and *Hiroshima* (1948). *Hiroshima* begins: "At, exactly fifteen minutes past eight in the morning on August 6, 1945, Japanese time, at the moment when the atomic bomb flashed above Hiroshima, Miss Toshiko Sasaki, a clerk in

In 1980, Congress amended the Act, adding two provisions, that by implication indicated that programs could be copyrighted. One provision defined a "computer program" as "a set of statements or instructions to be used directly or indirectly in a computer in order to bring about a certain result." The second one provided that "it is not an infringement for the rightful possessor of a copy of a computer program," when doing so is an essential step in actually using the program. The Courts agreed that these provisions showed congressional intent to extend copyright to programs, and now it is firmly established that copyright law cover computer programs. The protection extends to such things as word processors, digital photography systems, computer operating systems, and even smaller blocks of code.

One of the first cases to consider extending copyright to software was *Williams Electronics, Inc. v. Artic International, Inc.*, 685 F.2d 870 (3d Cir.1982). Williams claimed that Artic had copied its video game program. Such a program creates an output which a human fully understands. Two years later, in *Apple Computer, Inc. v. Franklin Computer Corp*, 714 F.2d 1240 (3d Cir.1984) the same circuit considered whether Act also would protect a computer operating system, a type of software which does not communicate to a human. Thus, it raised the type of issue that triggered John Hersey's dissent. The Court ruled that it did.

> Both types of programs instruct the computer to do something. Since it is only the instructions which are protected, a "process" is no more involved because the instructions in an operating system program may be used to activate the operation of the computer than it would be if instructions were written in ordinary English in a manual which described the necessary steps to activate an intricate complicated machine. There is, therefore, no reason to afford any less copyright protection to the instructions in an operating system program than to the instructions in an application program.[42]

The Third Circuit's decision became a leading case, and it has been followed by a host of others which accept that all forms of software may be a subject of copyright.

---

the personnel department of the East Asia Tin Works, had just sat down at her place in the plant office and was turning her head to speak to the girl at the next desk."

42. Apple Computer, Inc. v. Franklin Computer Corp, 714 F.2d 1240, 1251 (3rd Cir. 1984), cert. dismissed, 464 U.S. 1033, 104 S.Ct. 690, 79 L.Ed.2d 158 (1984). The Ninth Circuit came to the same conclusion later that year. Apple Computer, Inc. v. Formula Int'l Inc., 725 F.2d 521, 524–25 (9th Cir.1984).

It is difficult to reconcile copyright protection of a functional work, like an operating system, with a basic provision of the Act: "In no case does copyright protection for an original work of authorship extend to any idea, procedure, process, system, method of operation, concept, principle, or discovery, regardless of the form in which it is described, explained, illustrated, or embodied in such work."[43] The Courts have faced numerous cases that require them to decide whether an essentially functional program is protected or not. The decisions have focussed on the exclusion of ideas, rather than the exclusion of processes, systems and methods of operation.

One of the most helpful cases in understanding this issue is *Computer Assoc. Int'l, Inc. v. Altai, Inc.*, 982 F.2d 693 (2d Cir.1992). The program at issue was an internal control program called "ADAPTER" whose function "allows a computer user to change or use multiple operating systems while maintaining the same software."[44] The Court affirmed the District Court's decision that ADAPTER was not protectable by copyright. It discussed the difficulty of separating that which is subject to copyright from that which is not:

> The essentially utilitarian nature of a computer program further complicates the task of distilling its idea from its expression.... The variations of expression found in purely creative compositions, as opposed to those contained in utilitarian works, are not directed towards practical application. For example, a narration of Humpty Dumpty's demise, which would clearly be a creative composition, does not serve the same ends as, say, a recipe for scrambled eggs-which is a more process oriented text. Thus, compared to aesthetic works, computer programs hover even more closely to the elusive boundary line described in § 102(b).[45]

The Supreme Court has never addressed the issue. The closest it has come was affirming a Court of Appeals decision which had held that a series of key stroke commands could not be protected by copyright. There was no opinion by the Court other than to affirm the judgment below.[46]

To summarize: Copyright covers writings, songs, movies, photos, software—any fixed "expression." Unauthorized copying creates a *prima facie* case

---

43. 17 U.S.C. § 102(b).

44. 982 F.2d 693, 698.

45. 982 F.2d 693, 705. See also, Lexmark Int'l, Inc. v. Static Control Components, Inc., 387 F.3d 522 (6th Cir.2004).

46. Lotus Development Corp. v. Borland Intern., Inc., 49 F.3d 807, (1st Cir.1995), judgment aff'd by an equally divided court without opinion, 516 U.S. 233 (1996).

Table 3-2. Matrix of Copyright Liability

Fixed expression is immediately owned by copyright.
Copying the expression equals infringement; "*prima facie* case."
No liability if copying is judged to be fair use.
High statutory damages, preliminary injunctions, and "deep pocket" copyright owners, deter free exercise of fair use privilege.

of infringement. However, copying is completely legal when it is "fair use." We next examine the privilege of fair use.

Fair Use and Reverse Engineering

"Fair use" includes any reasonable use of copyrighted expressions in a way that does not undermine the value of the expression. The Supreme Court explained the basis of this broad privilege:

> From the infancy of copyright protection, some opportunity for fair use of copyrighted materials has been thought necessary to fulfill copyright's very purpose, "[t]o promote the Progress of Science and useful Arts. For as Justice Story explained, "[i]n truth, in literature, in science and in art, there are, and can be, few, if any, things, which in an abstract sense, are strictly new and original throughout. Every book in literature, science and art, borrows, and must necessarily borrow, and use much which was well known and used before." ... Similarly, Lord Ellenborough expressed the inherent tension in the need simultaneously to protect copyrighted material and to allow others to build upon it when he wrote, "while I shall think myself bound to secure every man in the enjoyment of his copy-right, one must not put manacles upon science."[47]

The law refines the term, "fair use," and explains its conditions, yet seeks to achieve the balance expressed above.

The fair use privilege has been codified at 17 U.S.C. § 107, which the Supreme Court states "continues the common-law tradition of fair use adjudication and

---

47. Campbell v. Acuff-Rose Music, Inc., 510 U.S. 569, 575 (1993).

requires case-by-case analysis rather than bright-line rules." The statute lists four factors to help evaluate fairness:

- the purpose of the copying,
- the nature of the copied work,
- the amount copied, and
- the effect that copying has on market for the copied work.

The factors are not exclusive. Any circumstance which bears on fairness may be considered. The congressional report which accompanied the bill stated:

> Although the courts have considered and ruled upon the fair use doctrine over and over again, no real definition of the concept has ever emerged. Indeed, since the doctrine is an equitable rule of reason, no generally applicable definition is possible, and each case raising the question must be decided on its own facts. On the other hand, the courts have evolved a set of criteria which, though in no case definitive or determinative, provide some gauge for balancing the equities.[48]

Many types of copying are protected by this concept of fairness. In fact, modern communications depend on copying to in order to relay information. On a regular basis email users copy and mail items to each other for comment. Teachers copy items so students may see and refer to them in discussion. Quotations copied for comment, excerpts passed around to discuss, film clips shown for illustration are all very likely to be covered by fair use.

The Ninth Circuit Court of Appeals has provided the following suggested jury instruction on fair use:

> One who is not the owner of the copyright may use the copyrighted work in a reasonable way under the circumstances without the consent of the copyright owner if it would advance the public interest. Such use of a copyrighted work is termed fair use. The owner of a copyright cannot prevent others from making a fair use of the owner's copyrighted work.[49]

The Copyright Office offers the following guideline on its website:

> Under the fair use doctrine of the U.S. copyright statute, it is permissible to use limited portions of a work including quotes, for pur-

---

48. H.R. No. 94–1476 (1976). 17 U.S.C. § 107.

49. Ninth Circuit Model Civil Jury Instructions 17.18 Copyright—Affirmative Defense—Fair Use (17 U.S.C. § 107). http://www.ce9.uscourts.gov.

poses such as commentary, criticism, news reporting, and scholarly reports. There are no legal rules permitting the use of a specific number of words, a certain number of musical notes, or percentage of a work. Whether a particular use qualifies as fair use depends on all the circumstances.[50]

While the concept of fair use is intentionally broad, a provision allows a copyright owner to collect either actual damages or statutory damages, which require no proof of any harm. If a copyright owner shows that the infringement was in some sense "willful," it may collect massive damages without proving any actual harm. In such a case, the Act provides that the owner must be awarded at least $750 and up to $150,000 for each infringement, without proving a penny of actual loss.[51] For example, in 2009, a jury returned a verdict of two million dollars against a Minnesota woman, Jammie Thomas-Rasset, who had shared twenty four songs through an online service.[52] The jury was within its authority in giving this disproportionate award. The trial judge, Michael Davis, stated that he had "labored to fashion a reasonable limit on statutory damages" reduced it to a still staggering $54,000 which he stated remained "significant and harsh."

In 2010, a District Court in Washington, DC ruled that a $670,000 statutory damage award against a willful infringer who downloaded thirty songs violated the due process clause of the Constitution. The Judge, Nancy Gertner, reduced the award to $2,250 per infringed work. Statutory damages continue to be available against infringers, unless the statute is amended or the Supreme Court strikes down the provision. Rulings in one federal district do not bind other federal courts.[53]

Software raises new questions concerning fairness. One of these is compatibility or the ability to get components to work together. A typical desk lamp illustrates compatibility. If the bulb burns out, one needs a replacement

---

50. See Fair Use, and Circular 21, Reproductions of Copyrighted Works by Educators and Librarians. U.S. Copyright Office—Can I Use Someone Else's Work? Can Someone Else Use Mine? (FAQ)—http://www.copyright.gov/help/faq/faq-fairuse.html. The url may change, but the Copyright Office continues to maintain such general guidance.

51. 17 U.S.C. §504 (c).

52. On June 19, 2009, the London Times reported that Ms. Rasset is a single mother with four children. Times Online, http://technology.timesonline.co.uk/tol/news/tech_and_web/article6534542.ece.

53. Sony BMG Music Entertainment v. Tenenbaum, 2010 WL 2705499, 93 U.S.P.Q.2d 1867 (D.Mass. 2010). The Judge reduced the award to $2,250 per infringed work. The case will likely be appealed.

Figure 3-2. Plugs as Interface

that will fit into the socket. The components of household light fixtures and lamps were standardized close to a hundred years ago. Thus, when one re-places a bulb or repairs a standard old fashioned lamp, one can usually pick up needed parts without much difficulty.

Computers and other digital products require additional forms of compat-ibility. Not only must they be able to connect physically, but their software must be compatible, as well. For example, a computer and a printer must have a cable that will connect to each of the two devices In addition, the software that controls the computer must be able to send commands back and forth to the software that controls the printer, called the "printer driver." The public benefits from compatibility, and so do many manufacturers. Some manufac-turers, however, derive greater profits if their products are compatible only with products that they make of license.

The video game industry provides an example of a struggle over software compatibility. Video games generate avid players and communities of players. These games can be designed to be played on either a computer or on a spe-cial console. The console type of game can offer more complete sound and sight effects, plus sensations, such as vibrations. A popular console maker might make more money if the public must buy only games that it produces or licenses. That is, it may profit by restricting the electronic compatibility of its console.

Sega Enters. Ltd. v. Accolade, Inc., 977 F.2d 1510 (9th Cir. 1992), tested the limits of the incompatibility strategy. In the 1980s, Accolade, a California computer game company, produced video games that ran on a variety of computers available at that time, including the Commodore 64, Atari 800, the Amiga, Apple II and IBM compatible PCs. Around that time, many of these computer platforms began to disappear from the market, while the market for games played on video game consoles soared. In the 1990s, Accolade responded to that shift and decided to move its game development into the production of games that would run on the popular Genesis computer game console produced by Sega Enterprises.

Sega's game consoles were designed with a digital lock that allowed them to play only games produced or licensed by Sega. Accolade decided to try to enter the Sega game market by producing Genesis compatible games without obtaining a license from Sega. To succeed the Accolade compatibility would have to be as smooth and seamless as playing a CD on a CD player. In effect, it had to provide a key to unlock the digital lock. To do that it would have to study the code and develop its own software key.

However, Accolade faced a hurdle in studying the code that was embodied in the Sega games. That code was in the electronic equivalent of ones and zeros. Thus, it was virtually impossible to "read" the code in order to study it. Accolade's solution was to "reverse engineer" Sega game cartridges. Reverse engineering is the equivalent of taking a watch or radio apart to see how it works. The Court described the reverse engineering process:

> Accolade transformed the machine-readable object code contained in commercially available copies of Sega's game cartridges into human-readable source code using a process called "disassembly" or "decompilation." Accolade purchased a Genesis console and three Sega game cartridges, wired a decompiler into the console circuitry, and generated printouts of the resulting source code. Accolade engineers studied and annotated the printouts in order to identify areas of commonality among the three game programs. They then loaded the disassembled code back into a computer, and experimented to discover the interface specifications for the Genesis console by modifying the programs and studying the results. At the end of the reverse engineering process, Accolade created a development manual that incorporated the information it had discovered about the requirements for a Genesis-compatible game. According to the Accolade employees who created the manual, the manual contained only functional descriptions of the interface requirements and did not include any of Sega's code.[54]

---

54. 977 F.2d 1510, 1514–15.

The decompilation process included making an unauthorized copy of Sega's code. After the decompilation and subsequent study, other Accolade engineers were able to write new code of their own code, including a "key" that would allow compatibility.

Sega sued Accolade and was granted a preliminary injunction. The injunction enjoined Accolade and its agents from "assembling, translating, converting or adapting the copyrighted object code in SEL's game programs in any manner whatsoever." That injunction would effectively have put Accolade out of business.

Accolade appealed. The Court of Appeals held that disassembly to achieve compatibility is privileged by the fair use doctrine. It ruled that copyright law does not grant the holder a monopoly over games that will play on a machine it produces. Accolade did not market any of the copied code, it simply used its knowledge to develop competing different games. The Court stated that "Accolade's identification of the functional requirements for Genesis compatibility has led to an increase in the number of independently designed video game programs offered for use with the Genesis console. It is precisely this growth in creative expression ... that the Copyright Act was intended to promote."[55]

In 1998, Congress enacted the Digital Millennium Copyright Act (DMCA).[56] A major feature of the DMCA is to make digital locks of the kind used by Sega legally enforceable. If a piece of software or database contains some copyrightable work, circumventing a digital lock may create severe civil and criminal liability.[57] This liability is independent of the traditional copyright liability we have discussed so far.

The DMCA provides a reverse engineering privilege, allowing one to copy portions of a digital lock in a computer program if one has legally obtained a copy of the program and "the sole purpose of identifying and analyzing those elements of the program that are necessary to achieve interoperability of an independently created computer program."[58] In addition, the DMCA provides that nothing in the anticircumvention provisions "shall affect rights, remedies, limitations, or defenses to copyright infringement, including fair use" in the Copyright Act.[59]

We now turn to other considerations of fair use, specifically transforming expressions into an essentially new work.

---

55. 977 F.2d 1510, 1523.
56. 17 U.S.C. §1201 *et seq.*
57. 17 U.S.C. §1201 (a).
58. See Davidson & Assocs. v. Jung, 422 F.3d 630 (8th Cir. 2005).
59. 17 U.S.C. §1201 (c).

Parody and Transformation

Roy Orbison composed and recorded the song "Oh, Pretty Woman" in 1964. In the late 1980s, Luther Campbell wrote a song "Pretty Woman." His rap group, 2 Live Crew, soon recorded and released the song. The first bars of the music are unmistakably a rendition of Orbison's song. The similarity of the two works prompted Acuff Rose Music, owner of the "Oh, Pretty Woman" copyright, to sue for infringement. The trial court found that Campbell's song was a parody entitled to be privileged as fair use. The Supreme Court affirmed that decision.[60]

The first twenty seconds of each song sound nearly identical. They have the same beat and general feel.[61] After that, Campbell's ballad diverges in sound and content. The song style becomes rap, rather than smooth. Different voices sing each verse. The entire group performs a chorus. The music, lyrics and performance all depart from the original. The trial judge commented on the lyrics:

> The physical attributes of the subject woman deviate from a pleasing image of femininity to bald-headed, hairy and generally repugnant. To complete the thematic twist, at the end of the parody the "two-timin" woman turns out to be pregnant. The phrase, 'the baby ain't mine' is completely inconsistent with the tone and story of the romantic original. In sum, 2 Live Crew is an anti-establishment rap group and this song derisively demonstrates how bland and banal the Orbison song seems to them.[62]

The Supreme Court ruled unanimously that a judge or jury could readily find that the spoof was fair use. That determination for all practical purposes decided the case in favor of 2 Live Crew. "Parody needs to mimic an original to make its point," the Court said. Copying was clear and extensive, but there could be no liability if the use was fair. Parody, "like any other use, has to work

---

60. Acuff-Rose Music, Inc. v. Campbell, 754 F. Supp. 1150, (M.D. Tenn. 1991); Campbell v. Acuff-Rose Music, Inc., 510 U.S. 569 (1993).

61. "The parody also employs a number of musical devices that exaggerate the original and help to create a comic effect. 2 Live Crew uses the same drum beat and bass riff to start its song. But unlike the original, only five seconds into the song and immediately following the bass riff, 2 Live Crew inserts a heavily distorted "scraper," indicating a significant disparity in style.... In addition, four times during the parody, 2 Live Crew repeats Orbison's bass riff over and over again, double the number of times on the original, until the riff begins to sound like annoying scratch on a record." 754 F. Supp. 1150, 1155 (M.D. Tenn.1991)

62. 754 F. Supp. 1150, 1155.

Figure 3-3. "Pretty Woman" Parody

its way through the relevant factors, and be judged case by case, in light of the ends of the copyright law."[63]

The "Pretty Woman" case emphasizes transformation of one work into an essentially different one. If a new work substantially transforms a work it copies,

---

63. Campbell v. Acuff-Rose Music, Inc., 510 U.S. 569 (1993).

Table 3-3. Pretty Woman (Verse 2)

Orbison	2 Live Crew
Pretty woman, won't you pardon me Pretty woman, I couldn't help see Pretty woman That you look lovely as can be Are you lonely just like me Wow	Big hairy woman, you need to shave that stuff, Big hairy woman, you know I bet its tough. Big hairy woman, all that hair ain't legit, cause you look like cousin it. Big hairy woman

it may be judged a fair use. Because the reward for copyright is commercial advantage, courts have often presumed that a commercial copying is unfair. The lower court in the "Pretty Woman" case had reasoned that because "the use of the copyrighted work is wholly commercial, ... we presume that a likelihood of future harm to Acuff-Rose exists." The Supreme Court rejected that idea. It stated that if the second use is transformative then the harm to the original is less likely. When "the second use is transformative, market substitution is at least less certain, and market harm may not be so readily inferred."[64]

Derivative Works

The owner of a copyright also owns works that are based on the original. These are called "derivative works."[65] Thus, in a case like the "Pretty Woman" case, a plaintiff might claim that it should win anyway, because it owned the transformation! While logical, such a claim should be rejected, as it would have the effect of reducing the statutory privilege to a nullity.[66] Instead, the right to claim ownership of a derivative work should also be limited by fair use privilege. The following case illustrates an example of the limitations of a derivative work claim.

In 2001, Alice Randall wrote *The Wind Done Gone (TWDG)* retelling *Gone with the Wind (GWTW),* but from a slave's point of view.[67] Suntrust Bank, the

---

64. 510 U.S. 569, 591.

65. 17 U.S.C. §106 gives a copyright owner the exclusive right to "to prepare derivative works based upon the copyrighted work." The act defines a derivative work: "a work based upon one or more preexisting works." 17 U.S.C. §101.

66. The Supreme Court, however, did not address that matter. The question before it was whether 2 Live Crew's version infringed, not who was the rightful owner of the parody. The Court commented that it was unlikely that one would lampoon one's own work. 510 U.S. 569, 591.

67. Suntrust Bank v. Houghton Mifflin Co., 268 F.3d 1257 (11th Cir. 2001), Rehearing and Rehearing *en Banc* denied 275 F.3d 58 (2001).

owner of the *GWTW* copyright sued Randall's publisher, Houghton Mifflin for copyright infringement, particularly urging that *TWDG* was an unauthorized derivative work. At the outset, the court noted that *Gone with the Wind* "has become one of the best-selling books in the world, second in sales only to the Bible." Randall had used the plot, characters, scenes, relationships, and verbatim dialogues and descriptions in her book. However, the Court of Appeals stated that Randall "persuasively claims that her novel is a critique of *GWTW*'s depiction of slavery and the Civil-War era American South." The Court dissolved an injunction which the District Court had entered and sent the case back for further proceedings. It concluded that Houghton Mifflin had established a clear basis for proving its claim that Randall's use of extensive details was protected by fair use.

Internet

The Internet is like an electronic spider web cast around the globe. The network depends on physical infrastructure such as telephone lines and fiber optics.[68] The messages are sent through many alternative routes, much like city streets. Email is one of the simplest forms of Internet communication, as it simply sends messages back and forth among fixed addresses. The World Wide Web (WWW or the Web) provides a mass of data that can be accessed from anywhere in the world. This worldwide data base generates needs and problems to be resolved. These include: How does one find what one wishes? Who will control access? How will the infrastructure and effort involved be paid for? With such a mass of connections among computers and their databases, one would be overwhelmed trying to find things if there were no tools to help.

The perfection of "hypertext" aided in the creation of the searchable system of communications we now know as the Web. Hypertext is a system that encodes words, phrases, or images, making them "hyperlinks." When one clicks on a hyperlink, one is immediately connected to another source. By convention, hypertext links appear in a different color from the rest of the text.

Hypertext makes it easier to jump from one Internet location to another in order to find data. It also raises copyright issues of the kind that we have see in other software applications. Each time one downloads, sends, or links an item

---

68. The physical infrastructure is enormous, complex, and It is constantly changing. It is subject to physical damage, and demands huge amounts of energy. See Connecting the Globe: IX. The Internet http://www.fcc.gov/connectglobe/sec9.html.

on the Internet, an electronic version is transmitted from computer to computer over the Web. Thus, multiple copies of fixed works are created immediately. Capturing data in the RAM (random access memory) or volatile memory of a computer fixes a work for copyright purposes.

A 1995 case illustrates the immediate fixing that occurs in a computer environment. A computer manufacturer, MIA, sued an unauthorized repair service, Peak, alleging that Peak temporarily copied its operating system during the repair process. The Ninth Circuit ruled that loading a software diagnostic system into a computer's RAM fixed the program into a medium, even though the "copy" was temporary.[69] One can readily see that copyright and DMCA issues constantly arise in such an environment. In fact, one finds the full range of intellectual property issues will arise.

Perfect 10, Inc. v. Amazon.com, Inc., 508 F.3d 1146 (9th Cir. 2007), illustrates copyright issues that arise. Perfect 10 operates a website that features young nude women. To access the site, one must pay for a password at a fee of $99.50 for six months. The greeting page offers a come-on "tour" of shots of some women, and assures the viewer that by joining the service one can view pictures of thousands of nude women. Google's search engine enables Internet users to search for images of Perfect 10 models and view them in reduced resolution called "thumbnails." One can then click on the thumbnail to view and copy a full resolution image of a women. The full resolution views are ones which have been downloaded by other computer users from Perfect 10 sites. "Google does not store the images ... does not communicate the images to the user; Google simply provides HTML instructions directing a user's browser to access a third-party website."[70] Those third parties have no permission to republish the images. Perfect 10 sued Google for copyright infringement for this practice. In brief, Google's use of thumbnails lets one browse for and retrieve a full-sized view from third party databases. The Court concluded "Perfect 10 has made a *prima facie* case that Google's communication of its stored thumbnail images directly infringes Perfect 10's display right."[71] Thus, Google's storing of reduced resolution images would form the basis for liability, but the

---

69. The Court stated, "by showing that Peak loads the software into the RAM and is then able to view the system error log and diagnose the problem with the computer, MAI has adequately shown that the representation created in the RAM is 'sufficiently permanent or stable to permit it to be perceived, reproduced, or otherwise communicated for a period of more than transitory duration.'" MAI Sys. Corp. v. Peak Computer, Inc., 991 F.2d 511, 518 (9th Cir.1995).

70. 508 F.3d 1146, 1156.

71. 508 F.3d 1146, 1160.

access to full-resolution images not stored by Google would not. However, there would be no liability, if Google's activities constituted fair use.

The Court then turn its attention to the fair use defense. It held that after balancing all the factors, Google's creation, display and use of the smaller thumbnail images was a fair use. The Court emphasized the value of the search engine to users and concluded that the use was "transformative." The Court explained:

> Google's use of thumbnails is highly transformative.... a search engine provides social benefit by incorporating an original work into a new work, namely, an electronic reference tool. Indeed, a search engine may be more transformative than a parody because a search engine provides an entirely new use for the original work, while a parody typically has the same entertainment purpose as the original work.[72]

Without search and reference tools, one gets lost in the mass of information on the Web. Solving that problem was a major factor in determining that Google's activity was fair use.

Practical Guidelines

Copyright cuts across many different fields of endeavor. Here are some practical guidelines:

1. The same basic questions arise whether one seeks to protect one's own work or to avoid liability for infringement of another's work. In either case, one needs to determine what the work expresses. One cannot own ideas, plots, or other building blocks. One needs to be objective when assessing what is expressed and what is taken from other sources. Discuss the problem with a colleague, and when need be, engage an attorney. You do not need to spend an "arm and a leg" getting advice.

2. If you know you are copying another's work, then admit it, and ask: "What am I going to do about this?" "Fair use" is a broad privilege that allows one to copy another's expression in a parody, in a critique, and in a range of other ways. The key is overall fairness. Once again, go over the matter with someone you can trust. Use the factors stated in 17 U.S.C. § 107 as guides: What is my purpose? What type of work am I copying? How does that serve my work? Am I taking more than necessary? What effect will my work have on the market of the other fellow's work? In addition, there are other consid-

---

72. 508 F.3d 1146, 1165–66.

erations of fairness, such as creation of a parody, transforming a work, or providing a necessary service, like a Web search tool.

3. These rules leave great room for anyone to use ideas and make fair use of copyrighted expressions. This allows for a dynamic creative environment. However, the severe consequences of statutory damages and injunctions force one to make tough choices. One cannot "run off and see an attorney" each time a question comes up. Thus, one needs to get a basic grasp of copyright, then exercise judgment on a day-to-day basis. A consultation with an attorney should include setting up guidelines that apply to one's work, then use those guidelines in making day-to-day decisions. When a copyright controversy heats up, get legal advice fast.

4. Copyright owners with deep pockets can afford to bring and defend lawsuits where others cannot. This is a defect in the system, but one which must be reckoned with. An attorney's advice is needed as soon as you perceive that you face an adversary able and willing to employ superior financial resources.

Concluding Observations

Like patent law, copyright is intended to reward creativity that provides benefit to the public at large. In the case of copyright, the degree of creativity required is not high. So long as a minimum of originality is achieved, the copyright to an expression comes into being as soon as the expression is captured in some medium. It extends to all forms of expressions, including software. Public access rights and private control are balanced by two general requirements: A copyright holder must prove that another copied the expression in his work, or did some other statutory equivalent. The alleged infringer enjoys generous privileges of fair use, reverse engineering, and transformation.

Table 3-4. Copyright Guidelines

General Rule	Comment	Source
Subject matter. Any *expression* in any form—a book, song, photo, software, compilation, and derived works.	The manner of portrayal or setting things forth is what is protected, not the underlying facts or principles.	17 U.S.C. §§ 102, 103
"Fixed." The work has to be put into some medium permanent enough to be copied.	Placing something in a transitory RAM computer chip is "permanent" enough.	17 U.S.C. § 101 & § 102 ("fixed")
What rights? Protects against copies or derivative works without permission.	The statute actually lists six separate rights. Core concept is protection against copying.	17 U.S.C. § 106
How long? A very long time. Lifetime plus 70 years for individuals; 95 years for corporations.	The 1976 (works created after 1978) and 1909 (before 1978) provide very different long terms. Compare term with the 20 years for patents.	17 U.S.C. §§,101, 104, and 201, 302–305
Cannot own ideas or systems. Only *expressions* are protected—not the underlying ideas or customary ways of expressing a thing.	Extremely important in things like software. Technology claims are conditioned by public right to use knowledge and unpatented methods.	17 U.S.C. § 102 (b); *Baker v. Selden*, 101 U.S. 99
Fair use. Broad privilege to copy portions (especially for non-commercial uses); "reverse engineering" software.	Basic rule favors uses that do not undermine the value of the work; many specific instances of fair use listed in the statute.	17 U.S.C. § 107; (and §§ 180–182)
Automatic. No filing required; as soon as fixed it is copyrighted.	One must register the work before bringing a law suit and to qualify for some remedies.	17 U.S.C. §§ 401, 411, 101, 106A
Who owns? Author or someone to whom copyright is transferred in writing.	A work made by an employee which is done as part of assigned work belongs to employer.	17 U.S.C. § 201
Original. Must contain a degree of originality, not be a commonplace.	Must originate from author's conception, not be common usage like alphabetical list.	U.S. Const. art I, § 8, *Feist* case
Published or unpublished.	Both receive copyright under 1976 Act.	17 U.S.C. § 104
Registration. Deposit form and copies with Copyright Office. Pay fee.	Easy, inexpensive. Contact Copyright Office. Constitutes evidence of copyright.	17 U.S.C. §§ 408–412
Notice. The familiar © notice is useful, but not required under the current law.	Works created before 1978 and ones not published until 1989 do require notice.	17 U.S.C. §§ 302, 401

Table 3-4. Copyright Guidelines, *continued*

General Rule	Comment	Source
Infringement. A substantial copying. It is judged generally by looking for "substantial similarity."	Access and copying. Mostly a question of fact. Independent creation is not copying. Award of damages, injunctions, attorney fees.	17 U.S.C. §§ 501–513
How to avoid trouble. Check with a thoughtful critic. Ask an attorney in important cases.	Copyright relies on factual judgments about what is expressed, what is copied, and what may be fair use.	17 U.S.C. §§ 102, 107
Major purpose. Reward creativity in cultural works—books, music, etc.	Contrasts with patent which rewards for new useful things and processes.	17 U.S.C. § 102; 35 U.S.C. § 101

Chapter Four

Trademarks

Introduction

A trademark is a mark or symbol used to identify the origin of goods. A service mark is the same thing, but identifies the provider of a service. For convenience, both are generally referred to as trademarks. Each provides a public benefit in the form of identifying a source that one can rely on for quality.

Any identifying word or symbol or other means of identification may be used to mark one's goods. This has been extended to include such things as a single color, a musical phrase or a distinctive restaurant décor. The last item, ambience, décor, or appearance is called "trade dress." The key concept is use *of the mark to identify sources of goods or services. The identifying feature must not serve any function other than identification of source. A carrying handle on a cushion cannot be the cushion maker's trademark, because the handle serves as a means of carrying the cushion. On the other hand, a distinctive nonfunctional design of the handle may serve as a trademark. The point is to distinguish one's product from those of others.*

No application or registration is needed to gain trademark protection under federal or state law, but state or federal registration of a mark provides advantages. For example, a trademark registered on the federal "Principal Register" is presumed valid and becomes incontestable after five years of continuous use.

In addition to protecting a trademark as a means of identifying the source of goods and services, legislation has added special protections for "famous" brands. Such names are now protected against use of the name by others in ways that "dilute" the value of the trademark.

These concepts produce a fluid body of law. A given case may be governed by federal or state law, or a combination of the two. In addition, outcomes of cases are influenced by such transitory things as consumer expectations.

Part I. Concepts

Trademark law originated with simple marking of goods and services with a distinctive mark of some kind. For the most part these were obvious marks and were clearly separate from the goods and services themselves. The law has evolved from that modest origin to include much more than that. The first part of this chapter sets out the evolution of this body of law and the scope of its concepts. The evolution is interesting in itself, and it is essential background for the practical applications which are covered in Part II.

Origins

The origins of Anglo-American trademark law trace to medieval times when merchants marked goods so they would not be lost or taken. The marks would also serve as a form of proof if there were some sort of controversy over ownership. This simple marking practice continued on for centuries. For example, a South Carolina case from 1840 recognized that cattle branding statutes "looked to the preservation of the right of property, against thieves, or open trespassers."[1]

Merchants became aware that marking goods and services would help with transactions in the marketplace. Bakers need high quality, clean flour. Identifying a source would help the bakers find that flour. At the same time a merchant selling the flour would gain by being recognized as a ready source to fill the need.

Building trust and reliance lies at the core of trade. The effort to build reliable trade arrangements extends even further back in time. Herodotus describes an approach taken by ancient Phoenicians when they first arrived on the coasts of West Africa many centuries before the Common Era:

> On reaching land, 'the Carthaginians unload their goods, arrange them in orderly fashion along the beach, and send a smoke signal.' The natives, Herodotus writes, come to examine the goods, 'place on the ground a certain quantity of gold in exchange', then retreat. The Carthaginians 'come ashore and assess the gold. If it is a fair price for their wares, they collect it and depart. If the gold seems too paltry, they go back to their ships and wait for the natives to add more gold.' The system is 'perfectly honest', he adds, 'for the Carthaginians do not

---

1. State v. Smith Chev. 157, 1840 WL 2006 S.C. App. Law 1840.

touch the gold until it equals the goods' value and the natives never touch the wares until the gold is taken'.... Herodotus' report suggests that the Carthaginians and Africans expected repeat visits.[2]

From early on, merchants recognized the power of reputation in the marketplace. That importance grew as markets grew and trade blossomed.

Touting wares likely made an early appearance, too. In England, early advertising took the form of simple signs, including such things as a sandwich board worn to attract attention to the shops of haberdashers, clockmakers, and tea merchants. In 1843, historian Thomas Carlyle had lampooned such "English puffery":

> Consider, for example, that great Hat seven-feet high, ... The Hatter in the Strand of London, instead of making better felt-hats than another, mounts a huge lath-and-plaster Hat, seven-feet high, upon wheels; sends a man to drive it through the streets; hoping to be saved thereby. He has not attempted to make better hats, as he was appointed by the Universe to do, and as with this ingenuity of his he could very probably have done; but his whole industry is turned to persuade us that he has made such![3]

Advertising has burgeoned in the intervening decades. "Branding" has taken on a new meaning, as well. Jay Gronlund, a marketing consultant describes the phenomenon:

> "Branding" is one of the hottest trends in business today. As businesses become more competitive, they increasingly rely on branding to distinguish their product or service. Traditionally it has been the domain of consumer marketers, as they try to build loyal relationships with their customers. However, today the concept of branding is being used for more than just consumer products—corporations, countries, wars ("Desert Storm").[4]

Law professor Laura Heymann comments: "Millions of dollars are spent on advertising campaigns that encourage consumers to create not only an association between the brand and the product but also an association between the

---

2. Adrienne Mayor "Pacesetter," LONDON REVIEW OF BOOKS Vol. 32, No. 12, 24 June 2010, page 30.

3. The Project Gutenberg EBook of Past and Present, by Thomas Carlyle, http://www.gutenberg.org/files/13534/13534.txt.

4. Jay Gronlund, *How Employer Branding Can Foster Trust and Loyalty*, 12-SPRING INT'L HR J. 6 (2003).

brand and the brand's meaning: not only that 'Ford,' means one kind of automobile as opposed to others but also that 'Ford' means, say, patriotic, or nos-
talgic, or dependable."[5] Advertising efforts include indirect influences, such as
product placement, where one may see a movie character working on an Apple
MacBook, while sipping a Pepsi. Since 1976, advertising has been protected
as an exercise of freedom of speech.[6]

In sum, several concepts have evolved and influence modern trademark
usage and law. "Branding," such as was done with cattle, originally meant
simply "these goods belong to me." When the goods got to market, the brand
also served as a convenient way to identify the source of goods one might
purchase. The "brand" became a "mark," a trademark. Today, both branding
and marking have new significances. "Branding" indicates a means of creating appetites or image among consumers. A trademark can capture the ap-
petite or image and thus become a valuable thing in itself. The trademark
then becomes a form of agglomerated wealth, or capital. Many famous marks
have book values in the billions of dollars. The value is just in the name itself; it does not guarantee any origin, producer, or quality. These phenomena have been conflated in much of the scholarly examination of trademark
law and practice.

The advantage of a good business reputation is often referred to as "goodwill."[7] Reputation can be captured in a trademark, and a popular trademark
can become a major asset in business. In addition to marking the goods, trademarks serve as a public image. A mark may develop a certain cachet that will
influence some people to choose it on the basis of brand name alone.

Although marks were used much earlier, English courts appear to have
begun to protect them in the eighteenth century. The first reported English
decision involved a playing card maker who sought to prevent a competitor
from using the mark "Great Mogul" on its cards. Apparently, the plaintiff's
claim of right to the trademark was based on a charter granted by Charles the
First.[8]

---

5. Laura A. Heymann, *Metabranding and Intermediation: A Response to Professor Fleis-
cher,* 12 HARV. NEGOT. L. REV. 201, 203 (2007). See, also, Mark P. McKenna, *Testing Modern Trademark Law's Theory of Harm,* 95 IOWA L. REV. 63, 92–93 (2009).

6. Virginia State Board of Pharmacy v. Virginia Citizens Consumer Council, Inc., 425
U.S. 748 (1976).

7. "Goodwill—the established reputation of a business regarded as a quantifiable asset,
e.g., as represented by the excess of the price paid at a takeover for a company over its fair
market value." Apple Dictionary.

8. Mark P. McKenna, *Normative Foundations of Trademark Law,* 82 NOTRE DAME L.
REV. 1839, 1852 (2007).

Framework of Trademark Laws

Trademarks are created by using a mark to identify a source of goods or services. They are protected by state common law and statutes and by a federal law, the Lanham Act.[9] This dual protection differentiates this area of law from patents and copyrights, which are governed only by federal statutes.

The Lanham Act is broad in its coverage. It defines a trademark as "any word, name, symbol, or device or any combination thereof" used by any person "to identify and distinguish his or her goods, including a unique product, from those manufactured or sold by others and to indicate the source of the goods, even if that source is unknown."[10] Trademarks can be registered with the United States Patent and Trademark Office or under statutory provisions in many states. Federal trademark cases often involve trademarks that developed locally, then were used in interstate trade of some kind. *Use* of a mark is the essential starting point. Thus, trademark protection varies depending on whether a name is protected by state law, federal law, or both. Trademark holders may sue in state and federal courts.[11]

Attorneys and courts apply trademark law in two different ways. The first or "traditional" approach insists that trademark laws serve *only* to assure accurate designation of the origin of goods or services. The second or "modern" approach expands beyond this and allows trademark owners to protect their trademark, even when there is no wrongful or confusing designation of the source of goods. In recent years trademark law has expanded to include the protection of the "fame" of certain brands.[12] These modifications allow trademark law to be used as a basis for legal actions that extend well beyond the

---

9. A working definition of a trademark is: A mark that identifies the source of a good or service. As we shall see, the legal definition depends on state law or the Lanham Act, when federal law applies. The Lanham Act is codified at 15 U.S.C. §§ 1051, *et seq.*

10. 15 U.S.C. § 1127.

11. The Lanham Act allows one to sue to protect any mark against confusing uses so long as the business activity has some significant relation to interstate or foreign commerce. The mark does not have to be federally registered.

12. Mark P. McKenna, *Normative Foundations of Trademark Law*, 82 Notre Dame L. Rev. 1839, 1849–50 (2007) discusses the origins of the "traditional" approach. In another article, Professor McKenna concludes: "Trademark law is in desperate need of a reliable limiting principle.... source indication, like virtually everything else in trademark law, can be determined only from the perspective of consumers. In fact, it is precisely this reliance on consumer understanding, and not courts' failure to apply a robust trademark use doctrine, that is responsible for trademark law's perpetual expansion." Mark P. McKenna, *Trademark Use and the Problem of Source*, 2009 U. Ill. L. Rev. 773, 828 (2009).

borders of misidentification of the source of a product or service. Both of these approaches are in use today.

These two approaches represent a sharp contrast in public policy. The traditional principle recognizes that trademarks are useful to those who provide goods and services and to those who utilize them. Source identification helps create reliability. That reliability seldom, if ever, interferes with one's liberty to engage in a lawful business or profession. However, expanding trademark protection beyond source identification readily interferes with this liberty and creates or contributes to monopoly power.[13] The "modern" approach allows trademarks to become valuable in themselves, apart from their identification function. Popularity and catchiness are rewarded as social values.

Trademark infringement can be redressed through a full range of remedies available in both state and federal courts.[14] The remedies include monetary damages, injunctions, and attorney fee awards. The scope of the remedies differs depending on the nature of the case and which laws are applied. Texas attorney, Richard A. Fordyce, has summarized the differences:

> Most of us, when we think "trademark," tend to think "federal case." There are sound reasons for this: the federal Lanham Act is familiar, offers an unusually wide array of possible remedies for infringement or dilution, and comes with books full of precedent to guide us.... Though the two regimes' injunctive remedies are mostly similar (with state law perhaps having a slight statutory edge), the monetary remedies differ drastically. Both regimes offer actual damages for infringement claims, but only federal law offers the further possibilities of disgorging the defendant's unjust profits or obtaining attorney's fees.[15]

Registration is not required in order to have trademark protection. Registration under state laws facilitates the protection of one's mark by providing for notice to be given to potential infringers.[16] A trademark used in interstate commerce may be registered with the United States Patent and Trademark Office.

---

13. Courts and legislatures have favored trademark claims by creating presumptions that favor trademark holders, by making injunctions readily available, and by expanding the scope of trademark protection.

14. Unlike patent and copyright, the states are free to establish trademark laws and have done so. There are also two separate court systems. The remedies provided in federal and states courts are similar, but nothing requires that they be the same.

15. Richard A. Fordyce, *Trademark Remedies in Texas: Not Necessarily a Federal Case*, 45 THE ADVOC. (Texas 2008) 53.

16. *E.g.*, Cal. Bus. & Prof. Code § 14245 (2009).

If the mark is accepted for registration on the "Principal Register" the owner is entitled to a presumption that it is incontestable after five years of continuous use. Registration also allows the owner to collect enhanced damages, attorney fees, and obtain remedies against infringing imports.[17] The registration can also be filed with the Customs Service to stop infringing imports from entering the United States. For many trademark users, the effect of the ® registration symbol is the greatest practical advantage. The symbol warns others that the mark belongs to the owner. It is permissible to label goods with the ® symbol only after the mark has been registered.[18] The often observed ™ symbol notifies others that one claims a trademark, as well, but that symbol has no recognized legal effect.[19] Because of this lack of legal effect one will do just as well omitting it when it interferes with the appearance of one's labeling.

Trademark disputes present two basic questions: Did the plaintiff use a distinctive mark? Did the defendant use the same or a very similar mark? In answering these questions, one looks at objective things, such as the distinctiveness of the mark, whether it was applied to a line of goods, whether the defendant's mark was the same or similar. Modern trademark law allows an additional more subjective question to enter and dominate much litigation: Did the defendant's markings or use of terms confuse consumers?

In 2009, Professor Mark McKenna noted that much legal scholarship criticizes modern trademark law. He attributes this to the "easy acceptance" of extending trademark protection to a wide variety of consumer confusion. He explains:

> Modern scholarship takes a decidedly negative view of trademark
> law.... beneath all of this criticism lies overwhelming agreement that
> consumer confusion is harmful. This easy acceptance of the harm-

---

17. One applies United States Patent and Trademark Office (USPTO) for registry to the "Principal Register" pursuant to 15 U.S.C. §1052. "The application is checked for compliance with technical trademark rules, as well as substantively, to see that the mark is not confusingly similar to another registered mark and that it is distinctive, not merely descriptive, among other things." Anne Hiaring Hocking, *Basic Principles of Trademark Law,* Practising Law Institute,1009 PLI/Pat 77 (2010). If the mark is not accepted for the Principal Register, it may be registered on the "Supplemental Register" if it is capable of distinguishing goods or services.

18. 15 U.S.C. §1111; Copelands' Enterprises, Inc. v. CNV, Inc., 945 F.2d 1563 (C.A. Fed.1991).

19. See Ann E. Sartwell and Jolyn Pope, *Braving the Waters: A Guide for Tennessee's Aspiring Entrepreneurs*, 8 Transactions: Tenn. J. Bus. L. 243, 289 (2007). The author has discovered no legal effect of the symbol ™. Legislation or common law could change this.

fulness of confusion is a problem because it operates at too high a level of generality, ignoring important differences between types of relationships about which consumers might be confused. Failure to differentiate between these different relationships has enabled trademark owners to push the boundaries of trademark protection, as they have been able to characterize virtually every use of their marks in consumer confusion terms.[20]

The following matrix identifies basic concepts that apply in trademark law and practice today.

Table 4-1. Trademark Law Basic Concepts

A property right
Use of a mark (word or symbol) which identifies the source of goods or services
Virtually any distinctive word, symbol, or other designation will serve as a trademark
Use of the mark to identify is the key factor of traditional trademark coverage
Modern trademark scope includes protection against confusion and other rights
Trademarks can be established under state or federal law
Registration is not required—but is useful
Long term protection—can continue as long as mark is used
Full range of remedies for infringement

Marking Goods and Services

Traditional trademark law protects a mark to the extent it is used to identify the source of goods or services.[21] The first user may sue a second user for the harm that user causes by using the mark.[22] This principle remains intact and covers most trademark disputes. However, trademark scope has greatly

---

20. Mark P. McKenna, *Testing Modern Trademark Law's Theory of Harm,* 95 Iowa L. Rev. 63, 75–82 (2009).

21. Professor J. Thomas McCarthy summarizes the rule: "The role that a designation must play to become a "trademark" is to identify the source of one seller's goods and distinguish that source from other sources." 1 McCarthy on Trademarks and Unfair Competition §2:1 (4th ed.).

22. "Trademark rights traditionally have been defined by a party's use." Mark P. McKenna, *Trademark Use and the Problem of Source,* 2009 U. Ill. L. Rev. 773, 779 (2009).

expanded, and in recent decades legislation has added protections that depart widely from the principle.

Hanover Star Milling Co. v. Metcalf, 240 U.S. 403 (1916), illustrates this basic principle. In *Hanover Star*, two flour milling companies claimed the right to use the name "Tea Rose" as a brand name for flour. Each party claimed the right to use that name in the same geographic area. The name was appealing. Perhaps the originator noticed that "flour" and "flower" are pronounced the same, and that identifying flour with a cultivated garden rose provides a pleasant association. The Court summarized the common law purposes of trademark:

> The primary and proper function of a trademark is to identify the origin or ownership of the article to which it is affixed. Where a party has been in the habit of labeling his goods with a distinctive mark, so that purchasers recognize goods thus marked as being of his production, others are debarred from applying the same mark to goods of the same description, because to do so would in effect represent their goods to be of his production and would tend to deprive him of the profit he might make through the sale of the goods which the purchaser intended to buy.[23]

The circumstances of the case emphasized that marks are intended to aid parties who seek goods based on identifying a source. One contender for the "Tea Rose" mark had built up its trade north of the Ohio River, while the other had done so south of that river in Georgia, Florida, Alabama, and Mississippi. Thus, "I will buy Tea Rose flour, because it is reliably good," might mean one company's product in one region, and another company's product in a different region. The Court agreed that the use of a mark deserved protection. However, that protection should not mean "that the proprietor of a trademark, good in the markets where it has been employed, can monopolize markets that his trade has never reached, and where the mark signifies not his goods, but those of another."[24] Reliance on the identity of the source of goods at the time of purchase is the essence of trademark under the traditional view. "Goodwill" is earned by performance. Trademarks simply point to the source of goods and services. As a result they provide a reward to a producer or merchant that earns a good reputation. If the public is not fooled at the time of purchase, there should be no trademark infringement.

---

23. Hanover Star Milling Co. v. Metcalf, 240 U.S. 403, 412 (1916).
24. *Id*. 416.

Misidentification of a source by use of another's trademark is the basis for liability in most cases. However, it is not the only basis for trademark liability. Today, one may be held liable under trademark law for activities even when one has not mislabeled the origin of goods or services. The next case illustrates the extent to which modern trademark allows for claims other than misidentifying a source.

In *Hermès Int'l v. Lederer De Paris Fifth Avenue, Inc.*, 219 F.3d 104, 108 (2d Cir. 2000), defendants Lederer and Artbag ran boutique stores that sold replicas of expensive designer purses at fashionable locations on Madison Avenue in the Upper East Side of Manhattan, New York. They included copies of purses which had been manufactured by Hermès. The copies were apparently as faithful to the originals as the defendants could make them. They were expensive, but the customers had been seeking replicas, and they were not expecting to buy the "real thing."[25]

Hermès asked the Court to enjoin the defendants from selling the purses. The judge declined, finding that Hermès "had offered no proof that defendants deceptively attempted to 'pass off' or 'palm off' their products as genuine Hermès." They had openly disclosed that the purses were not Hermès, but were copies.[26] The defendants had built up successful businesses selling replicas. They were not fobbing off any purses as Hermès purses. The purchasers had not claimed to be fooled. Apparently, Hermès had known of this activity for years, perhaps decades and had done little or nothing about it. In sum, the buyers were not fooled, the seller's business was openly conducted, and Hermès had not given any notice of displeasure until shortly before the suit.[27]

The judge was not convinced that a public interest was harmed. Hermès might be harmed because the cachet of its brand might be diminished. However, the judge reasoned that trademark law did not reach that kind of harm, because there was no confusion at the point of sale: "While defendants' exploitation of the possibility of post-sale confusion may increase their sales at the expense of Hermès, I am not convinced that defendants' activity harms

---

25. It is common for people to make and seek to buy replicas. For instance, there is a large legitimate market for replicas of Stradivarius violins. Only a few hundred genuine Stradivarius violins,violas and cellos exist today.

26. The trial court ruling in the case is reported at Hermès Int'l v. Lederer De Paris Fifth Ave., Inc., 50 F. Supp. 2d 212, 225 (S.D.N.Y. 1999).

27. One is left to speculate on why Hermès delayed. In Court some explanation was offered: "Hermès claims that until the time of the filing of this suit, infringement of Hermès leather products in the United States was limited in scope.... In addition, Hermès worries that with the presence of the Internet, the formerly local problem has now expanded into a national and perhaps international problem." 50 F. Supp. 2d 212, 218.

the *public* in the post-sale context. While Hermès' potential high-end customers may be confused in the post-sale context, these highly sophisticated purchasers will not be confused at the point of sale."[28]

The Court of Appeals overruled the District Court on the matter of the interests to be served by trademark law. The Court held that even when there is no confusion as to the identity of the source of the purses at the time of purchase, the trademark holder should be protected. The Court reasoned that "a loss occurs when a sophisticated buyer purchases a knockoff and passes it off to the public as the genuine article, thereby confusing the viewing public and achieving the status of owning the genuine article at a knockoff price."[29]

Modern Commerce and Trademarks

Trademark law has evolved based on changes in commerce and the influence that commerce has in society. Professor McKenna notes that apparent consumer perceptions play an important role in current interpretations of trademark law. "Almost every significant limitation in trademark law—from the existence of protectable rights to the scope of those rights and the availability of defenses—depends on consumer understanding. In itself this renders trademark law inherently unstable."[30] Consumer expectations and perceptions are influenced by media such as radio, television, the Internet, and various social networking media, such as Facebook and Twitter.[31]

Some trademarks not only mark products and services, but have become products in themselves. Some people will purchase a Louis Vuitton purse over a less expensive better one in order to tote that name. Others might order a Coca Cola from habit or association with the name, rather than for a superior flavor or capacity to quench thirst. Coca Cola's rival, Pepsi Cola, marketed its

---

28. *Id.* page 227. Delay and inattention to one's legal rights is a basis for denying an injunction in cases. This is called "laches."

29. Hermès Int'l v. Lederer De Paris Fifth Avenue, Inc., 219 F.3d 104, 108 (2d Cir.2000).

30. Mark P. McKenna, *Trademark Use and the Problem of Source*, 2009 U. ILL. L. REV. 773, 776 (2009).

31. In one form or another social engineering and social networking have throughout history. What has changed is the technical capacity to span time and distance and link with each other. "The art form know as *social engineering* is often used to manipulate individuals or social groups through the use of conversation, digital coercion, or other deceptive techniques. These tactics are commonly employed to persuade people to perform actions or divulge information they would not under normal circumstances." Brian Anderson and Barbara Anderson, *Seven Deadliest USB Attacks,* p. 177 (Syngress, Elsevier, 2010).

product for years with the slogan "Be sociable, have a Pepsi." The name itself is the product.

Consumers today often purchase products with little attention to their actual source. Products of a given brand may be produced anywhere in the world and under any circumstances. The average consumer, for example, likely does not know who produced the can of Coke he or she may be drinking. A franchising website describes the production of Coca Cola: "In general, The Coca-Cola Company and/or subsidiaries only produce syrup concentrate which is then sold to various bottlers throughout the world who hold a Coca-Cola franchise. Coca-Cola bottlers, who hold contracts with the company, produce finished product in cans and bottles from the concentrate."[32]

The market appeal of certain marks has allowed them to acquire a high capital value. For example, a 2007 ranking of top valued brand names placed Coca Cola at the top with a capital valued at 65 billion dollars. Second ranked was Microsoft with a capital valued at 58 billion dollars.

The success of a product or service rides in the wake of the image created by branding. Federal and state laws provide some restraints on fraud and misleading information. These, however, tend to be rather modest. One can sue for active frauds which cause personal harm. Trademark laws allow competitors seek redress for misleading statements concerning the origin of goods. However, trademark laws do not generally control advertising or govern claims "unfair competition." For example, the Supreme Court has ruled that the federal Lanham Act "can never be a federal 'codification' of the overall law of 'unfair competition.' "[33] Nevertheless, we shall see that recent extensions of trademark law allow trademark owners to obtain legal remedies in a large array of circumstances where no confusion of source has occurred.[34] In addition,

---

32. Coca Cola Bottling Franchise—http://www.dailyfranchises.com/franchises/Coca_Cola_Bottling_Franchise.htm.

33. Dastar Corp. v. Twentieth Century Fox Film Corp., 539 U.S. 23, 123 S.Ct. 2041, 156 L.Ed.2d 18 (2003). "[T]he Lanham Act prohibits actions like trademark infringement that deceive consumers and impair a producer's goodwill. It forbids, for example, the Coca-Cola Company's passing off its product as Pepsi-Cola or reverse passing off Pepsi-Cola as its product." *Id.* at 32. Actions by consumers for fraud depend on general common law or special statutes, such as those governing real estate disclosures. See, e.g., Cal. Civ. Code § 1102.6.

34. "Mark owners are able to characterize almost every conceivable use of their trademarks in consumer confusion terms, and because courts have simply equated confusion with harm, they have lacked the tools to resist novel confusion claims." Mark P. McKenna, *Testing Modern Trademark Law's Theory of Harm*, 95 Iowa L. Rev. 63, 67 (2009). Professor McKenna teamed with another prominent trademark scholar, and they concluded: "Not

Figure 4-1. Arm & Hammer

owners of "famous" trademarks have rights to protect against the "dilution" of the value of those marks.

What Qualifies as a Trademark

To qualify as a trademark, the mark must be distinctive. Otherwise, it would not function to identify a source. For example, Arm & Hammer is a familiar brand of baking soda. The name and image of a strong arm wielding a hammer have remained basically the same for 150 years. Neither the name nor the image describes or refers to the product, baking soda. They create an arbitrary association with the product, which is a simple molecule, sodium bicarbonate. A generic term, such as "*Soda!*," will not suffice as a trademark for that

---

history, nor economics, nor logic support giving the owner of a mark in one market the power to control all uses of that mark everywhere." Mark A. Lemley and Mark P. McKenna, *Owning Mark(et)s*, 109 MICH. L. REV. 137, 189 (2010).

product. The Second Circuit explained the rule with an example: "'Ivory' would be generic when used to describe a product made from the tusks of elephants but arbitrary as applied to soap."[35]

Virtually any distinctive symbol will suffice, so long as it is not "functional." The shape of a Coca Cola bottle, the three note succession announcing an NBC broadcast, and a flower scent applied to sewing thread are examples. The functionality limitation means that the symbol cannot not also serve a useful or aesthetic function.[36] For instance, the design of a handle for a purse might serve as a trademark, but if that design also makes it easier to carry the purse, the design should no longer be protectable as a trademark. Similarly, if the design of the handle is part of the aesthetic appeal of the purse, then it is serving to attract, rather than identify.[37] For example, a handle shaped like the letter "Q" could mark the brand of handbag, or perhaps the word "handle" on the handle. Neither would appear to be functional.

The Supreme Court has addressed the scope of the Lanham Act in a series of cases. The plaintiff in *Qualitex Co. v. Jacobson Products Co., Inc.*, 514 U.S. 159 (1995) marketed dry cleaning press pads, the commercial equivalent of ironing board covers. It claimed that the greenish gold color of its dry cleaning press pads were its trademark.

The Ninth Circuit denied its claim. "In this case, we confront the issue of whether to follow the majority of circuits in holding that color alone cannot form the basis for a trademark, ... We conclude that the better rule is that a trademark should not be registered for color alone."[38] The Supreme Court reversed the Ninth Circuit in a unanimous opinion. The Court noted that the Lanham

---

35. Abercrombie & Fitch Co. v. Hunting World, Inc., 537 F.2d 4, 9 (2d Cir.1976), footnote 6.

36. "The functionality doctrine prevents trademark law, which seeks to promote competition by protecting a firm's reputation, from instead inhibiting legitimate competition by allowing a producer to control a useful product feature." Qualitex Co. v. Jacobson Products Co., Inc., 514 U.S. 159, 164 (1995).

37. Aesthetics as a functional quality is discussed in Qualitex Co. v. Jacobson Products Co., Inc., 514 U.S. 159 at 169–70. A Ninth Circuit model jury instruction states: "A functional design has aesthetic appeal, or increases the utility or practicality of the product, or saves the consumer or producer time or money." United States Court of Appeals for the Ninth Circuit, http://www.ca9.uscourts.gov (visited 2010).

38. Qualitex v. Jacobson Products Co., Inc., 13 F.3d 1297, 1302 (9th Cir. 1994). Some Circuit courts had allowed color to be a trademark, while others denied it. Each Circuit is the end of the line within its jurisdiction. A Circuit Court is free, even obligated to interpret an Act of Congress according to its own best reasoning, rather than merely copy the result from another Circuit. The Supreme Court may decide to grant review in order to create a uniform national interpretation. The situation is the same under the Copyright

Figure 4-2. Dry Cleaning Press Pad

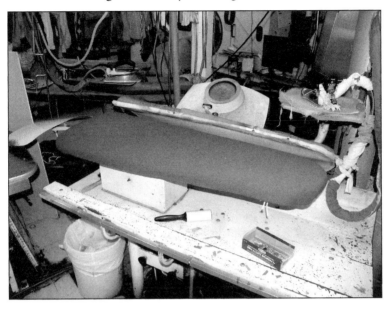

Act allows "any word, name, symbol, or device, or any combination thereof" to function as a trademark. "Since human beings might use as a 'symbol' or 'device' almost anything at all that is capable of carrying meaning, this language, read literally, is not restrictive."

Though the scope of trademark is broad, the Court stressed that a trademark should not be allowed to control the features of goods. "It is the province of patent law, not trademark law, to encourage invention by granting inventors a monopoly over new product designs or functions for a limited time, ... after which competitors are free to use the innovation."[39] If trademark protection were extended to cover the attractiveness of goods, it would intrude on the functions of copyright law. Copyright protects expressions for a long yet limited period of time. Trademark protection can last for as long as a mark is used. If trademark extended to utilitarian or expressive features of the goods themselves, then the trademark owner would achieve a kind of super patent or super copyright protection. The Court concluded that a distinctive color can be a trademark, if it functions as an identifier rather than an attribute of the goods. "We

Act. However, the Federal Circuit has exclusive jurisdiction to decide appeals on matters involving construction of the Patent Act.

39. 514 U.S. 159 at 162.

cannot find in the basic objectives of trademark law any obvious theoretical objection to the use of color alone as a trademark, where that color has attained 'secondary meaning' and therefore identifies and distinguishes a particular brand (and thus indicates its 'source')."[40]

A combination of attributes can be claimed as a trademark and is called "trade dress." The breadth of this concept makes it difficult, perhaps impossible, to separate the mark from the product or service offered. In *Two Pesos, Inc. v. Taco Cabana, Inc.*, 505 U.S. 763 (1992), Taco Cabana claimed the appearance and ambience of its restaurants to be protected trade dress. It described its trade dress: "a festive eating atmosphere having interior dining and patio areas decorated with artifacts, bright colors, paintings and murals.... The stepped exterior of the building is a festive and vivid color scheme using top border paint and neon stripes. Bright awnings and umbrellas continue the theme."

When Two Pesos adopted a similar overall look for its restaurants, Taco Cabana sued. At trial the judge had explained the law to the jury in an instruction: "'Trade dress' is the total image of the business. Taco Cabana's trade dress may include the shape and general appearance of the exterior of the restaurant, the identifying sign, the interior kitchen floor plan, the decor, the menu, the equipment used to serve food, the servers' uniforms and other features reflecting on the total image of the restaurant."[41] Based on the instructions, the jury returned a verdict that Two Pesos had infringed a trademark. The Supreme Court affirmed the verdict, but it did not provide definite guidelines. As we have seen, the Lanham Act allows almost any feature to stand as a trademark, so long as it links the product or service to the provider, without being part of a function. Decoration and ambience can be distinctive, and a jury had found that they were in this case.

The *Two Pesos* situation illustrates difficulties of allowing a party to own décor or ambience by use of trademark law. Different things motivate people to choose a restaurant. One of these is ambience. Everything in Taco Cabana's description of its "trade dress" was something that would be part of the visual and physical experience of being there. Rather than simply being the mark, those attributes, festive, bright colors, awnings, umbrellas were part of the experience itself. Trademark law is intended to protect only the identifying aspect, not to grant ownership of the thing which is identified. The Court has recog-

---

40. 514 U.S. 159 at 163. Sounds can be trademarks, too. In the 1990s Harley Davidson made an amusing attempt to register its famous "vrvrum ... rum ... rum." It finally gave up. J. Thomas McCarthy, McCarthy on Trademarks and Unfair Competition §7:104 (2009).

41. 514 U.S. 159 at 765, footnote 1.

nized that copyright and patent law are designed to draw the lines as to what one may own with regard to expressions and methods. Trademark law is intended to filter out functional elements and protect only the mark. Under these criteria, one restaurant ought not to own a certain type of festive atmosphere. Yet the *Two Tacos* decision allowed precisely that result.

The Supreme Court returned to trade dress in *Wal-Mart Stores, Inc. v. Samara Bros., Inc.* 529 U.S. 205, (2000). "In this case, we decide under what circumstances a product's design is distinctive, and therefore protectable, in an action for infringement of unregistered trade dress under §43(a) of the Trademark Act of 1946 (Lanham Act)." The plaintiff Samara sued Kmart, Caldor, Hills, Goody's, and Wal-Mart for selling dresses which it claimed resembled the children's dresses it designed and manufactured. Its claim was that the design of the dresses identified the source of goods, as color did in *Qualitex* and ambience did in *Two Tacos*. The Court summarized the events leading up to the suit:

> Petitioner Wal-Mart Stores, Inc., is one of the Nation's best known retailers, selling among other things children's clothing. In 1995, Wal-Mart contracted with one of its suppliers, Judy-Philippine, Inc., to manufacture a line of children's outfits for sale in the 1996 spring/summer season. Wal-Mart sent Judy-Philippine photographs of a number of garments from Samara's line, on which Judy-Philippine's garments were to be based; Judy-Philippine duly copied, with only minor modifications, 16 of Samara's garments, ... In 1996, Wal-Mart briskly sold the so-called knockoffs, generating more than $1.15 million in gross profits.[42]

All defendants except Wal-Mart settled before trial. After a week long trial, a jury ruled in favor of Samara. In addition to a large jury verdict, Samara was granted an injunction and 1.6 million dollars in fees, costs, and interest. Wal-Mart appealed, and the Circuit Court affirmed the jury verdict. The Supreme Court granted review.

The Court acknowledged some of the difficulties presented by expanding trademark law to cover appearance and the like. "Consumers are aware of the reality that, almost invariably, even the most unusual of product designs—such as a cocktail shaker shaped like a penguin—is intended not to identify the source, but to render the product itself more useful or more appealing."[43] The Court's solution was to require a trademark claimant to prove that the public associates the design with it as a source. This requirement is called "secondary

---

42. 529 U.S. 205, 208.
43. 529 U.S. 205, 213.

meaning," that is, the distinctiveness must be associated "in the minds of the public … with the product's source rather than the product itself."[44] That means that when one sees a dress, automobile, or restaurant, one thinks of the brand name, not of the pleasing aspects of the thing itself.

Protection of Name Per Se

Some companies spend a lot to promote a name or mark. That effort could be put into improving the product instead. They do what Carlyle spoke of in his Great Hat commentary — "instead of making better felt-hats than another, [the hatter] mounts a huge lath-and-plaster Hat, seven-feet high, upon wheels."[45] Coca Cola's history provides a classic example.

Coke's efforts to build its brand included vigorous efforts to suppress what it considered infringing trademarks. During the first half of the twentieth century the company brought suits seeking to suppress competitors' uses of names, graphics, and packaging. Many of these decisions and decrees up to 1938 are collected in a three thousand page, three volume work which the company published itself. The books are bound in a fashion that closely resembles the "trade dress" of the official United States Supreme Court Reports. Names it sought to squelch include "CoCo Lime," "Celery Cola," "Pure Cola," "Roxa Cola," "Dope Cola," "Champion Cola," "Crown Cola," "Rye-Ola," "High Grade Cola." Coke won some, lost some. Surprising wins for Coke included the suppression of the word brands "Crown Cola," and "High Grade Cola." Coke must have made a deep impression on potential competitors — "Watch out; we're watching you!" No business wants to face the devastation of a lawsuit by a determined company, especially one with deep pockets.

In 1925, Coke sued a little company in northern Ohio formed by three men who called themselves the Lake Erie Bottling Works. One of their trade names

---

44. 529 U.S. 205, 205–206. "*Two Pesos* unquestionably establishes the legal principle that trade dress can be inherently distinctive, … but it does not establish that product-design trade dress can be. *Two Pesos* is inapposite to our holding here because the trade dress at issue, the decor of a restaurant, seems to us not to constitute product design." 529 U.S. 205, 215. In TrafFix Devices, Inc. v. Marketing Displays, Inc. 532 U.S. 23 (2001), the Court ruled unanimously that a wind resistant traffic sign design which had been the subject of an expired patent could not be protected by trade dress. The case does not shed much light on the scope of trade dress.

45. In some instances, this includes actively "policing" the use of their brand names. For example, Coca Cola sends agents to restaurants and bars to order a "Coke." If served some other brand, the agent may admonish the server or recommend some other action.

Figure 4-3. Coca Cola vs. Dope Cola

was the word "Cola" in a circle and the other was "Dope" in a circle along with other words. It seems to have been one of the rare cases that Coke lost. The judge said he was unpersuaded that Coke had established a case for a preliminary injunction. Coke's case was "not so clearly established, and the danger ... of irreparable injury is not so serious as to justify ... a preliminary injunction." If the Court had issued the injunction, Lake Erie Bottling would have had the right to have a trial on whether the order should become permanent. However, many small entities, Lake Erie might have been forced to fold before going to trial. The small company would have faced the expense of trial, and at the same time would have been unable to pursue their normal marketing due to the injunction.[46]

Coca Cola Co. v. Koke Co. of America, 254 U.S. 143 (1920), gives a more accurate view of the success of Coke's legal crusade. In that case, a California Federal District Court had granted an injunction against a competitor's use of the name "Koke" and its use of packaging that was intended to be similar to that of Coca Cola. The Ninth Circuit Court would readily have affirmed the injunction, except that a long standing rule denied a trademark owner an injunction if its labeling misleads the public. Coca Cola's name and its use of pictures of coca leaves and cola nuts did mislead the public, for the drink no longer contained those ingredients. Furthermore, based on the ingredients, Coke had long advertised its drink as a " 'valuable brain tonic,' an 'ideal nerve tonic and stimulant,' as a cure of 'headache, neuralgia, hysteria, and melancholy,' and 'of nervous afflictions.' " On this basis, the Ninth Circuit set aside the injunction.

When the case reached the Supreme Court, Justice Holmes agreed that a misleading name ought not be protected: "Of course a man is not to be protected in the use of a device the very purpose and effect of which is to swindle

---

46. The decision gave the company breathing space, though we do not know how long it survived.

the public." That rule against enforcing fraudulent and misleading trademarks continues today.[47] However, Justice Holmes was not persuaded that the advertising did mislead. Coke, he said, had become a popular drink and not a medicine. He added:

> The name now characterizes a beverage to be had at almost any soda fountain. It means a single thing coming from a single source, and well known to the community. It hardly would be too much to say that the drink characterizes the name as much as the name the drink. In other words 'Coca-Cola' probably means to most persons the plaintiff's familiar product to be had everywhere rather than a compound of particular substances.[48]

The Supreme Court reinstated the District Court's injunction in a modified form. Coke adopted Holmes' phrase "a single thing coming from a single source, and well known to the community" as a slogan and claimed the Court's imprimatur in promotional literature.

Holmes' comment in 1920 that "Coca Cola is a thing" identified a phenomenon which would shift trademark from traditional to modern protection. A 1927 article by Frank Schechter summarized a shift in trademark law over time that echoes Holmes' comments:

> Four hundred years ago a trademark indicated either the origin or ownership of the goods to which it was affixed. To what extent does the trademark of today really function as either? Actually, not in the least! ... Over twenty years ago it was pointed out by the Circuit Court of Appeals for the Seventh Circuit that "we may safely take it for granted that not one in a thousand knowing of or desiring to purchase 'Baker's Cocoa' or 'Baker's Chocolate' know of Walter Baker & Co., Limited."[49]

Schechter concluded that trademark should be protected as a valuable item in itself, rather than as a source identifier, because it functions as "a valuable, though possibly anonymous link between [the trademark owner] and his con-

---

47. 15 U.S.C. §1052 denies federal registration to misleading marks. Glendale Intern. Corp. v. U.S. Patent & Trademark Office, 374 F. Supp. 479 (E.D. Va. 2005).

48. Coca Cola Co. v. Koke Co. of America, 254 U.S. 143, 146 (1920).

49. Frank I. Schechter, *The Rational Basis of Trademark Protection,* 40 Harv. L. Rev. 813 (1927), 814–815.

Figure 4-4. Justice Holmes

Source: Library of Congress.

sumer." Professor Robert Bone credits Schechter with being the originator of the body of trademark law that now protects against diluting trademarks.[50]

---

50. Professor Bone concludes: "In the 1920s and 1930s, ... Frank Schechter's pragmatic style of argument had considerable force, but it no longer satisfies those trademark schol-

Fame and Dilution

In 1996 Congress passed the "Federal Trademark Dilution Act of 1995" to create new federal protection for famous trademarks. The House Committee that had reported the bill to Congress explained its conception of the function and need for the legislation:

> The protection of marks from dilution differs from the protection accorded marks from trademark infringement. Dilution does not rely upon the standard test of infringement, that is, likelihood of confusion, deception or mistake. Rather, it applies when the unauthorized use of a famous mark reduces the public's perception that the mark signifies something unique, singular, or particular. As summarized in one decision:
>
> > Dilution is an injury that differs materially from that arising out of the orthodox confusion. Even in the absence of confusion, the potency of a mark may be debilitated by another's use. This is the essence of dilution. Confusion leads to immediate injury, while dilution is an infection, which if allowed to spread, will inevitably destroy the advertising value of the mark.[51]

The owner of a "famous mark" would be entitled to an injunction against any party who "commences use of a mark or trade name in commerce that is likely to cause dilution by blurring or dilution by tarnishment of the famous mark, regardless of the presence or absence of actual or likely confusion, of competition, or of actual economic injury." Fame is achieved when a mark has become "widely recognized by the general consuming public of the United States as a designation of source of the goods or services of the mark's owner."[52] The dilution act departs from traditional rationales for trademark law. It protects the fame of the name, rather than the name as a designation of source of a service or product.[53]

The Committee Report stated that the "bill defines the term 'dilution' to mean 'the lessening of the capacity of a famous mark to identify and distinguish

---

ars today who demand that dilution be justified by a more careful accounting of its social costs and benefits." Robert G. Bone, *Schechter's Ideas in Historical Context and Dilution's Rocky Road*, 24 Santa Clara Computer & High Tech. L.J. 469, 505 (2008).

51. House Report No. 104-374.

52. 15 U.S.C. § 1125 (c).

53. A number of legal scholars have criticized the Act, now named Trademark Dilution Revision Act of 2006 ("TDRA"), 15 U.S.C.A. § 1125(c). See e.g. Clarisa Long, *Dilution*, 106 Colum. L. Rev. 1029 (2006). Kenneth L. Port, *The Congressional Expansion of American Trademark Law: A Civil Law System in the Making*, 35 Wake Forest L. Rev. 827 (2000).

goods or services regardless of the presence or absence of (a) competition be-tween the parties, or (b) likelihood of confusion, mistakes, or deception.' Thus, for example, the use of DUPONT shoes, BUICK aspirin, and KODAK pianos would be actionable under this legislation." To the extent that the statute de-fines "dilution," it does so indirectly, stating "dilution by blurring or dilution by tarnishment of the famous mark" is actionable.

Part II. Practical Applications

Infringement and Remedies

Attorneys, judges, and commentators commonly refer to two general classes of trademark cases, infringement and dilution:

1) Infringement. These cases involve claims that a competitor used one's mark to divert business to himself. It is what has been referred to as a "tradi-tional" claim. One can recover for such claims today, if the marking of goods confuses consumers. For example, a flour supplier who owns the "Tea Rose" may prevail against another who use "Hybrid Rose" in the same market if he shows that the mark confused buyers."[54]

2) Dilution. In a dilution case, the owner sues because another uses the name in some way that undermines the value of the name.[55] The use does *not* necessarily mislabel the source of a good or service. In fact, there need be no competition between the trademark owner and the offender at all. If "Tea Rose" flour were to have achieved the name recognition of, say Coca Cola or Nike, its trademark owner might use the dilution theory to sue "Hybrid Rose" for producing silly T-shirts with roses on them that might be similar to the "Tea Rose" logo. Such a claim would have been preposterous at the time that *Hanover* was decided. People who want to buy T-shirts do not rely on flour suppliers to make or supply good shirts.[56]

Professors Lemley and McKenna emphasize that at the heart of both types of cases lies the matter of confusing the public: "With some significant excep-

---

54. Rose lovers refer to hybrid garden roses to as "hybrid tea roses" or "tea roses."

55. The bifurcation is confusing. "Infringement" means a violation of a right, but has this specialized limitation in the parlance of trademark law.

56. Trademark law's development is explained thoroughly in a trio of articles—Robert G. Bone, *Schechter's Ideas in Historical Context and Dilution's Rocky Road*, 24 SANTA CLARA COMPUTER & HIGH TECH. L.J. 469, 497 (2008), Mark P. McKenna, *Testing Modern Trade-mark Law's Theory of Harm*, 95 Iowa L. Rev. 63, 75–82 (2009), and Frank I. Schechter, *The Rational Basis of Trademark Protection*, 40 HARV. L. REV. 813 (1927).

tions, the basic rule of trademark law is that a defendant's use of a mark is illegal if it confuses a substantial number of consumers and not otherwise."[57] In an infringement case, the confusion is regarding the source; in dilution cases, the confusion is regarding the affiliation.[58]

3) Control of distribution. In addition to the two major classes of cases mentioned above, the Lanham Act has been used to control the way that goods or services are distributed. The mechanics of this form of liability are discussed below.

A judge or jury may decide the factual questions in a trademark case. As in all cases, this depends on whether a party has asked for a jury trial. When a jury is used, the essential questions are posed to a jury by instructions that state the law in an understandable fashion. For example, the Ninth Circuit's Model Jury Instruction on trademark infringement informs the jury that, "[a] trademark is a word, a name, a symbol, a device, or a combination of them that indicates the source of goods. The owner of a trademark has the right to exclude others from using that trademark." The model instructions then ask the jury to decide whether the defendant used a mark similar to the plaintiff's trademark "without the consent of the plaintiff in a manner that is likely to cause confusion among ordinary purchasers as to the source of the goods."[59]

Once a case of infringement has been proved, a trademark owner has a full panoply of legal remedies, including damages, injunctions, and seizure of items by customs officials. These remedies include liberal use of injunctions. Courts have often presumed that a preliminary injunction is justified once a trademark owner shows that it is likely that it will show ownership and infringement of the mark at trial. A critical element in the decision of whether to grant an injunction is showing that the harm done by the infringement cannot be compensated by monetary damages alone, therefore, the plaintiff has suffered "irreparable harm." This has led courts in the past to presume irreparable damage. This presumption is unlikely to hold in future cases, and plaintiffs will probably have to prove that element to obtain an injunction.[60]

---

57. Mark A. Lemley & Mark McKenna, *Irrelevant Confusion*, 62 STAN. L. REV. 413, 414 (2010).

58. A brand name can be tarnished by being associated with bad things. It is reminiscent of Groucho Marx's quip: "I don't care to belong to any club that will have me as a member."

59. United States Court of Appeals for the Ninth Circuit, http://www.ca9.uscourts.gov/ (visited 2010). However precisely drawn a juror is like to understand such an instruction to mean: "Did the defendant's use confuse buyers?" Similarly, in dilution a juror is likely to understand an instruction to mean: "Did the defendants dilute the value of the trademark?"

60. Judges have discretion to issue injunctions *before* a full trial. A Supreme Court case, Ebay Inc. v. MercExchange, LLC, 547 U.S. 388 (2006), casts doubt on presuming "irreparable

Some trademark infringements are quite obvious. For example, one can easily find fake Rolex watches for sale in large cities or on the Internet. These obvious instances are called "knock offs" or "counterfeit goods." The Lanham Act defines a counterfeit as "a spurious mark which is identical with, or substantially indistinguishable from" a trademark owner's mark.[61] Infringement in such cases is usually relatively easy to prove.

Use of Marks to Control Distribution

Suppliers of goods sometimes use trademark law to control the distribution of goods in a given market. For example, a company might license its trademark to be used on men's clothes manufactured in China for sale in China, but not elsewhere. The supplier can prevent importation of those clothes into the United States. The goods are not counterfeit or "black market" goods, because the goods have been marked with the trademark owner's consent. They are referred to as "gray market" goods or parallel imports.[62]

Some producers also seek to control how goods, wherever produced, are sold in the United States. For example, some brands will sell only through their own stores or specified outlets, as is the case with "Louis Vuitton" stores. At other times, these brands seek to control how independent outlets market their goods. The control mechanism is: "You are using our trademark—these are our restrictions."

Tempur-Pedic, Inc. manufactures and distributes a fairly popular line of mattresses and pillows. It sued Brand Named Beds, LLC (BNB), a company which sold Tempur-Pedic mattresses online. The Court described Tempur-Pedic's method of marketing:

> Tempur-Pedic maintains an "authorized network" of sellers for its TEMPUR-PEDIC® products. This network includes Tempur-Pedic itself, physicians and other health care professionals, general bedding retailers, and other retailers such as Brookstone. To ensure quality control throughout this network, Tempur-Pedic monitors these re-

---

injury," federal trademark cases. The matter is far from settled. A 2010 a District Court judge in Connecticut stated "illogical if trademark was the only intellectual property regime holding harm inherent in a *prima facie* case of infringement." People's United Bank v. Peoplesbank, 2010 WL 2521069 (D.Conn. 2010). Remedies are discussed further in Chapter Six.

61. 15 U.S.C. §1127.

62. See K Mart Corp. v. Cartier, Inc., 486 U.S. 281 (1988). Other theories, especially copyright are employed in "gray market" cases, as well. See Omega S.A. v. Costco Wholesale Corp., 541 F.3d 982 (9th Cir. 2008).

tailers and trains their staff on the proper use and care of Tempur-Pedic's products; the retailers are instructed to pass this information on to consumers. Territory Sales Managers visit authorized retailers' stores after initial retail training in order to "ensure that retailers in each sales territory incorporate the Tempur-Pedic training and are actually providing correct information to consumers."[63]

The defendant, BNB, claimed that it "does not modify, alter, or change any of the Tempur-Pedic products it buys before it sells them to consumers," and that "Tempur-Pedic products sold by Brand Name Beds are identical in all respects to those sold by Plaintiffs and all other Tempur-Pedic dealers." Tempur-Pedic responded that a mattress might arrive in a different condition, and that there could be differences in the warranty. These might make a "material difference" between the product which Tempur-Pedic marks and the product delivered by BNB. The Court determined that, if proved, these differences were sufficient to allow a jury to conclude that BNB violated trademark rights under applicable New York and federal trademark laws.

Parody and Fair Use

Louis Vuitton Malletier v. Haute Diggity Dog, LLC. 507 F.3d 252 (4th Cir. 2007), pitted a large luxury item manufacturer against a small boutique provider of dog toys. Louis Vuitton is a French company that manufactures and retails luxury handbags and luggage. A 2007 business survey, Top 100 Brands, ranked Vuitton number seventeen on a worldwide list of most valuable brands. It gave the brand a capital value of 20 billion dollars. A Vuitton signature is a stylized LV which often appears as the motif in its designs. Louis Vuitton handbags range in price from several hundred to several thousand dollars.

Haute Diggity Dog is a small marketer of dog toys and accessories. The company described itself on its original website: "HAUTE DIGGITY DOG is the brain puppy of Pamela Reeder and together with partner Victoria Dauernheim, Haute Diggity Dog has quickly grown from a fun idea to a successful line of popular parody dog toys, unique collars, carry bags, and must have dog accessories."

---

63. Dan-Foam A/S v. Brand Named Beds, LLC, 500 F.Supp. 2d 296, 301 (S.D.N.Y. 2007).

One of Haute Diggity's creations is Chewy Vuiton, a small ten dollar dog chew toy that resembles a Louis Vuitton handbag retailing for about $1200. The resemblance aroused Vuitton's ire, and in 2006 it sued Haute Diggity and its owners, Reeder and Dauernheim, for copying its design. Vuitton complained that Chewy infringed Vuitton's trademark, diluted the trademark, counterfeited the trademark, infringed trade dress, and violated Vuitton's copyright. Each side filed a motion for summary judgment. The Court's ruling on the motions began: "This 'dog of a case' gave the court a great amount of facts to chew upon and applicable law to sniff out. Nevertheless, having thoroughly gnawed through the record ... the Court will deny Plaintiff's motion and grant Defendants' motion."[64]

Vuitton appealed. The Court of Appeals stated, "The marks are undeniably similar in certain respects. There are visual and phonetic similarities. [Haute Diggity Dog] admits that the product name and design mimics LVM's [Louis Vuitton Malletier] and is based on the LVM marks."[65] The Court affirmed the District Court decision that Vuitton had failed to make out a case on any count. Let us focus on Vuitton's infringement claim first. Later we will return to another aspect of the case—fame.

To win an infringement case, a plaintiff must prove that it owns a valid and protectable mark, that the defendant used a copy or a colorable imitation without consent, and that the use is likely to cause confusion. Ownership and copying of the mark had been admitted, so the court addressed whether Chewy was likely to confuse the public. Might one mistake a Chewy for a Louis Vuitton? Haute Diggety argued that Chewy had to imitate Louis in order to create its whimsical product. Chewy is a parody of an overpriced handbag. "It is necessary for the pet products to conjure up the original designer mark for there to be a parody at all." The Court discussed the parody:

> No one can doubt that LVM handbags are the target of the imitation by Haute Diggity Dog's "Chewy Vuiton" dog toys.
> At the same time ... the differences are immediate, beginning with the fact that the "Chewy Vuiton" product is a dog toy, not an expensive, luxury LOUIS VUITTON handbag. The toy is smaller, it is plush,

---

64. Louis Vuitton Malletier v. Haute Diggity Dog, 464 F.Supp. 2d 495, 497 (E.D Va. 2006). As is often the case, the plaintiff urged many different theories of liability, including trademark, trade dress, and copyright. The judge explained the reasons for his ruling in a detail in a forty page opinion.

65. Louis Vuitton Malletier v. Haute Diggity Dog, LLC. 507 F.3d 252, 259 (4th Cir. 2007).

Figure 4-5. Chewy Vuiton vs. Louis Vuitton

and virtually all of its designs differ. The toys are inexpensive; the handbags are expensive and marketed to be expensive: The furry little "Chewy Vuiton" imitation, as something to be *chewed by a dog,* pokes fun at the elegance and expensiveness of a LOUIS VUITTON hand-bag, which must *not* be chewed by a dog.[66]

Even though Chewy was a parody, it must not appear to be created by Louis Vuitton. In this aspect, The Court viewed Louis Vuitton's fame as an immediate tip-off that a cheap dog toy is not likely from Vuitton. Chewy's "differences are sufficiently obvious and the parody sufficiently blatant" that a potential consumer would not view Vuitton as the source. Vuitton's exclusive marketing methods worked against it, as well. Haute Diggity sells over the Internet, in pet stores, and in occasional department stores. Vuitton sells only through its own stores or boutiques.

The Chewy Vuiton case falls into a category of cases in which an alleged infringer raises a defense that the use or reference to a trademark is fair. For example, one may refer to another's mark for purposes of comparison, but must avoid making false statements in the comparison.[67] Professor William McGeveran, notes that often the courts protect fair uses, but that the net practical result is little real protection. He explains: "The lethal combination of uncertain standards with lengthy and costly litigation creates a classic chilling effect upon the unlicensed use of trademarks to facilitate speech, even when such uses are perfectly lawful. Markholders policing their portfolios send cease-and-desist letters attacking virtually any unlicensed use of their trademarks."[68] The fear of being sued and the expense of litigation deter many creative users of language and image from forging ahead with their projects.

The second part of the *Vuitton* case was a dilution claim. First the Court considered: Did the chewy toy blur or tarnish the Louis Vuitton trademark? Blurring refers to undermining the distinct impression given by the mark, while tarnishment refers to creating a harmful association with the mark. The Court concluded that the Chewy Vuiton toy was a successful parody that would not blur the reputation of an entirely different product. The Court stated that

---

66. 507 F.3d 252, 260–261.

67. Attorney Charlotte J. Romano observes that "80% of all television advertisements, and 30% to 40% of all advertisements, contained comparative claims in the United States in the early 1990s." Charlotte J. Romano, *Comparative Advertising in the United States and in France*, 25 Nw. J. Int'l L. & Bus. 371 (2005). "Use of another's trademark to identify the trademark owner's product in comparative advertising is not prohibited by either statutory or common law." Smith v. Chanel, Inc., 402 F.2d 562, 565–66 (9th Cir.1968). Regarding avoiding false statements, see, Castrol, Inc. v. Quaker State Corp., 977 F.2d 57 (2d Cir. 1992).

68. William McGeveran, *Rethinking Trademark Fair Use*, 94 Iowa L. Rev. 49, 52 (2008).

no extended discussion was needed to show that no tarnishment had occurred either. It gave short shrift to the feeble argument that "that the possibility that a dog could choke" on a toy tarnished the Louis Vuitton name. A composite picture emerged, as well: The spoof was obvious, yet it was clear that while it called attention to Vuitton, it did not indicate that the dog toy was an expensive purse, let alone one made by Vuitton. Chewy is a dog toy, and it is having some fun with the reputation of the handbag.[69]

The Internet

The Internet plays a powerful role in commerce and in daily lives. People commonly "google" on a computer to get a recipe for fish, to order a machine part, or to find a factoid that will clinch an argument. The Internet's technology and infrastructure influence trademark usage, and trademark practices play a reciprocal role shaping the Internet and its contents. The latter is especially true with regard to the influence of strong corporate entities, such as Google.

The growth of Google illustrates the economic and technological interplay. Google's basic software was devised as a research project in 1996 by Larry Page and Sergey Brin, a pair of graduate students at Stanford. They incorporated Google Inc. in 1998, using a garage in Menlo Park, California, as a home base. In 2010 its market capital evaluation was in excess of 100 billion dollars. Google gets its primary revenue from sales of advertising and services to businesses. It also gains revenue from Internet sale of goods and charges for access to its constantly growing database of information which includes books, magazines, recordings, and personal and demographic data.[70]

The Internet is an application of computer technology with the following dominant features: sending, retrieving, classifying, and storing data. Its infrastructure comprises a vast array of computers and communication equipment spread around the world. Commerce and advertising rely on delivering data, products, and persuasion. Thus the Internet's technologies and structure have a direct influence on commerce. A business needs to know how to get the word out and deliver services. Thus, they need to comply with the technical demands of the Internet.

---

69. Louis Vuitton Malletier v. Haute Diggity Dog, LLC. 507 F.3d 252, 263 *et seq.* (4th Cir. 2007).

70. About Google, http://www.google.com/intl/en/about.html. August 29, 2010.

For example, if a company, KidBookz, markets children's books and videos online, it will need to comply with the technical protocols that allow users all over the world to gain access to, find, and retrieve information.[71] At each step of the way, the user's computer must comply with the demands of the computer system that searches for the information and sends it back. A user who wishes to buy a Wimpy Kid or Harry Potter book online will need to find it, pay for it, and get it delivered. Also, these "goods" are often available in a digital format that can be delivered in a data stream over the Internet. The technical requirements include ability to exchange messages in a computer code such as HTML (Hypertext Markup Language) and provide passwords when needed.

Trademark's influence on the Internet is more indirect and nuanced. Individuals and corporations exercise power over the content of messages that flow over the Internet in proportion to their economic power. The catchiness of a message, in turn, has an effect on gathering economic power. Apple Computer, Inc. provides a good example. Its computers triggered its original success, because they were easy to use. Equally part of the business success is Apple's ability to create style in its design, naming, image, and feel. Apple products are considered "cool," whether iPods, iPhones, iPads, or slim computers. The image effect is carried to design of stores. Its store in New York City is maximum cool—an icy clean glass cube juts up at the corner of 59th street and Fifth Avenue right across from Central Park. This expensive projection is nothing but a housing for a futuristic feeling stair case, taking one down into the bustling store, which is itself underground.

Let us combine all these features in the case of the hypothetical Kidbookz. The company wants to succeed online. To do so, it must follow the Internet rules and become well known. The Internet structure provides the technology, while trademark plays a role in creating popularity. If Kidbookz were to become popular or control some popular item, such as the copyright to Harry Potter literature or the Harry Potter trademarks it might exercise *de facto* control in a valuable market.[72]

---

71. "Kidbookz" is used as a hypothetical. Not surprisingly, many names one can think up have been tried or used on the Internet. A number of websites list the status of domain names. Kidbookz was listed among expired domains. However, other online suppliers of books, videos, games, etc. exist with names that include the terms "kidz" or "bookz."

72. Actual ownership of the array of Harry Potter marketed items is complicated. The author, J.K. Rowling, apparently owns the United States copyright of the Potter books. Warner Brothers apparently owns Potter trademarks. Warner Bros. Entm't Inc. v. RDR Books, 575 F.Supp. 2d (S.D.N.Y.2008). An online white pages telephone book search indicated that there are more than 100 people named Harry Potter in the United States.

The Internet Address

The addressing system is the core technical feature of the Internet. That system is also the most prominent arena of reciprocal relations between the Internet and trademark.

An email address or a website is an identifier that allows one to find, send, and receive information by way of the Internet and the World Wide Web (WWW or "the Web"). It allows a precise point to point delivery of information. In short, it is an electronic address that functions like a mailbox or street address.[73] As with a physical address one can receive actual goods and services, too, since many of those are in electronic form today. For example, one can send and receive movies, music, and computer programs by way of email.

A joke that originated at the time that fax machines first became popular illustrates the method involved in email and other electronic transmissions. It seems that a young attorney in Washington, DC tried to fax a document to an attorney in New York City. After the young attorney had tried to do this for an hour or so, the attorney in New York called him and said, "Hey, why do you keep sending me this same fax?" The young attorney replied, "Well, I keep putting the document in the machine, and it keeps coming back out!"

The domain name portion of an Internet address, has become a matter of strong personal and commercial interest. In an email address, the domain name is that part of an address after the "@" symbol and which ends with .com, .org, .net, etc. The Internet presence of the publisher of this book, Carolina Academic Press, provides an example. The Website is http://www.cap-press.com; an email address within that domain reads "orderstatus@cap-press.com." The domain is the "cap-press" part and is identical in a Website and an email address. Thus, the domain is like a big building with lots of mailboxes in it. The domain name system is a hierarchical structure designed to assure that one address (or number) attaches to one single account. Thus, the hypothetical address "monkeybusiness@toves.com" would identify one and only one email recipient account within the toves.com domain.[74]

---

73. An actual Internet address is a string of integers in a format such as: 123.45.678.901. That string is converted into a format which is easier to use, such as mypal@everywhere.com.

74. Based on Lewis Carroll's "Jabberwocky"in Chapter One of *Through the Looking Glass and What Alice Found There*— "Twas brillig, and the slithy toves / Did gyre and gimble in the wabe: / All mimsy were the borogoves, / And the mome raths outgrabe."

I made up the name while writing the book. I have since discovered that Toves.org is apparently a registered domain. An Internet search showed "The Domain TOVES.COM was Successfully Registered with Joker.com." Toves might also establish a website, in which case it would establish Uniform Resource Locator (URL) identifaction such as http://toves.com.

Figure 4-6. Carolina Academic Press

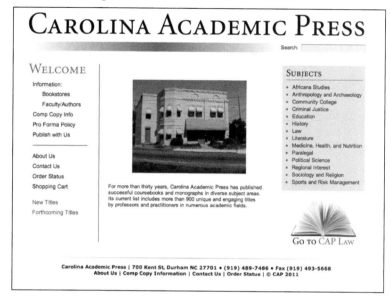

The system of obtaining a domain assignment functions for the most part smoothly. Information on how to register a domain can be found on the Internet. One such resource lists companies (registrars) one may contact to obtain the domain. It explains that once one makes the contact with the registrar, "the registrar you choose will ask you to provide various contact and technical information that makes up the registration. The registrar will then keep records of the contact information and submit the technical information to a central directory known as the 'registry.'"[75] Below this surface, however, lies a complicated arrangement. The complications are inherent in the system which has been set up, largely by delegation of authority from the United States government.

The Domain Name System (DNS) comprises a loosely formed layer of corporations that assigns domain names. For example, if one wants the name "toves.com," one applies to a company that assigns ".com" domain names.

The Internet Corporation for Assigned Names and Numbers (ICANN) has been delegated the authority to administer the Internet addressing system.[76]

---

75. Non-legal guidelines to the DNS system can be found online, e.g., InterNIC | FAQs on the Domain Names, Registrars, and Registration, http://www.internic.net/faqs/domain-names.html.

76. A 2008 article described the overall authority of ICANN: "As it now stands, day-to-day control over the DNS resides with ICANN, a California non-profit corporation with an

ICANN accredits the companies that provide the registrations. In effect, the corporation rules the most pervasive worldwide communications medium today. Domain name assignments are ruled by the policies of ICANN together with the contracts made at the time of assignment of a domain name. ICANN is not a government agency, yet it controls a vast communications system. It exercises a kind of power that one associates with a government. However, constitutional rights, such as freedom of speech, do not rule the conduct of private entities, as they do in the case of government agencies.[77]

ICANN policy also controls disputes concerning domain names. Its website describes the process:

> All registrars must follow the Uniform Domain-Name Dispute-Resolution Policy (often referred to as the "UDRP"). Under the policy, most types of trademark-based domain-name disputes must be resolved by agreement, court action, or arbitration before a registrar will cancel, suspend, or transfer a domain name. Disputes alleged to arise from abusive registrations of domain names (for example, cybersquatting) may be addressed by expedited administrative proceedings that the holder of trademark rights initiates by filing a complaint with an approved dispute-resolution service provider.
>
> To invoke the policy, a trademark owner should either (a) file a complaint in a court of proper jurisdiction against the domain-name holder (or where appropriate an in-rem action concerning the domain name) or (b) in cases of abusive registration submit a complaint to an approved dispute-resolution service provider.

---

explicit mandate in its Articles of Incorporation to "operate for the benefit of the Internet community as a whole, carrying out its activities in conformity with relevant principles of international law and applicable international conventions and local law." Christopher M. Bruner, *States, Markets, and Gatekeepers: Public-Private Regulatory Regimes in an Era of Economic Globalization*, 30 MICH. J. INT'L L. 125, 154–55 (2008).

77. "One of the main debates regarding the formation of ICANN was the question of whether the Department of Commerce had the authority to delegate Internet governance to a private, nonprofit organization.... As Michael Froomkin argued ... giving regulatory power to a non-profit organization meant relinquishing government sovereignty and delegating the federal government's Constitutional powers to a non-governmental entity.... Froomkin's advice remained unheeded.... [T]he heated debate concerning the legitimacy and structure of ICANN and the role of the United States continues." Jay P. Kesan & Andres A. Gallo, *Pondering the Politics of Private Procedures: The Case of ICANN*, 4 J. L. & POL'Y FOR INFO. SOC'Y 345, 352–355 (2008).

A domain name can become a hot commodity in itself, because the name can attract attention. A 2004 news items reported that, "a small Austin marketing firm has paid $2.75 million for CreditCards.com. Despite the rocky history of high-priced domain sales, participants say it was a fair price, and the sale may signal a new gold rush for Internet address speculators."[78] A domain incorporating an element of fame like "@cocacola.com" or "@vuitton.com" will likely draw attention and "hits."

Domain Name Disputes

Salient features of the domain address system include: A domain is not a trademark. It is an electronic address. The address is assigned by contract with a private company. Contracts assigning a name contain a provision which requires disputes to be resolved under the Uniform Domain Name Dispute Resolution Policy (UDRP).[79] A name used in the domain may be a trademark, if used to identify the source of goods or services. A name used in a domain name may infringe a trademark, if it is likely to create confusion. A famous trademark appearing in a domain name might blur or tarnish the mark's fame.

The World Intellectual Property Organization (WIPO) is a major administrator of the dispute process (UDRP). The current UDRP provides that a complaining party (e.g., Julia Roberts or Bruce Springsteen discussed below) must prove each of the following:

- the domain name is "identical or confusingly similar" to a complaining party's trademark;
- the party who holds the domain has no "legitimate interests" in the domain name; and
- the domain was registered and is being used in bad faith.

It also provides that ICANN itself does not participate, that the UDRP can be changed at any time, and that parties may choose to go to court or other tribunals instead of pursuing arbitration. Disputes beyond the scope of domain registration may go to any court or competent tribunal. The WIPO rules concerning the process provide for notice to parties, selection of a panel to deter-

---

78. Tech and gadgets—msnbc.com, http://www.msnbc.msn.com/id/5467584.

79. ICANN | Uniform Domain-Name Dispute-Resolution Policy—http://www.icann.org/en/udrp/udrp.htm.

mine the dispute, and case administration.[80] With these features in mind let us now turn to the resolution of two cases involving celebrities, the registrations of juliaroberts.com and brucespringsteen.com.

In 2000, actress Julia Roberts learned that Russell Boyd had registered "juliaroberts.com" in his name, and he claimed "ownership" to the address. Ms. Roberts filed a complaint with the WIPO Arbitration and Mediation Center.[81] From what we have learned so far, what does Julia Roberts have to complain about? The domain is just an address. "Julia Roberts" is the name of an actress; it refers to her. Many other women are named Julia Roberts in the United States.[82] The actress gained her celebrity for acting, not for being a brand of goods or services. Someday her name will become a brand as in the instances of Coco Chanel and Louis Vuitton. However, we know that the law recognizes such names because they are used to mark the source of goods or services, not because the person is famous. Even in the case of dilution, the marking aspect must come before fame is protected.

Russell Boyd appears to have speculated on the potential value of the domain name, juliaroberts.com. This resembles other economic speculation such as purchasing real estate near a planned freeway exit. Under usual business practices, there is nothing wrong with seizing such an opportunity. Obtaining property or commodities for resale drives much of the economy. Boyd's actions might be called "entrepreneurial" by some, "cybersquatting" by others.[83] Perhaps Boyd *did* think about selling later to the actress. Why not? That, after all, is how CreditCards.com got its name—it bought it. Or perhaps some other Julia Roberts would like to have the domain. Boyd then might resell the name to any one of them.

The WIPO panel that considered the Julia Roberts case consisted of one member appointed by WIPO and one selected by each party. Providing practically no analysis or explanation, the panel determined that "Roberts has rights in common law trademark or sufficient rights to ground an action for passing off." It noted that Boyd "admits that he has registered other domain names including several famous movie and sports stars. Such actions necessarily pre-

---

80. The WIPO rules are found at: World Intellectual Property Organization Supplemental Rules for Uniform Domain Name Dispute Resolution Policy, http://www.wipo.int/amc/en/domains/rules/supplemental/#2.

81. Julia Fiona Roberts, WIPO Domain Name Decision: D2000-0210, http://www.wipo.int/amc/en/domains/decisions/html/2000/d2000-0210.html. See also World Intellectual Property Association (WIPO), Domain Name Dispute Resolution—http://www.wipo.int/amc/en/domains/index.html.

82. An online white pages search for indicated that there may be over 300 people named "Julia Roberts" in the United States.

83. Federal legislation on cybersquatting is discussed below.

vent Complainant from using the disputed domain name and demonstrate a pattern of such conduct." The panel found Boyd acted in "bad faith" as required by the policy and awarded the domain to Ms. Roberts.

Some months after the Roberts case, Bruce Springsteen brought a WIPO complaint to wrest registration of brucespringsteen.com. from its registrant, Jeff Burgar. However, Springsteen lost his case. The WIPO panel was a three person panel set up by the same selection process as that of Roberts. The panel described Springsteen as "the famous, almost legendary, recording artist and composer." The panel distinguished Springsteen's case from Robert's, briefly discussing the lack of proof of a "distinctive secondary meaning" in Springsteen's claim.

> It appears to be an established principle from cases such as Jeanette Winterson, Julia Roberts, and Sade that in the case of very well known celebrities, their names can acquire a distinctive secondary meaning giving rise to rights equating to unregistered trade marks, notwithstanding the non-registerability of the name itself. It should be noted that no evidence has been given of the name 'Bruce Springsteen' having acquired a secondary meaning; in other words a recognition that the name should be associated with activities beyond the primary activities of Mr. Springsteen as a composer, performer and recorder of popular music.

The panel noted that Springsteen had a solid website without owning the brucespringsteen.com domain: "Nothing that has been done by Mr. Burgar has prevented Bruce Springsteen's official website at 'brucespringsteen.net' being registered and used in his direct interests."[84] The analysis sparked a dissent from the third panelist: "Complainant's name has acquired secondary meaning, has come to be recognized by the general public as indicating an association with the Complainant, and is the source of enormous goodwill towards the Complainant. Accordingly, Complainant has common law trademark rights in his name."[85]

The Springsteen and Roberts cases provide some guidance on future arbitrations, at least before WIPO panels. A famous celebrity is likely to be recognized as having priority to regain a domain assignment. Over time, the panels' rulings on domain disputes may develop a body of interpretation of the ICANN

---

84. Bruce Springsteen v. Jeff Burgar, WIPO Domain Name Decision: D2000-1532—http://www.wipo.int/amc/en/domains/decisions/html/2000/d2000-1532.html.

85. These references to "secondary meaning" do not withstand analysis if one applies United States law. The Supreme Court makes clear in the *Qualitex* case, secondary meaning *only applies* when that meaning identifies a source of products or services. One does not acquire trademark rights to a name because the name "has an association" with oneself!

policy. ICANN itself retains power to change its policies. The UDRP and its enforcement are limited. The system is pervasive and important, but it remains a contractual arrangement. The dispute resolution process is "incorporated by reference into your Registration Agreement, and sets forth the terms and conditions in connection with a dispute between you and any party other than us [the registrar]." The remedies do not go beyond awarding "ownership," that is, control, of the given domain registration.

The WIPO panel rulings cannot extend to any party who is not part of the contract, although, by contract one might agree to conditions that are "incorporated by reference" into all other contracts and make every other party bound, too. That is essentially what happens in gated communities and condos. ICANN has many attributes of being a gated worldwide "Internet Turnpike." A problem with such arrangements is that civil rights, such as those in the United States Constitution do not usually apply to limit the power of "private" arrangements.[86] Nor are the panels bound to follow the established law of any legal system in determining matters such as the meaning of a common law trademark. For example, in the Supreme Court decision in the *Samara* case, prior precedents were examined and their dynamics analyzed. The appearance of the Samara brand children's clothing could not be both "trade dress" and the fashion appeal of the clothing itself. Such an effort at rigor does not appear in these panel decisions.

Domain Names in Court

So far, the situation with regard to domain names presents a patchwork. Fame is not "property" in a legal sense. Yet privacy has been protected by common law and statute, and this protection has been extended to commercial fame.[87] Congress has given famous brands special protections. Domains are not trademarks. Yet certain people have successfully claimed special rights to own or control domains that use their names. Some domains like CreditCards.com command a high price. Finally some entrepreneurs (or cybersquatters) snap up domains that might become valuable. They behave like real estate speculators.

By the late 1990s, claims that domain names interfered with trademarks began to elbow their way into courts. One of these involved Avery Dennison, a modestly well known maker of paper products, adhesives, and other products.

---

86. In general the Constitution does not limit private actions (as opposed to governmental actions) that, e.g., deny speech or discriminate on the basis of sex or race.

87. Rights of privacy and publicity are discussed in Chapter Six.

Avery Dennison sued Jerry Sumpton and his business, Freeview Listings, Ltd., for trademark dilution and sought an order to force them to relinquish registration of the domains "avery.net" and "dennison.net." The Federal District Court found that Avery Dennison was famous, granted summary judgment in its favor, and ordered Sumpton and Freeview to relinquish their registration of the two names and ordered Avery Dennison to pay Sumpton and Freeview $600.

The trial judge began the decision by characterizing the defendants:

> Defendants are "cybersquatters," as that term has come to be commonly understood. They have registered over 12,000 internet domain names not for their own use, but rather to prevent others from using those names without defendants' consent. Like all "cybersquatters," defendants merely "squat" on their registered domain names until someone else comes along who wishes to use them.[88]

The description condemns the activity, yet speculation in real estate, stock, commodities, and so forth is routinely accepted.[89] What exactly was wrong here? A contemporaneous WIPO decision found that Sumpton's business had been set up to rent out email boxes to people who have the relevant surname and that it did not operate in any sort of bad faith.[90]

Sumpton appealed the trial court decision. The Ninth Circuit opened its opinion by noting that it was "the third panel of this court in just over a year faced with the challenging task of applying centuries-old trademark law to the newest medium of communication—the Internet." The Court found that Avery Dennison utterly failed to prove dilution or cybersquatting. It reversed the summary judgment in favor of Avery Dennison and ordered summary judgment to be entered in favor of Sumpton.[91] It remanded the case to the trial

---

88. Avery Dennison Corp. v. Sumpton, 999 F.Supp. 1337, 1338 (C. D. Cal. 1998); reversed Avery Dennison Corp. v. Sumpton, 189 F.3d 868 (9th Cir.1999).

89. "An extensive economic literature discusses the phenomenon of speculation. The exact meaning of the term, however, has proven remarkably elusive. Theorists generally use the word "speculator" to refer to someone who purchases an asset with the intent of quickly reselling it, or sells an asset with the intent of quickly repurchasing it." Lynn A. Stout, *Why the Law Hates Speculators: Regulation and Private Ordering in the Market for OTC Derivatives*, 48 Duke L.J. 701, 735 (1999).

90. Fashion designer Emilio Pucci proceeded against Sumpton. Emilio Pucci SRL v. Mailbank.com, Inc., WIPO Domain Name Decision: D2000-1786, http://www.wipo.int/amc/en/domains/decisions/html/2000/d2000-1786.html. As of February 4, 2009, Jerry Sumpton's company, Mailbank.com, appeared to be thriving. See Mailbank.com. As of that date, it also held an active registered trademark, "NETIDENTITY," Serial Number 76195879.

91. Avery Dennison Corp. v. Sumpton, 189 F.3d 868, 971 (9th Cir.1999).

Figure 4-7. Domain Names

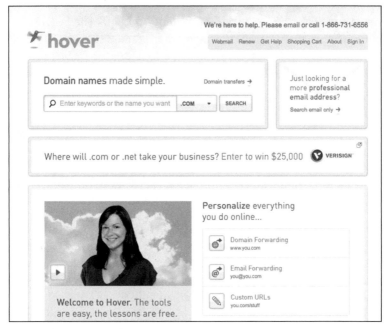

Note: Mailbank.com is now hover.com.

court only to determine whether attorney fees ought to be assessed against Avery Dennison on the basis that its case had been "groundless, unreasonable, vexatious, or pursued in bad faith."

After a number of cases like Avery Dennison had progressed through the courts, Congress began to take an interest. In 1999 the trademark law was amended to allow trademark owners to sue anyone who with a "bad faith intent to profit from that mark ... registers, traffics in, or uses a domain name" that is confusingly similar to the mark or dilutes the fame of a famous mark.[92] The Act referred to such activity as "cyberpiracy."

Utah Lighthouse Ministry v. Foundation for Apologetic Information and Research, 527 F.3d 1045, (10th Cir. 2008), involved a dispute among parties with conflicting views about the Church of Jesus Christ of Latter Day Saints (LDS). The case dealt with both trademark confusion and cybersquatting claims.

---

92. 15 U.S.C. §1125 (d), Cyberpiracy prevention, the Anticybersquatting Consumer Protection Act, Pub. L. 106–113. The neologisms "cyberpiracy" and "cybersquatting" are rife with connotation and tend to be used interchangeably in legislation and court opinions.

The plaintiffs in the case were Jerald and Sandra Tanner, disaffected Mormons who were sharply critical of their former church. They had organized a nonprofit organization in 1983, called the Utah Lighthouse Ministry (UTLM). With the advent of the Internet UTML built up a notable online presence. The website for the organization announces: "Utah Lighthouse™ Ministry (UTLM) is a Christian non-profit organization providing humanitarian outreach to the Community, and printing critical research and documentation on the LDS Church."[93]

The Tanners' criticism of Mormonism was strongly contested by another organization, Foundation for Apologetic Information & Research (FAIR), formed in 1997. Allen Wyatt, vice president and webmaster for FAIR, created a website for FAIR, the appearance and content of which were strikingly similar to those of UTLM. A striking similarity between the two websites caused the pitched religious disagreements to ripen into a trademark lawsuit. The mimicry was such that one would understandably confuse FAIR's website with the website of UTLM. The Court summarized the similarity:

> The design elements are similar, including the image of a lighthouse with black and white barbershop stripes. However, the words "Destroy, Mislead, and Deceive" are written across the stripes on the Wyatt website. Prominent text on the Wyatt website consists of a slight modification of the language located in the same position on the UTLM website. For example, the UTLM website states: "Welcome to the Official Website of the Utah Lighthouse Ministry, founded by Jerald and Sandra Tanner." In comparison, the Wyatt website states: "Welcome to an official website *about* the Utah Lighthouse Ministry, *which was* founded by Jerald and Sandra Tanner."(emphasis added.)[94]

Both organizations sold books. UTLM sold their books at a bookstore and online, while FAIR sold theirs only online. The two organizations offered thirty overlapping titles.

The Court determined that UTLM had failed to prove its case in three separate ways. It failed to provide adequate evidence that its Lighthouse display identified UTLM as the source of goods or services. UTLM also failed to show that the claimed Lighthouse mark was actually used to promote sales of goods or services. Finally, UTLM had failed to prove that FAIR's website would confuse consumers. Most instructive, the mimicry by FAIR successfully mocked

---

93. UTLM website—http://www.utlm.org/navaboutus.htm. Jerald Tanner died in October 2006.

94. Utah Lighthouse Ministry v. Foundation for Apologetic Information and Research, 527 F.3d 1045, 1049 (10th Cir. 2008).

Figure 4-8. UTLM vs. FAIR

Utah Lighthouse Ministry
PO Box 1884 Salt Lake City, UT 84110

Welcome to the Official Website of Utah Lighthouse™ Ministry,
founded by Jerald and Sandra Tanner.
The purpose of this site is to document problems with the claims of Mormonism and compare LDS doctrines with Christianity.

In Memoriam: Jerald Tanner

About Us
FAQs
What's New
Topical Index
Testimony
Newsletters
Online Resources
Online Books
Booklist
Order/Contact
Email
Special Thanks
Other Websites

Psalms 43:3
"O send out thy light and thy truth: let them lead me..."

John 3:21
"But he that doeth truth cometh to the light..."

John 8:12
Jesus said: "I am the light of the world: he that followeth me
shall not walk in darkness..."

"Come on! ye prosecutors! ye false swearers! All hell, boil over! Ye burning mountains, roll down your lava! for I will come out on top at last. **I have more to boast of than ever any man had.** I am the only man that has ever been able to keep a whole church together since the days of Adam. A large majority of the whole have stood by me. Neither Paul, John, Peter, **nor Jesus** ever did it. I boast that no man ever did such a work as I. The followers of Jesus ran away from Him; but

UTAH LIGHTHOUSE MINISTRY
SHADOW or Reality?

Welcome to an official Website about the Utah Lighthouse Ministry,
which was founded by Jerald and Sandra Tanner.
The purpose of this site is to document problems with the claims made by Jerald and Sandra Tanner under the guise of Christianity.

Click this
Lighthouse
to see
Reliable
Information
About the
LDS Church

Click the
Lighthouse's
base for
the Official
LDS Site

Titus 1:10-11
"For there are many unruly and vain talkers and deceivers...
Whose mouths must be stopped, who subvert whole houses,
teaching things which they ought not, for filthy lucre's sake."

2 Peter 3:3
"...there shall come in the last days scoffers, walking after their
own lusts."

John 8:32
"And ye shall know the truth, and the truth shall make you free."

Articles
about the
Tanners

Books
by the
Tanners

"For more than three decades, **Jerald and Sandra Tanner have devoted their lives to exposing and trying to destroy Mormonism.** They have succeeded in upsetting Mormons of various persuasions, largely because of their abrasive writing style, which is most nearly reminiscent of FBI undercover agents reporting back to J. Edgar Hoover on the terrible the UTLM website. "The fact that the Wyatt website is a successful parody weighs heavily against a finding of likelihood of confusion. A parody adopts some features of the original mark, but relies upon a difference from the original mark to produce its desired effect."[95]

The Court firmly rejected UTLM's claim that Wyatt had been "cybersquatting" when he registered a group of domain names utahlighthouse.com and utahlight-house.org, To prove a claim under the Act, UTLM would have to show that Wyatt had registered or used the domain names with a bad faith intent to profit from them. The Court of Appeals independently reviewed the evidence on this issue and concluded that the defendants lacked the necessary bad faith when they registered for the domains. Wyatt's belief that his use of any of these domains would have been legal as a parody militated against a finding of "bad faith."

Other Internet Issues

The Internet provides a space for commercial and productive activity. That space is "virtual," in the sense that it is a simulation of reality. For example, video games provide simulations of war or of urban living. However, the Internet is also a real place where events occur. This is the case when email provides the means of communication, when a software program is collaboratively developed by way of the Internet, and when an electronic product is delivered.[96]

The conflicts examined above show how important the addressing system is. "A domain name is a valuable resource, yet one which resists being classified as a form of property."[97] In addition to domain name issues, Internet technology presents conflicts based on its power to control events in a direct, physical sense. For example, "linking" is a basic feature of Internet technology. In a nutshell, linking refers to a word or image functioning as an immediate connection to something else. That ability forms the core of the functional aspect of the Internet called the World Wide Web (WWW). Click on a highlighted word, and the computer immediately connects to a linked reference.[98]

---

95. *Id.* 1057.

96. The simulations may very well compete with reality in many people's minds. This presents a growing social issue. In one type of involvement Internet users "live" a second reality online, as in "Second Life," http://secondlife.com.

97. H. C. Anawalt, IP STRATEGY—COMPLETE INTELLECTUAL PROPERTY PLANNING, ACCESS AND PROTECTION §1:133 (Thomson West 2010). §1:133. See Dorer v. Arel, 60 F. Supp. 2d 558 (E.D. Va. 1999).

98. Linking is discussed further in the Chapter on Copyright and in the Appendix, An Internet Case Study.

We conclude our inquiry into Internet issues with a case that pitted Google against a small computer service provider named Rescuecom. *Rescuecom Corp. v. Google Inc.*, 562 F.3d 123 (2nd Cir. 2009). The core of the conflict involved the use of links. The linking involved had the potential of diverting commercial traffic away from Rescuecom's services and redirecting it to competitors.

The Google search service is so commonly used that many readers will have used it routinely. "To google" has become a common verb. Google's business has been built on the searching and finding capacity of the Web. It does not charge any user; its use is "free." However, Google does get paid handsomely. It generates income in at least two ways. It sells advertising which automatically reaches the user. It also sells the use of hyperlinked words that guide users to certain sources in accordance with a ranking system. Google determines the ranking. Its software in effect tells the reader where to go first.

Rescuecom provides computer and systems repairs. It does so by licensing others to do these repairs under its name, presumably under standards of performance that it requires. "Rescuecom" is a registered trademark of the company.[99] Google had identified "rescuecom" as a useful word to tag. That is, Google had turned the term "rescuecom" a hyperlink which would automatically refer to other sites.[100] Google allowed other businesses to purchase the use of that tag and thus direct Internet inquiries to their websites. According to the allegations in the case, Rescuecom's competitors were able to purchase use of the term. The Court explained:

> Many of Rescuecom's competitors advertise on the Internet. Through its Keyword Suggestion Tool, Google has recommended the Rescuecom trademark to Rescuecom's competitors as a search term to be purchased. Rescuecom's competitors, some responding to Google's recommendation, have purchased Rescuecom's trademark as a keyword in Google's AdWords program, so that whenever a user launches a search for the term "Rescuecom," seeking to be connected to Rescuecom's website, the competitors' advertisement and link will appear

---

99. "Since 1998, 'Rescuecom' has been a registered federal trademark, and there is no dispute as to its validity." 562 F.3d 123, 125.

100. Note on terminology: As I understand the matter, "metatag" and "hyperlink" each refer to code that cause a word to *function* rather that just be read. However, "hyperlink" generally refers to code that will cause the search to jump to another (perhaps unrelated) item. "Metatag" generally refers to a function which makes a word of text more "visible" on the Web. The latter has become much less important in Web usage. See Meta element, http://en.wikipedia.org/w/index.php?title=Meta_element&oldid=403453276 (last visited Dec. 24, 2010).

on the searcher's screen. This practice allegedly allows Rescuecom's competitors to deceive and divert users searching for Rescuecom's website.[101]

Google had argued that the inclusion of the name in its search function did not constitute a trademark use, as it was an internal, rather than a public usage. The court ruled, however, that the use of "Rescuecom", as a hyperlink (that is, as an active search function) constituted "use" of a mark for trademark purposes. It explained, "regardless of whether Google's use of Rescuecom's mark in its internal search algorithm could constitute an actionable trademark use, Google's recommendation and sale of Rescuecom's mark to its advertising customers are not internal uses."[102]

The Court differentiated permissible uses of another's trademark, for example, to draw attention to its own product solely for comparison. For example, bottles of generic pain reliever might be placed next to a brand name for comparison with a generic product. In such a case, one would escape liability not because of a lack of use, but because it is "a benign practice which does not cause a likelihood of consumer confusion." The Court stated, "we have no idea whether Rescuecom can prove that Google's use of Rescuecom's trademark in its AdWords program causes likelihood of confusion or mistake." Those would be matters to be proved in further proceedings.[103]

Linking and other message control issues will continue to arise in trademark practice. The Internet and the Web are integral to commerce, and commerce of today is directly concerned with all phases of branding and direction of consumer tastes.

Owning Language

Trademarks and their economic power have enormous influence on society. This is especially in the evident in economic power exercised by owners of powerful trademarks. As we close this chapter we will briefly consider the influence of trademarks on language and culture.

It is easy to become cranky about language and its so called "proper" use. In their book *Do You Speak American?*, Robert MacNeil and William Cran cau-

---

101. 562 F.3d 123, 126–27.
102. *Id.* 130.
103. *Id.* 130.

tion against this crankiness. The English language is a constantly evolving fabric and has been so from its beginnings. Proper usage really depends entirely on what we agree to. A dictionary is primarily a record of how words are in fact used. This said, even the most liberal or inclusive view of what our language is or should become draws the line at ownership: English (and its American variant) belongs to all of us. It should not be owned, dominated, or managed by a few or by a power structure, governmental or corporate.

Trademarks commercialize language. Marketers seize on slang and make it their own. A well known example is "just do it," a common expression which emerged sometime in the 1960s or 70s. That phrase was appropriated by Nike in the 1990s and is now a registered and famous trademark.[104] In addition certain trademarks function mainly to create image, rather than to identify a source or inform consumers. This function was noted by Justice Holmes nearly a century ago.

The word "olympics" provides an interesting example of the phenomenon of commercial language control. For most of us, "olympics" or "Olympics" in the plural refers to the Olympic Games, ancient or modern. That term derived from ancient Greek society. The Greek city-states would set aside their incessant wars and other conflicts in order to enjoy watching and participating in fine athletics. The same competition and enjoyment occurs today, though the circumstances have been altered enormously. Traditional elements that remain include the contest of fine athletes, the use of such games to divert a populace from pressing problems, and commitment of public resources, including stadiums. The changes include enhanced professionalization of athletes, use of dope, and above all domination by commercial activity and advertising. The trademark and brand "olympics" are both cause and effect in this phenomenon.

The word "olympic" is in certain contexts a protected trademark, controlled by the United States Olympic Committee. The Committee is a federally chartered corporation with a "perpetual existence." Among other things, the Act of Congress grants the U.S. Olympic Committee the exclusive ownership and control of the Olympic Games symbol (five interlaced circles) as well as the words "Olympic," "Olympiad," "Citius Altius Fortius," "Paralympic," "Paralympiad," "Pan-American," "America Espirito Sport Fraternite," or any combi-

---

104. Nike "owns valid and subsisting federal trademark registrations issued by the United States Patent and Trademark Office for its JUST DO IT mark, including Reg. Nos. 1,817,919 (registered on January 25, 1994) and 1,875,307 (registered on January 24, 1995)." Nike, Inc. v. Circle Group Internet, Inc. 318 F. Supp. 2d 688 N.D. Ill., 2004. The defendant in the Circle Group case did not dispute that the mark was famous.

nation of these words.[105] In addition, the Committee is entitled to an injunction against any person who uses those words or symbols to "promote any theatrical exhibition, athletic performance, or competition." Thus, the term "olympic" is far from free for all to use. Use of this ancient term is now for practical purposes controlled by a corporation.

In *San Francisco Arts and Athletics v. U.S. Olympic Committee*, 483 U.S. 522 (1987), the United States Supreme Court upheld the grant of sweeping trademark control to the Committee. The case arose due to the enthusiastic efforts of a portion of the San Francisco gay community during the 1980s.[106] The group wanted to establish a competition for that community. Its first choice was to call its event the "Gay Olympics." Why not? The name is a splashy, engaging way to call attention to athleticism and to assist in changing social mores that were harming a stigmatized group. In addition, the "Special Olympics" (for handicapped persons) had already been held for more than twenty years and had grown exponentially in those decades. The group incorporated and in 1981 began publicly promoting a forthcoming "Gay Olympic Games." In short order, the group was enjoined from using the name "Olympics" in its promotions. The injunction was sustained by the Supreme Court. The Court ruled that the term "Olympic" is not a generic term as to which Congress could not grant trademark protection.[107] Justice Brennan dissented, finding that the Act violated the First Amendment. "Language, even in a commercial context, properly belongs to the public, unless the Government's asserted interest is substantial, and unless the limitation imposed is no more extensive than necessary to serve that interest."[108]

Practical Guidelines

Virtually all businesses use trademarks. Use of marks by small or local businesses usually creates little risk of expensive conflict. On the other hand, aggressive marketing and advertising, especially by sizable corporations can create

---

105. Amateur Sports Act of 1978, 36 U.S.C. §220506. See also *Gold Meddling: How the U.S. Olympic Committee Overprotects the Olympics Brand* 5 DePaul J. Sports L. & Contemp. Probs. 57 (2008).

106. Federation of Gay Games: History, http://www.gaygames.com/index.php?id=28.

107. "Because Congress reasonably could conclude that the USOC has distinguished the word 'Olympic' through its own efforts, Congress' decision to grant the USOC a limited property right in the word 'Olympic' falls within the scope of trademark law protections, and thus certainly within constitutional bounds." San Francisco Arts and Athletics v. U.S. Olympic Committee, 483 U.S. 522, 535–36 (1987).

108. *Id.* at 573. Four justices dissented.

serious conflicts, as in the case of Chewy Vuiton. The following guidelines track that reality:

1. Most businesses use some sort of a trademark. Usually little needs to be done to continue one's use of the mark. When a mark makes a significant difference to a business, it is worthwhile to check with an attorney to see what steps, if any, ought to be taken to protect the mark. For example, if state registration is available, that might be useful. It should be easy to find an attorney to provide this basic advice at little cost. In general, if one uses an attorney in business planning, it is worthwhile to have a trademark review be part of that process.

2. When making a sizable investment in decor or marketing efforts, a consultation is also worthwhile. For example, one would not wish to invest in decorating a business, then be surprised by a "trade dress" lawsuit. Also, if one plans a business that will be interstate or operate by way of the Internet, consultation is useful.

3. If one receives a demand letter or other communication concerning a trademark, one ought to contact an attorney right away. A small amount of prevention may avoid difficulties. One should get early advice when famous brands or expensive advertising enters into the picture.

Concluding Thoughts

The core practical concept in trademark law is using a mark to identify one's goods. That identification function has remained in place during centuries of development of trademark law. However, since the industrial revolution, trademarks have assumed a more prominent place in the commercial landscape, especially in relatively affluent markets. Trademarks have become a part of a culture which is dominated by goods and marketing. In addition, the pervasiveness and power of Internet and other media have enhanced the influence of names and branding. Along with these changes in commerce and in consumer understanding of markets has come an alteration in trademark legal realities.

These changes in marketing have been accompanied by changes in how courts handle cases. These changes have led scholars to speak of "traditional trademark law" and "modern trademark law." When cases go to court, liability for trademark infringement appears to turn on a more general state of consumer confusion than on their particular confusion as to source. This allows judges and juries to find trademark infringement more easily than when the question of liability is more tightly drawn. Attorneys defending against trademark claims can counter such broad claims by tenaciously returning to the essential language of statutes such as the Lanham Act.

Table 4-2. Trademark Guidelines

General Rule	Comment	Source
Subject matter. Any mark or symbol used to identify the source of goods or services.	*Use* to *identify* is central concept. Service marks identify services, but "trademark" commonly refers to both.	Common law; 15 U.S.C. §1125
Registration. No registration is necessary to enforce trademarks. May register under state and federal law.	Marks on "Principal Register" presumed valid; can become incontestable after five years continuous use.	37 C.F.R. PART 2, §2.21; fees to file
What rights? Remedies against another's use of one's mark.	The core concept is to prevent confusion as to the origin of goods or services.	17 U.S.C. §106
How long? One may preserve a trademark for as long as one uses it.	One maintains a mark by using it; loses it by lapse of use.	Common law; 15 U.S.C. §1125
Serves only as mark. Functional or aesthetic features are not permitted.	Marks are to identify, but do not allow ownership of functions, aesthetics.	*Qualitex* 514 U.S. 159
Mark must not mislead.	One purpose of trademark is to help the consumer make informed choices.	*Koke* 254 U.S. 143
Trade dress and color. An ambience or color which serves only to *mark* may qualify as a trademark.	The trade dress must not be functional and must have acquired a marketplace meaning ("secondary meaning").	*Wal-Mart* 529 U.S. 205
Famous trademarks. Brands like Coca Cola protected against blurring or tarnishment without showing confusion.	Fame does not immunize from commentary or parody.	State statutes, 15 U.S.C. §1125 (c)
Domain names. These are addresses. However, use of a domain name may infringe a trademark.	Domain names are established by contract; contract disputes are governed by an ICANN defined process, the UDRP.	*UTLM* case, 527 F.3d 1045
"Gray Market." Trademark owner can use law to restrict sale of properly marked goods when sold outside approved channels.	Owner must prove that the goods sold by defendant are "materially different" from one owner authorizes for sale.	See *K Mart Corp.* 486 U.S. 281
Fair use. Broad freedom to comment, spoof, parody.	Defendant needs to show, e.g., parody and show lack of confusion.	Common law; 15 U.S.C. §1125

Chapter Five

Trade Secrets

Introduction

Any commercially valuable information one guards well may be treated as a trade secret. While there is there is general acceptance of basic propositions across the United States, the law of each individual state determines the extent and protection of trade secrets. An exception to this is a federal statute, the Economic Espionage Act of 1996 which creates federal criminal liability in some cases.

The notion of "secrecy" can be misleading, however. Secrecy disappears once one reveals a secret. What the law enforces is reasonable efforts to limit access to the ideas one considers important. One needs to keep the information to oneself or within the confines of established confidential relationships. Some confidential relationships are established by law. For example, matters revealed to an attorney during a legal consultation are generally confidential. However, what one says to another at a party does not become confidential simply because that person is an attorney. The conversation must be part of a private legal consultation, not conversation at the dinner table with guests. Employment or service on a board of directors are examples of circumstances which may create a trade secret obligation. Other confidential relationships can be established by a contract or conduct that makes it reasonably clear that one expects confidentially concerning what is about to be revealed. Thus, some simple guidelines emerge: Establish a confidential relationship first. Then reveal the secret. When revealing matters, one needs identify what is secret clearly enough, so the confidant may safeguard it.

The first case in the chapter the California Supreme Court put the matter bluntly: "The idea man who blurts out his idea without having first made his bargain has no one but himself to blame for the loss of his bargaining power."

Ace in the Hole

In the 1951 movie, *Ace in the Hole,* a newspaper reporter, Chuck Tatum (Kirk Douglas) is in Mexico doing a story on a rattlesnake hunt when he learns of a man trapped in a cave he has been excavating for artifacts to sell at his struggling tourist restaurant. Tatum connives with a local sheriff to slow down rescue efforts, so he can build the drama of the story and milk the story for his advantage. The movie helped vault Billy Wilder into prominence as a director. It also embroiled Wilder and Paramount Films in a controversy with an actor, Victor Desny, who claimed that Wilder had made off with a story that was rightfully his. The controversy blossomed into a case which went to the California Supreme Court.[1]

The *Desny* case provides a segue from copyright concepts to trade secret law. The Court summarized the facts as follows:

> In November, 1949, plaintiff telephoned Wilder's office. Wilder's secretary ... answered, and plaintiff stated that he wished to see Wilder. At the secretary's insistence that plaintiff explain his purpose, plaintiff 'told her about this fantastic unusual story.... I told her that it was the life story of Floyd Collins who was trapped and made sensational news for two weeks ... and I told her the plot.... Plaintiff sought to send Wilder a copy of the (sixty-five page) story but ... she stated that Wilder ... wanted stories in synopsis form ... Two days later plaintiff, after preparing a three or four page outline of the story, telephoned Wilder's office a second time and told the secretary the synopsis was ready. The secretary requested plaintiff to read the synopsis to her over the telephone so that she could take it down in shorthand, and plaintiff did so. During the conversation the secretary told plaintiff that the story seemed interesting and that she liked it. 'She said that she would talk it over with Billy Wilder and she would let me know.' Plaintiff on his part told the secretary that defendants could use the story only if they paid him 'the reasonable value of it ... I made it clear to her that I wrote the story and that I wanted to sell it.... I naturally mentioned again that this story was my story ... and therefore if anybody used it they will have to pay for it ... She said that if Billy Wilder or Paramount uses the story, 'naturally we will pay you for it." Plaintiff did not remember whether in his first telephone conversation with the secretary anything was said concerning his purpose of selling the story to defendants. He did not at any time speak with defendant Wilder.[2]

---

1. Wilder won a number of Academy Awards and nominations for his screenplays and directing. Desny appears to have been a working actor who appeared in many movies, but without screen credit.

2. Desny v. Wilder, 46 Cal.2d 715, 727 (1956).

The film followed the lines of Desny's synopsis. Desny consulted attorneys, and they determined that he had a case. But *what* case? The secretary's stenography could qualify as "fixation" of his synopsis, for copyright purposes. However, he had asked her to take dictation, thus he had consented to her having the copy which she would share with her boss. If that synopsis had been used in preparing the film, it would seem that only ideas rather that expression were used by Wilder. Thus, his attorneys did not cast his case as a copyright claim, but as some other form of wrongful taking of a work without compensating for it. If Wilder or Paramount knew that Desny had offered a valuable writing, a "property," on the condition that he be paid for it, then Wilder ought to pay.[3]

The Court accepted the conclusion that Wilder had used the synopsis in making the movie. The movie "closely resembles plaintiff's synopsis. Ergo, plaintiff's synopsis appears to be a valuable literary composition." The Court ruled that Wilder might have a legal obligation to pay for what he used depending on the answers to the following questions: "Did he (Desny) submit the composition to the defendants for sale? Did the defendants (Wilder and Paramount), knowing that it was offered to them for sale, accept and use that composition or any part thereof? If so, what was the reasonable value of the composition?"[4]

The Court observed that Desny had not shown violation of a property right, such as copyright.[5] Nor could he require others to pay him because he passed on valuable ideas. The court put the matter bluntly: "The idea man who blurts out his idea without having first made his bargain has no one but himself to blame for the loss of his bargaining power." But if ideas are revealed under circumstances where one could reasonably expect to be paid, then the law may imply an obligation to compensate, even when no specific bargain has been struck. However, a heavy burden rests on any party claiming such a right.

---

3. The Court viewed the case as "threading a maze." "Among the questions are these: 'Is the plaintiff seeking to recover for (a) the conveyance of an abstract idea or (b) the sale of a literary property? Or (c) is he clutching at both theories? (d) Does plaintiff's evidence tend to show an express or implied contract or (e) facts from which the law might impose a so-called quasi-contractual obligation, as to either the idea or the synopsis?' " 46 Cal.2d 715, 724.

4. 46 Cal.2d 715, 744.

5. There is general consensus on this point. "The influential formulation in §757 of the RESTATEMENT OF TORTS (1939), reporting that the property conception 'has been frequently advanced and rejected,' concluded that the prevailing theory of liability rests on 'a general duty of good faith.' " RESTATEMENT (THIRD) OF UNFAIR COMPETITION §39 (1995). That, however, does *not* prevent any state from treating or analyzing trade secret cases as property right cases. "The dispute over the nature of trade secret rights has had little practical effect on the rules governing civil liability for the appropriation of a trade secret." *Id.*

Some companies establish policies of refusing to consider unsolicited ideas in order to fend off Desny type claims. For example, Apple Inc. publishes the following policy on its website:

> Apple or any of its employees do not accept or consider unsolicited ideas ... Please do not submit any unsolicited ideas, ... if, despite our request that you not send us your ideas, you still submit them, then regardless of what your letter says, the following terms shall apply to your submissions.... You agree that: (1) your submissions and their contents will automatically become the property of Apple, without any compensation to you; (2) Apple may use or redistribute the submissions and their contents for any purpose and in any way; (3) there is no obligation for Apple to review the submission; and (4) there is no obligation to keep any submissions confidential.

The policy is likely useful in discouraging both submissions and claims made on them. However, simply publishing a boilerplate statement on a website will not create any form of agreement, let alone that contents of a submission "will automatically become the property of Apple." A submission to Apple in California takes the first step into the murky zone of the *Desny* case. Trade secret law seeks to provide clearer guidance concerning the actual legal obligations.

* * *

A Pause

A key practical concept in trade secrets is keeping information to oneself or sharing it with trusted persons. Trade secret law enforces the confidentiality of such relationships. A practical definition of a trade secret is: A right to require certain others to keep information confidential. The legal definition of a trade secret depends on state law, with few exceptions. Trade secret law does not create a form of "property." This invites a comparison of the four doctrines, patent, copyright, trademark, and trade secret. The first three protect a form of property; trade secret does not. Instead, trade secret protection stems from a civil obligation to respect certain relationships. Classification of a right as property usually gives added advantages, such as ease of obtaining a preliminary injunction. Those are discussed further in Chapter Seven.[6]

---

6. See Charles Tait Graves, *Trade Secrets as Property: Theory and Consequences*, 15 J. Intell. Prop. L. 39 (2007).

Table 5-1. A Comparison of Rights

Patent	Copyright	Trademark	Trade Secret
A property right.	A property right.	A property right.	A civil obligation or tort.
Patents clearly define rights, not conditioned by fair use, independent creation not a defense.	Copyrights cover "expression," thus are indefinite; subject to fair use, independent creation is not a copy.	Intent to eliminate confusion only; increased protection of big "famous" brands.	Law protects efforts to keep confidential rather than "property"; but some states do classify as a property right
Recognized circa 1620.	Recognized circa 1710.	Recognized circa 1740.	Recognized in 19th century.

There are some exceptions to the generalization that a trade secret is not a property right. Some states have decided to treat trade secrets as property rights. States have power to do that, just as they do with regard to creating institutions such as marital community property. Also, the United States Constitution protects individuals and corporations against a taking of property without due process and just compensation. The Supreme Court has ruled that trade secrets must receive this constitutional protection.[7]

Secrecy and Confidentiality

When Desny called Wilder's secretary, he had his own "ace in the hole," a possibly valuable sketch for a movie.[8] The value of the sketch lay in being able to use or market the sketch. If one continues with an analogy to an ace in the hole, a hidden card in a game of stud poker, one tries to keep other players from knowing about that ace. If other players know, they can design their play so they avoid or minimize the influence of your ace! A good player with the ace

---

7. Ruckelshaus v. Monsanto Co., 467 U.S. 986, 1003 (1984) explains why "a trade secret is property protected by the Fifth Amendment Taking Clause." The *Monsanto* case determines that government must compensate when takes a trade secret, but does not classify a trade secret as property for any other purpose.

8. In stud poker some cards are dealt face up and others face down. An "ace in the hole" refers to an ace which is face down and hidden from other players. A poker player's trade secret!

will not help the others out; he will likely keep a "poker face." The value of Desny's sketch lay in large part in keeping it secret. If he told Wilder, then Wilder would not only know about the ace, but he would have it, too! The first method in protecting the value of a trade secret is to keep it secret—just like in a game of poker.

The secretary had pushed Desny into a tight spot. She made it clear that he would have to provide a synopsis or there was no chance of a deal. Desny essentially threw himself on Wilder's goodwill. In a poker game, one does not expect the other players will bail one out. The whole point of the game, whether for fun or profit, is to take thoughtful risks and take advantage of others' mistakes. However, trade secret law differs from poker in a important way. Trade secret law allows one to restrict others from using information under certain circumstances. Generally one needs to identify what is secret and assure the existence of a relation of confidentiality in order to protect a secret.[9]

In order to use most valuable information, one must share it with others. Desny's situation is a case in point. To profit from his story ideas he would need to move ahead with them. He might dig in and write a short story, then publish it. However, the publication of the story would reveal his story line or theme, and he might not want to do that. For example, the expressions in the published story would be protected by copyright, but the component ideas would not. At some point, Desny will have to engage others and share his ideas. That is why he went to Wilder's office.

By the time Desny saw his attorneys, he had lost his ace, but he wanted to be paid for it anyway. He left his attorneys to scramble for some legal theory that would aid him. Trade secret law does allow a means of sharing information under conditions that protect it. The basic method is to share the secret with someone else, but to do so under conditions of confidentiality. Laws establish certain confidential relationships. For example, one can usually require an attorney, doctor, or priest to decline to give evidence in court of information revealed during a professional consultation.[10]

One can also create a special relationship. We do that often enough when we create friendships. We expect our friends not to abuse confidences or take

---

9. I asked a friend, "what does this sentence mean?" She said, "This is a secret. I'll show you, if you agree to keep it confidential." That is a good summary of trade secret law.

10. These are three types of legal relationships commonly protected by rules of evidence: attorney/client, doctor/patient, and "priest/penitent." Another such privilege available in litigation is communications between spouses. These privileges are not absolute, and they do not create trade secrets. They provide good examples of legal protection of certain established relationships.

advantage of us. But some friends do, and friends are not legally bound to maintain confidences. The relationship entered into must have ingredients that make it legally binding to preserve information. In most instances, one will have to show an on-going relationship that implies a degree of confidentiality. Often this will arise in an employment relationship. At other times the specific communications among parties give rise to an enforceable confidential relationship.

Desny had done little or nothing to create a relationship. Basically he forced his story on the secretary and did so from the beginning. He failed to satisfy either of the classic prongs of trade secret law—hide the information or create a relationship. However, Desny did win his appeal because he had presented a strong enough case for him to go to trial and have a judge or jury hear his story. Wilder and Paramount eventually settled, perhaps because they worried about the outcome, or perhaps because the case was a nuisance.

It is difficult to isolate definitive legal principles that bind in trade secret cases. This contrasts sharply with patent and copyright law, where the basic requirements are stated firmly in United States statutes. Everyone, including the Supreme Court, is bound to follow the rules laid down in those statutes. In trade secret law, each of the fifty one jurisdictions (the states plus the District of Columbia) is free to define its own limits as to what will be protected. Even within a given state jurisdiction, courts and legislatures have difficulty drawing clear lines.

Trade secret law resists definitive statement, but several practical considerations are widely shared throughout the United States. First, it is generally agreed that ideas in themselves cannot be owned. The *Desny* court quoted Justice Brandeis on this point: "The general rule of law is, that the noblest of human productions—knowledge, truths ascertained, conceptions, and ideas— become, after voluntary communication to others, free as the air to common use." If one wants to keep a secret one must guard it. Second, it is impractical to work with ideas without sharing them with others. That is, as a practical matter one cannot literally keep a secret, if one wants to use it. Third, legal protection for trade secrets requires the creation of conditions of confidentiality.[11]

---

11. The United States Supreme Court described the area of trade secret law as driven by commercial ethics: "The maintenance of standards of commercial ethics and the encouragement of invention are the broadly stated policies behind trade secret law. 'The necessity of good faith and honest, fair dealing, is the very life and spirit of the commercial world.'" Kewanee Oil Co. v. Bicron Corp., 416 U.S. 470, 481–82 (1974). *Desny* and the *DuPont* case (discussed below) represent unusual situations where courts have allowed a basis of recov-

Efforts to State General Rules

In the 1920s a group of legal academics, attorneys and judges established the American Law Institute (ALI). One of its major projects was an effort to make general summaries of major principles of law for all fifty states. One of those efforts, the First Restatement of Torts, set forth a provision which has deeply influenced trade secret law across the country. Section 757 provides:

> One who discloses or uses another's trade secret, without a privilege to do so, is liable to the other if
> (a) he discovered the secret by improper means, or
> (b) his disclosure or use constitutes a breach of confidence reposed in him by the other in disclosing the secret to him, or
> (c) he learned the secret from a third person with notice of the facts that it was a secret and that the third person discovered it by improper means or that the third person's disclosure of it was otherwise a breach of his duty to the other, or
> (d) he learned the secret with notice of the facts that it was a secret and that its disclosure was made to him by mistake.

The authors explained their rule as follows: "The subject matter of a trade secret must be secret.... The (secret holder) may, without losing his protection, communicate it to employees involved in its use. He may likewise communicate it to others pledged to secrecy. Nevertheless, a substantial element of secrecy must exist, so that, except by the use of improper means, there would be difficulty in acquiring the information."

Many cases which have been decided in the intervening years have been influenced by the concepts stated in section 757. A more recent restatement adopted by the American Law Institute in 1995 contains a similar statement of principles. It provides that liability should be imposed for gaining trade secrets by improper means including "theft, fraud, unauthorized interception of communications, inducement of or knowing participation in a breach of confidence, and other means either wrongful in themselves or wrongful under the circumstances of the case."[12] A piece of model legislation, the Uniform Trade Secrets Act (USTA), has also contributed to uniformity among the state laws. Neither the restatements, nor the Uniform Act create binding laws. Instead, they provide invitation to state legislatures to adopt similar principles or

---

ery absent either substantial efforts to preserve secrecy or existence of a confidential relationship.

12. Restatement (Third) of Unfair Competition § 43 (1995).

laws. By 2009 the USTA or a similar statute had been adopted by forty-two states.[13]

Valuable Information

Any valuable information may be protected under trade secret law. The current Restatement summarizes the scope as follows: "A trade secret is any information that can be used in the operation of a business or other enterprise and that is sufficiently valuable and secret to afford an actual or potential economic advantage over others."[14] Frequently claimed secrets include: processes of manufacture, formulas, business plans, design projects, customer lists and information. The value refers to what is commercial or marketable, as opposed to something personal.

Sometimes the secret is something definite such as a formula. In other instances, it may be something evanescent, such as timing for the release of a product. An example is the reputed secrecy of the recipe for Coca Cola. In a 1985 case, a federal judge stated: "The complete formula for Coca-Cola is one of the best-kept trade secrets in the world. Although most of the ingredients are public knowledge ... the ingredient that gives Coca-Cola its distinctive taste is a secret combination ... and is known by only two persons within The Coca-Cola Company ('the Company'). The only written record of the secret formula is kept in a (bank) security vault ... which can only be opened upon a resolution from the Company's Board of Directors."[15]

A key element in secrecy cases is to identify what is secret. The burden to do that rests with the one who claims the secret. If a court does not know what is claimed, it will not know how to judge the case. In Desny's case the matter appeared to have been straightforward—the story. Yet at trial he would have been hard pressed to explain exactly what parts were secret. The story was based largely on public events.

A Minnesota Supreme Court case, *Jostens, Inc. v. National Computer Systems, Inc.*, 318 N.W.2d 691 (Minn. 1982), illustrates practical constraints of

---

13. The Restatements continue to be written today and are the product of the American Law Institute (ALI). See Patrick J. Kelley, *The First Restatement of Torts: Reform by Descriptive Theory*, 32 S. Ill. U. L.J. 93 (2007). Neither restatements, nor model laws, such as the USTA, constitute the law of any state. Their concepts or provisions may become law if adopted by the legislature or courts of a state.

14. Restatement (Third) of Unfair Competition §39 (1995).

15. Coca-Cola Bottling Co. of Shreveport, Inc. v. Coca-Cola Co., 107 F.R.D. 288 (D. Del. 1985).

Figure 5-1. Coke and Diet Coke

maintaining secrecy. The Jostens company began as a small watch repair company set up by Otto Jostens in Owatonna, Minnesota, in 1897. The company evolved into jewelry manufacture in the early 1900s. It currently lists its products as including "yearbooks, class rings, graduation products and products for athletic champions and their fans." Among those are Super Bowl rings.

Originally Jostens' rings were designed by skilled artisans who created molds for the rings. In the early 1970s Jostens became interested in using computerized processes, CAD/CAMS (computer-aided design and computer-aided manufacturing systems), to produce the ring designs. An engineer at Jostens, John Titus, spearheaded the effort to computerize the business. By 1974 it was in operation and provided Jostens with a strong advantage over other ring makers.

In 1975, Titus and two other employees (Henderson and Hoagberg) left Jostens, apparently amicably, to go to work for NATIONAL COMPUTER SYSTEMS, INC. (NCS), a systems design company. The Court described the situation: "In about January 1978, Jostens lost its position as the sole class ring manufacturer with a computerized mold-making system, when respondent National Computer Systems, Inc., designed and sold a similar computer system to L.C. Balfour Company, a competing ring manufacturer. That sale triggered this lawsuit."[16] Jostens claimed that the system contained trade secrets misappropriated from Jostens.

The Court stated that the trial had been "long and complex." It emphasized Jostens' lack of clarity in identifying its secret: "It is not always easy to follow Jostens' contentions because its claim of a trade secret is rather elastic." That lack of clarity dogged Jostens throughout the case.

The Court summarized four characteristics governing a Minnesota trade secret case: "(1) the matter involved is not generally known or readily ascertainable, (2) it provides a demonstrable competitive advantage, (3) it was gained at expense to the plaintiff-owner, and (4) the plaintiff-owner intended to keep it confidential." Applying those, the Court agreed with the trial judge that Jostens' case was riddled with holes. Much of the Jostens' software and hardware were "both generally known and readily ascertainable." While a new combination of known techniques can be a secret, the combination must add some element that others cannot easily find out for themselves: "Clearly, the CAD/CAM system as such, as the combination of three generally known subsystems, does not achieve the degree of novelty or 'unknownness' needed for a trade secret."

Jostens also failed to keep its information to itself. Reasonable steps to keep a secret suffice, but Jostens had allowed tours of its plant, approved publication of an article describing the system, and failed to identify for itself or others crucial elements of any potential secret. The Court compared this behavior with various forms of reasonable efforts, such as protecting sensitive information with passwords and explaining to employees which items are important secrets.

The Court also ruled on a contract claim: "A confidence may be imposed contractually as well as by employment status, so Jostens also asserts a separate claim that defendants Titus and Henderson are liable for breach of their employment agreements." The agreement had been entered as follows:

> Four years after Titus began his employment with Jostens and two years after Henderson began his, they each signed the following agreement:
>> All papers and apparatus relating to Jostens' business, including those prepared or made by me, shall be the property of Jostens and except as required by my work, I will not reveal them to others nor will I reveal any information concerning Jostens' business including its inventions, shop practices, processes and methods of manufacturing and merchandising.

---

16. 318 N.W.2d 691, 694.

Again, Jostens had failed to carry its burden in the case. To prevail on the contract claim case, Jostens would have to show that the employees had received a *quid pro quo* called "consideration" in contract law. Jostens urged that the employees received consideration in that they had been permitted to continue their employment. The court rejected that claim. Jostens had not established a new and uniform employment condition for employees of a certain classification, but had singled out these individuals. The Court stated "where other employees with similar access were not asked to sign, the mere continuation of employment for Titus and Henderson is not enough."

The *Jostens* case comes as close as any case will do to provide clear and direct guidelines to what it takes to create relatively reliable trade secret protection: Identify what is important clearly enough. Take reasonable steps to protect that particular information. In other words, let people know what information is secret. Finally, establish clear confidential relationships *before* the sensitive information is released. None of this can be accomplished by "boilerplate" agreements.[17] Established relationships, such as employment, help show a relation of confidentiality. However, the mere fact of employment does not indicate what the particular employees are obliged to keep secret. Likewise, contractual agreements that cover secrecy can be helpful. They, too, need to identify what is secret and what are the obligations in order to be effective.[18]

Kewanee Oil Co. v. Bicron Corp., 416 U.S. 470 (1974), involved nuclear technology. Nuclear collisions and other events create radiation which can be detected and analyzed. Such analysis requires very specialized equipment, and it involves an ever advancing technological frontier.[19] The Court described the technology development as follows:

> Harshaw Chemical Co., an unincorporated division of petitioner (Kewanee Oil), is a leading manufacturer of a type of synthetic crystal which is useful in the detection of ionizing radiation. In 1949 Harshaw commenced research into the growth of this type crystal and was able to produce one less than two inches in diameter. By 1966, as

---

17. Secrets are not general; how can one expect that protections of them should be general?

18. This does not mean that a contract need be long or verbose. The goal is workability and clarity, both of which can often be accomplished by short statements as well as detailed ones. H. C. ANAWALT, IP STRATEGY—COMPLETE INTELLECTUAL PROPERTY PLANNING, ACCESS AND PROTECTION §§ 2:13–19 and §§ 2:45 & 46 (Thomson West 2010).

19. On the technologies and their role, see, e.g. Radiation Detection and Measurement, http://hyperphysics.phy-astr.gsu.edu/HBASE/nuclear/rdtec.html. See also, Johns Hopkins, Applied Physics Laboratory (APL), http://www.jhuapl.edu/areas/sciencetech/facilities.asp.

the result of expenditures in excess of $1 million, Harshaw was able to grow a 17-inch crystal, something no one else had done previously. Harshaw had developed many processes, procedures, and manufacturing techniques in the purification of raw materials and the growth and encapsulation of the crystals which enabled it to accomplish this feat. Some of these processes Harshaw considers to be trade secrets.

The company had not applied for a patent, but had opted to keep its process secret. The Court addressed the question whether that choice was permissible. The Court concluded that states have the power to create trade secrets for matters that also could be patented. "We conclude that the extension of trade secret protection to clearly patentable inventions does not conflict with the patent policy of disclosure." Thus, an inventor or controller of a new process has the option—protect by patent or by trade secret.

The Supreme Court reinstated a trial court judgment which had granted Kewanee a permanent injunction. Unlike *Jostens* where the technology was mainly off the shelf, it had taken the inventor more than sixteen years to perfect the crystal making process. The defendant Bicron had been able to produce such a crystal less than a year after employing the former Harshaw-Kewanee employees. That sort of leap fuels an inference that the information obtained from the employees had been valuable and kept secret.

In *E.I. du Pont deNemours & Co. v. Christopher*, 431 F.2d 1012 (5th Cir. 1970), the defendants moved to dismiss the case on the basis that the facts as alleged did not amount to misappropriation of trade secret under Texas law. The trial denied that motion, and the defendants appealed. The Circuit Court of Appeals began its decision with a summary of the allegations made in the complaint:

> This is a case of industrial espionage in which an airplane is the cloak and a camera the dagger. The defendants-appellants, Rolfe and Gary Christopher, are photographers in Beaumont, Texas. The Christophers were hired by an unknown third party to take aerial photographs of new construction at the Beaumont plant of E. I. duPont deNemours & Company, Inc. DuPont employees apparently noticed the airplane on March 19 and immediately began an investigation to determine why the craft was circling over the plant. By that afternoon the investigation had disclosed that the craft was involved in a photographic expedition and that the Christophers were the photographers.... DuPont subsequently filed suit against the Christophers, ... DuPont contended that it had developed a highly secret but unpatented process for producing methanol, ... The area photographed by the

Christophers was the plant designed to produce methanol by this secret process, and because the plant was still under construction parts
of the process were exposed to view from directly above the construction area.[20]

The case was in federal court because the parties were from different states. In
such cases, the federal courts have what is called "diversity jurisdiction." In
those cases, the court applies state law, in this case the law of Texas, where the
incident took place. This requires the judges to bone up on the law of the state.

Upon review of Texas law, the Court determined that the Texas Supreme
Court had specifically adopted the view of Restatement of Torts (First) §757
that any "improper" activity could amount to misappropriation of another's trade
secret. Since DuPont had tried to conceal its process, an attempt to pry by
means such as aerial photography could be viewed as improper.

The Court affirmed the denial of the motions and ordered further proceedings, which would include trial. However, the Court added comments
which would made a trial futile. It stated that the basic question was "whether
aerial photography of plant construction is an improper means of obtaining
another's trade secret. We conclude that it is and that the Texas courts would
so hold."

The Court explained its conclusion:

> In the instant case the Christophers deliberately flew over the DuPont plant
> to get pictures of a process which DuPont had attempted to keep secret.
> The Christophers delivered their pictures to a third party who was cer-
> tainly aware of the means by which they had been acquired and who
> may be planning to use the information contained therein to manufac-
> ture methanol by the DuPont process. The third party has a right to use
> this process only if he obtains this knowledge through his own research
> efforts, but thus far all information indicates that the third party has
> gained this knowledge solely by taking it from DuPont at a time when
> DuPont was making reasonable efforts to preserve its secrecy. In such a
> situation DuPont has a valid cause of action to prohibit the Christo-
> phers from improperly discovering its trade secret and to prohibit the undis-
> closed third party from using the improperly obtained information.

These comments effectively ended the case.

It is unfortunate that the Court of Appeals put its thumb on the scales in this
way. No one had heard any evidence so far in the case. The result is a lack of

---

20. 431 F.2d 1012, 1014.

clarity as to what activity was improper. If the Court had simply affirmed the decision without this dictum, then the attorneys would have been able to present the facts, brief the law, and create a basis for a clear decision. Here are some questions that might have been explored: Is it impermissible to engage a pilot to fly them over the site? The defense would surely argue that this cannot be the case. For example, they might urge that constructing a building does not permit one to restrict the use of airspace. If one can fly over the site, is one prohibited from looking out the windows? Again the defense attorneys could have a field day with this. If one can look out the windows, can one take notes? If one can take notes, why not make sketches? If sketches, why not photos? The Court of Appeals also observed that photographers' client "*may* be planning to use the information … to manufacture methanol." This, too, ought to have been subject to proof. Nor had there been proof of the photographers' knowledge of what the third party intended to do with the photos.

Many lines of inquiry would have been open. Most would have been appropriate, for in a trade secret case, the one who claims secrecy ought to be put to the task of showing what steps have been taken to preserve it. If something is so open as a view of a construction project, then perhaps there simply is no secrecy. In any event, the matters of fact ought to have been open to exploration.

DuPont had apparently not identified with any degree of clarity what parts of the visible construction were secret. The approach in the *DuPont* case differs greatly from the one *Jostens*, where the Minnesota Supreme Court expressed exasperation at Jostens' failure to clarify its secret. The Court's assertion that one may use only knowledge which one has researched contradicts a basic notion of secrecy: One may use what one sees, research or not. The normal burden lies on the secret claimant to define its secrets and take clear efforts to guard them. The *DuPont* interpretation of Texas law oddly reverses this, requiring that one avert one's eyes.[21]

Crime

The Court in the *DuPont* case assumes "badness" in the photographers' behavior. In effect, the Circuit Court said the photographers were spying, and to deny liability would be "accepting the law of the jungle as the standard of morality expected in our commercial relations." When behavior is viewed as repre-

---

21. One can imagine cases that might crop up today. Does the *Dupont* case oblige one not to look as a satellite view which is available today on a cellphone?

hensible, society often responds by making it a crime. Some states classify theft of trade secrets as a crime. For example, in 1986, Douglas Southard, a California prosecutor summarized the requirements of California's law as follows: "Like any criminal theft statute, trade secret theft has three elements: (1) object (trade secret), (2) specific intent, and (3) act. Proof beyond a reasonable doubt must be shown as to each element."[22]

Federal Legislation

When Congress enacted the Economic Espionage Act of 1996, the House committee reporting the bill noted that it "creates a new crime of wrongfully copying or otherwise controlling trade secrets." The committee painted a grim picture:

> This [trade secret] material is a prime target for theft precisely because it costs so much to develop independently, because it is so valuable, and because there are virtually no penalties for its theft. The information is pilfered by a variety of people and organizations for a variety of reasons. A great deal of the theft is committed by disgruntled individuals or employees who hope to harm their former companies or line their own pockets. In other instances, outsiders target a company, systematically infiltrate it, and then steal its vital information.[23]

Relying on the testimony of the Director of the FBI, the Committee concluded that a federal criminal law was needed.[24]

The Act makes it a crime to knowingly obtain, convey, or receive any trade secret information in connection with interstate or foreign commerce. The

---

22. Douglas K. Southard, *Trade Secrets and the Criminal Law: A View from Silicon Valley*, Practising Law Institute, 224 PLI/Pat 181 (1986). Mr. Southard is now a California Superior Court Judge in Santa Clara County; that is, Silicon Valley. He noted that California was an early state to adopt such a law. A majority of states now have some such trade secret crime statute.

23. H. R. Rep. No. 104-788, sec 3 (1996). Available online at, http://thomas.loc.gov/cgi-bin/cpquery/T?&report=hr788&dbname=104&.

24. One scholar comments: "Congress abandoned the approach of most states that bases civil and criminal trade secret laws on wrongful conduct, and justified the EEA on the view that trade secrets are property. As a result, under the EEA, more information qualifies as a trade secret, more conduct triggers legal action, and it is easier to establish that a trade secret exists. Unintended consequences of this enhanced protection are likely to undermine achievement of Congress's goals." Geraldine Szott Moohr, *The Problematic Role of Criminal Law in Regulating the Use of Information: The Case of the Economic Espionage Act*, 80 N.C. L. Rev. 853 (2002).

penalty is ten years in prison. 18 U.S.C. § 1832. An accusation can bring the full power of federal law enforcement to bear. Becoming a defendant in a civil trade secret case is time consuming, expensive, and wearing. A federal criminal investigation or indictment is more so. In 1986, Mr. Southard (quoted above) urged that the primary remedy for trade secret disputes should remain a civil action. He added, "nevertheless, selective prosecution of particularly egregious cases, where the proof is strong, can provide an effective remedy for the victim, appropriate punishment for the wrongdoer, and increased public awareness tending to establish a societal deterrent."[25]

In 1998, federal law also entered into the arena of protection of trade secrets by enacting the "digital lock" portions of the "Digital Millennium Copyright Act" (DMCA), 17 U.S.C. § 1201 *et seq.* These provisions are discussed in Chapter 6. In essence they provide stiff civil and criminal penalties for using a technological means to circumvent a software that is designed to prevent access to a program or data base.[26]

The cases we have reviewed contain common elements with variations. The parties disagree. Usually each party has some measure of justification for its position. Often it is difficult to identify the secret, and even attorneys and judges seem befuddled. Some of these cases turn out to be squabbles. Others involve genuine disagreements about contributions to a business. Probably few trade secret disputes nefarious behavior. Thus, prosecutors need to be especially sensitive in proceeding with prosecutions.

Concluding Points

Trade secret protection depends on careful assessment and identification of which matters are important enough to keep to oneself. It "relies primarily (and nearly exclusively) on the efforts of the developer to protect himself or herself."[27] Once one decides that information or plans are valuable enough to keep secret, one needs to establish effective safeguards, especially through creating reasonable arrangements with employees and business confidents.

---

25. 224 PLI/Pat 181 (1986).

26. See I.M.S. Inquiry Management Systems, Ltd. v. Berkshire, 307 F.Supp.2d 521, 531 (S.D.N.Y.2004) and H. C. ANAWALT, IP STRATEGY—COMPLETE INTELLECTUAL PROPERTY PLANNING, ACCESS AND PROTECTION (Thomson West 2010) § 1:56 *et. seq.*

27. H. Clarke Anawalt, IDEAS IN THE WORKPLACE, p. 23 (Carolina Academic Press, 1988).

Becoming obsessive about security carries its own risks. Too much emphasis on secrecy can stifle creativity and initiative. Approaching potential business associates with a heavy hand about secrecy may well send them away. Fair assessment and consideration of each party's needs can produce agreements that provide effective protection of what is truly important.

Practical Guidelines

Individuals and businesses often have information and plans that are better kept to themselves. Maintaining confidentiality involves creating a delicate balance.

1. Secrecy ought to be preserved without disrupting the work environment. Adopt effective procedures that do not "turn people off." Projects, sources, client lists, and other items that are confidential need to be identified, so that colleagues and employees can protect them. Some internal measures may need to be formalized. For example, non-disclosure obligations may need to be set up. Formalities should be assessed with attention to legal effectiveness and conduciveness of the environment.

2. A memorandum of understanding, such as a non-disclosure agreement, ought to be established before sensitive disclosures are made to those outside the business.[28]

3. It is valuable to learn the limitations of trade secrecy in one's work before problems arise. One usually can obtain legal consultation on these matters without great expense.

---

28. Agreements related to confidentiality are discussed in Chapter Six.

Table 5-2. Trade Secret Guidelines

General Rule	Comment	Source
Subject matter. Any idea, information, or organization which can be valued commercially.	The key is the preservation of secrecy or confidences; the ideas (subject) is not property.	State laws; influence of Rest.Torts §757.
Confidentiality. The subject protected is the activity (keeping secret) and the relationships (confidentiality).	Trade secret law is driven by "maintenance of standards of commercial ethics."	E.g., *Kewanee*, 416 U.S. 470, 481–482 (1974).
What rights? One may go to court and prove secrecy was carefully preserved, but as a practical matter one must rely on others and use reminders.	The core concept is creating and maintaining relationships of confidentiality.	Common law.
Who owns? The secret holder controls the secret and can convey his rights to others.	As noted, the right is not property, but a claim to a civil obligation.	Each state's laws.
How long does a trade secret last? The trade secret may be maintained so long as one maintains the secrecy.	The USTA provides that an action must be brought within three years of the misappropriation.	Each state's statutes.
Relationships. The requisite confidentiality can come from a relation like employment or a contract.	Contracts can create relationships. They create a basis for a contract claim and for related trade secret tort claims.	Each state's laws.
State Crimes. Many states punish trade secret "theft." The burden of proof rests sharply on the prosecutor.	Prosecutions are usually limited to "egregious" conduct, yet this leaves room for political considerations to weigh in.	Each state's statutes.
Federal Crime. The Economic Espionage Act punishes taking trade secrets in interstate or foreign commerce.	Prosecutions are usually limited to "egregious" conduct, yet this leaves room for political considerations to weigh in.	18 U.S.C. § 1832.
How does one avoid trouble? Create clear relationships. When changing employment or business, review what may be someone else's stuff.	Trade secrets cover any valuable idea. They also play a big role in starting or altering a business.	
Related doctrine. A "shop right" gives an employer a non-exclusive license to use inventions made on the job. Employees own what they invent, unless relatively clear job conditions show otherwise.	A contract or specific job assignment to invent may allow an employer to claim a right to be assigned ownership of an invention.	Each state's laws; *U.S. v. Dubilier*, 289 U.S. 178 (1933); Cal. Lab. Code 2860; 2870–2872.

Chapter Six

Other Legal Theories
and Remedies

Introduction

This Chapter introduces a variety of other legal theories that find a place under the umbrella of "intellectual property." Some of these doctrines grapple with defining the boundaries of what commerce and the public accept as "fair." One set of legal theories we look at deals directly with fairness. These theories include unfair competition, rights of privacy and publicity, and antitrust.

A second group is a potpourri—federal laws that deal with semiconductor mask works, boat hulls, plant variety protection, and the use of "digital locks" to protect copyrighted works. This chapter also covers the use of contracts in intellectual property transactions.

Finally, the chapter sketches the range of legal and equitable remedies available in intellectual property cases. In general, the same range of remedies applies to all the legal doctrines in this book. In a given case, depending on the facts, an injured party may receive a monetary award for damages, a court order (injunction), and an award for court costs and attorney fees.

Fairness

Intellectual property law works within the context of two general concepts. One is fairness among participants in commerce and industry. The other is overall service to the public good. This chapter focuses on the first of these, commercial fairness. Chapter Seven examines serving the public good. We begin with a case that presents an unusual question about fairness.

In the early 1900s Edward Tuttle built up a successful barbershop in Howard Lake, Minnesota. A wealthy banker, Cassius Buck, also from Howard Lake, equipped a barbershop, hired two barbers, paid them a salary, and had the in-

Figure 6-1. Ron Sorci, Barber

come from the shop paid to him. In short, he set up a competing barbershop.[1] However, Tuttle sued Buck complaining that Buck opened his shop "with the sole design of injuring the plaintiff, and of destroying his said business." A jury agreed with Tuttle and gave a verdict in his favor. Buck appealed.

The Minnesota Supreme Court affirmed Tuttle's verdict. The Court plainly had difficulty with the case. The opinion referred to English and American precedents to the effect that "mischievous motives make a bad case worse, but they cannot make that wrong which in its own essence is lawful." Actions and intentions to bring about certain consequences are relevant in determining what is lawful, but underlying motives are not. The majority of the justices agreed with that premise, but they also insisted that there are some fringe cases that cannot justly follow that limit. Tuttle's case was one of those.

---

1. The photograph is of Ron Sorci, the owner of Norm's Barber Shop in San Jose California. The shop is named after Ron's father. Dayton Duncan, a writer of contemporary United States history commented that barbers and hairdressers are among the last services that remain in a community before it becomes practically extinct. "Hairdressers, like video rentals, are part of the irreducible minimum. I came across only one county without both." Dayton Duncan, MILES FROM NOWHERE: IN SEARCH OF THE AMERICAN FRONTIER (Penguin, 1994).

To divert to one's self the customers of a business rival by the offer of goods at lower prices is in general a legitimate mode of serving one's own interest, and justifiable as fair competition. But when a man starts an opposition place of business, not for the sake of profit to himself, but regardless of loss to himself, and for the sole purpose of driving his competitor out of business, and with the intention of himself re-tiring upon the accomplishment of his malevolent purpose, he is guilty of a wanton wrong and an actionable tort.[2]

Tuttle's case falls far short of establishing a general rule. Buck had a lot of money, and the Court allowed a jury to decide that he could not use it just to run someone out of business. The jury's verdict decided only this case. It provided no rule for future cases.

Tuttle's case cannot be classified easily, if at all. If it contains any general rule it is that competing by offering lower prices is *fair* competition. Dean William L. Prosser described the barbershop case as part of a tort for interference with another's economic opportunity or advantage. The tort requires that one show an intent to interfere with some specific interest.[3] The Restatement (Third) of Unfair Competition (1995) includes the case as an example of "unfair competition." Section 1 of that Restatement defines unfair competition to include deceptive practices, trademark type infringements, misappropriation of trade secrets, and appropriation of another's "right to publicity." It also includes "other acts or practices of the actor determined to be actionable as an unfair method of competition, taking into account the nature of the conduct and its likely effect on both the person seeking relief and the public."

Privacy and Publicity

Common law and state statutes often protect aspects of one's private life or image. These protections are often labeled a "right of privacy," though some of

---

2. Tuttle v. Buck, 107 Minn. 145, 147, 119 N.W. 946 (Minn. 1909).

3. Prosser, PROSSER ON TORTS (4th ed. West Pub. Co. 1971); this is the last edition by Prosser himself) pp. 949–958. Among the early precedents is a nineteenth-century English case, Gregory v. Duke of Brunswick, 6 Man. & G. 953, (C.P. 1843) in which a group of defendants had conspired to have the plaintiff actor hissed off the stage. The California Supreme Court examines this tort in Della Penna v. Toyota Motor Sales, U.S.A., Inc., 45 Cal.Rptr.2d 436 (Cal. 1995).

them protect very public types of activities.[4] The tort encompasses a variety of harms from eavesdropping to protecting one's image. That aspect of the tort is sometimes called a "right of publicity."

Hugo Zacchini was a circus performer. In one of his acts he had himself loaded into a cannon and fired through the air to the oohs and aahs of his audience. One day when he was performing at a fair in Ohio, a freelance reporter filmed his act. The film was then broadcast on the evening news. Zacchini sued, claiming a violation of his right of privacy. The Ohio Supreme Court discussed the contradictory nature of his claim:

> It seems, of course, somewhat anomalous for the plaintiff, who regularly performs in public before large crowds, to claim a right of privacy. The very purpose of a performer is to lure people to come watch him, and certainly the plaintiff hoped not for privacy, but for crowds of thrilled spectators. But there is no real anomaly; the 'privacy' which the performer seeks is personal control over commercial display and exploitation of his personality and the exercise of his talents. In other words, performers and other public figures wish to keep the benefits of their performances private, or at least to retain control over them in much the same way that any individual would wish to keep control over his name and face. Judge Jerome N. Frank has aptly called this aspect of privacy 'the right of publicity.'[5]

The Ohio Court ruled that Zacchini had a valid claim under Ohio law. However, it also ruled that the First Amendment gave the news media a privilege to record and air the tape. The United States Supreme Court determined that the news broadcast was not protected by the Constitution.[6] The case went back to Ohio, and the Ohio Supreme Court sent it back to the trial court to determine if there was liability and if so, what damages.[7]

In another case, Bette Midler sued an advertising agency for using a "sound alike" rendition of her voice in its "Yuppie Campaign" commercials for Ford cars. The appeals court found that Midler had stated a valid claim for misappro-

---

4. Prosser attributed the rise of the doctrine to a law review article, Samuel D. Warren & Louis D. Brandeis, *The Right to Privacy*, 4 HARV. L. REV. 193 (1890).

5. Zacchini v. Scripps-Howard Broadcasting Co., 351 N.E.2d 454 (1976).

6. Zacchini v. Scripps-Howard Broadcasting Co., 433 U.S. 562, 578 (1977).

7. The United States Supreme Court *accepted* the Ohio Supreme Court's decision that Ohio law protects a "right of publicity." However, the United States Supreme Court reversed the Ohio court's decision that the Ohio right was trumped by a federal privilege based on freedom of the press. In sum: Ohio law defined the right of publicity; the Constitution defined any claim of a constitutional privilege for the press.

priating the particular qualities of her voice in its commercial. The Court stated: "The human voice is one of the most palpable ways identity is manifested.... We hold only that when a distinctive voice of a professional singer is widely known and is deliberately imitated in order to sell a product, the sellers have appropriated what is not theirs and have committed a tort in California."[8]

Midler's claim harkens back to a case that Professor Prosser noted to be the first United States case to deal with a privacy claim. In that case, *Robertson v. Rochester Folding Box Company,* 171 N.Y. 442 (1902), "the defendant made use of the picture of a pulchritudinous young lady to advertise its flour without her consent. In a four-to-three decision, with a vigorous dissent, the court flatly denied the existence of any right to protection against such conduct ..." Shortly after that decision, the New York legislature enacted laws "making it both a misdemeanor and a tort to make use of the name, portrait or picture of any person for 'advertising purposes or for the purposes of trade' without his written consent."[9]

Other Federal Claims

Unfair competition and the rights to privacy and control of publicity are based on state law. In addition, federal legislation has created special laws from time to time. Here are three created by the federal government.

The Semiconductor Chip Protection Act of 1984 (SCPA)[10]

A semiconductor chip is an array of miniscule transistors, circuits, and other components all laid out within a small chip made up largely of a semiconductor, most often one made of silicon. Over time the dimensions of these layouts keep getting smaller and smaller. The circuits are laid out on a two di-

---

8. Midler v. Ford Motor Co., 849 F.2d 460 (9 Cir. 1988).

9. Prosser on Torts (4th ed.) p. 803. *Id.*, p. 803. A suit by Vanna White, a quiz show celebrity, sparked a spirited dissent from Judge Alex Kozinski. Ms. White claimed that an ad with a robot impersonating her demeanor appropriated her image. Judge Kozinski commented: "Something very dangerous is going on here.... reducing too much to private property can be bad medicine. Private land, for instance, is far more useful if separated from other private land by public streets, roads and highways. Overprotecting intellectual property is as harmful as underprotecting it. Creativity is impossible without a rich public domain." White v. Samsung Elecs. Am., Inc., 989 F.2d 1512, 1512–13 (9th Cir.1993) (denial of rehearing en banc) (Kozinski, J., dissenting).

10. 17 U.S.C. §901 *et seq.* (1984).

mensional surface by a photographic or other process. Several of these surfaces are stacked on top of each other. The final result, the chip, may be likened to a building with each floor laced with circuitry rather than halls and rooms.

Some advances in chip technology can be patented, but the layout of a particular chip does not qualify for patent protection. That layout takes care and engineering, and it can easily be copied. Congress decided to protect these designs. The resulting act is a hybrid of patent and copyright concepts. The act protects the design of the chip as laid out in a "mask work." A mask work is defined as "a series of related images, however fixed or encoded." Thus, the mask work could be "fixed" on a piece of paper, on the chip itself, or in an electronic memory, such as a hard drive.[11] The protection of the layout resembles protection of an expression by a copyright. In particular, the protection is akin to protection of architectural works by copyright.[12]

To gain protection, one must register the mask work with the Copyright Office within two years of commercial exploitation. The Register exercises a minimal degree of judgment, i.e., "that the application relates to a mask work which is entitled to protection," before registration is allowed.[13] Protection lasts for a period of ten years. Others have a right to reverse engineer a mask work for the purposes of analysis or "to incorporate the results of such conduct in an original mask work which is made to be distributed."[14]

In *Altera Corp. v. Clear Logic, Inc.*, 424 F.3d 1079 (9th Cir. 2005), two producers manufactured chips that would perform specific processes. For example, a buyer might need a chip that would control a thermostat or other heat monitoring device. The two companies used distinctly different approaches to providing such chips. Altera produced programmable logic devices (PLDs) which are chips that a user can program to do a specific job. This offers the user flexibility. Clear Logic manufactures Application-Specific Integrated Circuits (ASICs). These chips cannot be reprogrammed, but they are cheaper. Thus, an Altera chip in a thermostat would be reprogrammable, but more expensive. A Clear Logic Chip would be inflexible, but cheaper.

Altera customers would use Altera chips for a while, then send the entire programming, including the Altera design, to Clear Logic. Clear Logic thus piggybacked on the work of both Altera and the customer. That worked to the advantage of Clear Logic and its customers, but not to Altera. The Court of Ap-

---

11. 17 U.S.C. §901.
12. 17 U.S.C. §§101, 102. Protection of architectural works is discussed in Chapter Three.
13. 17 U.S.C. §980 (e).
14. 17 U.S.C. §906.

peals summarized the case: "Faced with the loss of millions of dollars in business, Altera has challenged Clear Logic's business model. In the district court, Altera argued that Clear Logic infringed its rights under the SCPA by copying the layout design of its registered mask works for three families of chip products. Clear Logic denied the infringement and asserted an affirmative defense of reverse engineering. The jury returned a verdict in favor of Altera on the infringement claim."[15] The jury rejected a reverse engineering defense and found in favor of Altera. A judgment in excess of 36 million dollars was entered against Clear Logic. The judge also enjoined Clear Logic from any further such activity in relation to Altera's chips and designs. The Court of Appeals affirmed.[16]

Protection of Boat Hull Designs

17 U.S.C. § 1301. This act of Congress provides for a ten year period of protection of "an original design of a useful article which makes the article attractive or distinctive in appearance to the purchasing or using public." However, the act defines "useful article" to mean only a vessel hull. The design must be registered with the Copyright Office within two years of making it public. The act appears to be special legislation to aid a particular constituency. It was enacted to overrule an unanimous Supreme Court decision which had ruled that state laws could not protect such things as boat designs.[17]

---

15. 424 F.3d 1079, 1082.

16. The appeal focused on the accuracy of the jury instructions. The Court of Appeals found some inaccuracies in the instructions, but determined that they were clear enough to allow the jury to focus on the crucial question: Did the defendant engage in permissible study and adaptation or impermissible plain copying? 424 F.3d 1079, 1087–88.

17. Bonito Boats, Inc. v. Thunder Craft Boats, Inc., 489 U.S. 141 (1989). "By offering patent-like protection for ideas deemed unprotected under the present federal scheme, the Florida statute conflicts with the 'strong federal policy favoring free competition in ideas which do not merit patent protection.'" *Id.* p. 168.

Figure 6-2. Scout Boat Hull Registration

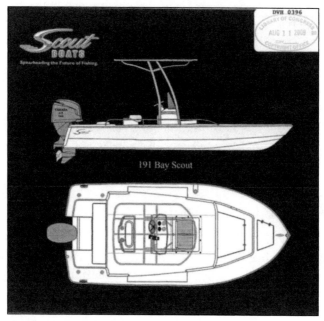

Source: U.S. Copyright Office.

Geographical Indications and Plant Varieties

Two forms of food production control fall under the umbrella of intellectual property. They have arisen from dramatically different policies.

Geographic Indications have roots in policies that favor conservation of culture. For example, Roquefort cheese is often called *"le roi de fromage"* in France. It is a sheep's milk cheese fermented in caves that originated in southern France.[18] To be sure, the fungus, *penicillium roqueforti* can be introduced into milk and a generally similar cheese produced anywhere. Granting a form of legal exclusivity to the label, "Rocquefort," was intended to preserve the integrity of this heritage. The United States, however, has a less forceful regime of protection than Europe. Such marks as "Roquefort" or "Idaho Potatoes" are protected as a type of trademark, called a "collective mark," under the Lanham Act. To reg-

---

18. A gentle joke about the difference between the English and French runs: "What is the difference between England and France? The English are a nation with three cheeses and three hundred religions. France is a nation of three religions and three hundred cheeses!"

ister and maintain such a mark, the "holder cannot be a producer of the certified products." The holder must not allow it to be used for anything but certification of the relevant products and must allow others who meet the standards of certification to use the mark.[19]

The Plant Variety Protection Act of 1970 (PVPA) was enacted to secure protection for those who develop new varieties of plants. The Act allows those who develop a distinct new variety to apply to the United States Department of Agriculture for a "Certificate of Plant Variety Protection" which grants a period of twenty years control over use of the seed.

There is a third approach to controlling living organisms, and that is to obtain a utility patent as discussed in Chapter Two. Thus, three legal regimes exist to grant legal control over reproduction of plant life in the United States. Originally, United States policy understood plants to be part of nature, thus not subject to species ownership.[20]

The Digital Millennium Copyright Act

In 1998, Congress enacted the Digital Millennium Copyright Act (DMCA). One part of the DMCA protects Internet service providers (ISPs) from liability when they merely send on content provided by others. To receive this "safe harbor" protection the ISP must set up procedures that deter repeat copyright infringers from continuing to infringe.[21]

Another section of the DMCA provides: "No person shall circumvent a technological measure that effectively controls access to a work protected under this title." 17 U.S.C. § 1201(a) (1) (A). These technological means include such things as passwords. This section means that one who bypasses or picks a "dig-

---

19. 15 U.S.C. § 1064. Justin Hughes, *Champagne, Feta, and Bourbon: The Spirited Debate About Geographical Indications,* 58 HASTINGS L.J. 299, 309–10 (2006).

20. "Before passage of the Plant Patent Act in 1930, it was the common perception that plants and other living organisms were not eligible for patent protection because living organisms were products of nature. This proposition was cited as the holding by the Commissioner of Patents in *Ex parte Latimer* [1889 Comm'n Dec. 123] in 1899, which held that the fiber from the needle of an evergreen tree was an unpatentable product of nature." Nicholas J. Seay, *Protecting the Seeds of Innovation: Patenting Plants,* 16 AIPLA Q.J. 418, 427–29 (1989).

21. The basic requirement is that the ISP show that is "has adopted and reasonably implemented, and informs subscribers and account holders of the service provider's system or network of, a policy that provides for the termination in appropriate circumstances of subscribers and account holders of the service provider's system or network who are repeat infringers." 17 U.S.C. § 512. Perfect 10, Inc. v. CCBill, LLC, 488 F.3d 1102 (9th Cir.), cert. denied, 552 U.S. 1062, (2007).

ital lock" protecting a database may be subject to substantial civil liabilities. The database must contain some copyrighted work in order for liability to apply. However, most databases will have something copyrightable in them. If a database lacks copyrightable content, its owner might make up a limerick and include it in the database to assure that it contains copyrightable material. This aspect of the DMCA is discussed further in Chapter Three.

Contracts

Contracts play a big role in intellectual property. A contract claim is neither a property right nor a general civil obligation. It is an enforceable agreement between parties. A typical example is an exchange like this: "You install a new roof on my house and I will pay you $5,000." Each party agrees to provide something for the other. Unless a rule requires it, a contract can be either oral or in writing. It is the agreement of "this for that" that makes the promises enforceable in a court. This is also called "consideration" in legal jargon. A contract allows parties to make rules that govern their relations to each other. For example, parties can agree to have an arbitrator decide disputes rather than rules of law. In effect, by contract, parties make law that governs their relations to each other concerning the transaction.

A major problem with an oral contract is recalling or proving what was agreed. As a result, it is a good practice to "get it in writing," and most business contracts are in writing. Also, state laws, called "statutes of fraud," generally require a writing for real estate contracts or contracts whose performance extends past one year. The copyright law also has a writing requirement. In order to transfer ownership of a copyright, including an exclusive license, the owner must put the transfer in writing.[22] That requirement became the central issue in *Effects Associates, Inc. v. Cohen*, 908 F.2d 555 (9th Cir. 1990), cert. denied, 498 U.S. 1103 (1991). The Court summarized the controversy:

> This started out as a run-of-the-mill Hollywood squabble. Defendant Larry Cohen wrote, directed and executive produced "The Stuff," a horror movie with a dash of social satire: Earth is invaded by an alien life form that looks (and tastes) like frozen yogurt but, alas, has some unfortunate side effects—it's addictive and takes over the mind of anyone who eats it. Marketed by an unscrupulous entrepreneur, the Stuff becomes a big hit. An industrial spy hired by ice cream man-

---

22. 17 U.S.C. §204.

ufacturers eventually uncovers the terrible truth; he alerts the American people and blows up the yogurt factory, making the world safe once again for lovers of frozen confections.

In cooking up this gustatory melodrama, Cohen asked Effects Associates, a small special effects company, to create footage to enhance certain action sequences in the film. In a short letter dated October 29, 1984, Effects offered to prepare seven shots, the most dramatic of which would depict the climactic explosion of the Stuff factory. Cohen agreed to the deal orally, but no one said anything about who would own the copyright in the footage.[23]

Cohen argued that the writing requirement did not apply to this transaction. The Court rejected the argument:

> Cohen suggests that section 204's writing requirement does not apply to this situation, advancing an argument that might be summarized, tongue in cheek, as: Moviemakers do lunch, not contracts. Cohen concedes that "[i]n the best of all possible legal worlds" parties would obey the writing requirement, but contends that moviemakers are too absorbed in developing "joint creative endeavors" to "focus upon the legal niceties of copyright licenses."…. Common sense tells us that agreements should routinely be put in writing. This simple practice prevents misunderstandings by spelling out the terms of a deal in black and white, forces parties to clarify their thinking and consider problems that could potentially arise, and encourages them to take their promises seriously because it's harder to backtrack on a written contract than on an oral one. Copyright law dovetails nicely with common sense by requiring that a transfer of copyright ownership be in writing.… Rather than look to the courts every time they disagree as to whether a particular use of the work violates their mutual understanding, parties need only look to the writing that sets out their respective rights.[24]

Since there had been no writing, Cohen could not claim any ownership rights in the footage. The case did have a slightly happy ending for Cohen. The trial court had found that he did obtain an implied permission or license to use the footage in his film.

Contracts are used in a variety of ways in intellectual property transactions. Their subject matter includes granting licenses, agreeing to assign inventions,

---

23. 908 F.2d 555, 555–56.
24. *Effects Associates, Inc. v. Cohen*, 908 F.2d 555, 557–558.

agreeing to disclose, agreeing not to disclose, agreeing to develop, and creating conditions of employment. Contracts can cover any legal subject. There are some restrictions. One cannot enforce a contract that violates a basic public policy. For instance, one cannot enforce an agreement to break the law.

Contracts may contain clauses that restrict people from pursuing their usual business, profession, or line of employment. Generally, state laws and court decisions will only enforce such restrictions when they are reasonable and pursue a recognizable business interest.[25] For example, it may be reasonable to enter an agreement that one will not compete with another party for a definite period of time in a given location. Such clauses are likely to be viewed as reasonable, if they are part of a sale of a business.

Often one side dictates conditions based on a strong economic position. Many states have statutes or common law that try to counter unfairness that unequal bargaining power may create. For example, California statutes protect against contracts that are so one-sided that they are "unconscionable."[26]

Varieties of Intellectual Property Contracts

Types of contracts and contract clauses used in intellectual property transactions include:

- Agreements to *apply for a patent.*
- Agreements to *assign* a patent or copyright. These create contract rights, but do not actually convey the patent to someone else.[27]
- *Nondisclosure* agreements (NDAs). These agreements create a contractual obligation not to disclose information to others. Thus, they aid efforts to protect trade secrets. It is necessary to be sufficiently clear about matters that the agreement covers. The concern with NDAs overlaps with matters discussed in the chapter on trade secrets.
- Agreements *to disclose* information. Sometimes common parlance confuses this sort of agreement with an NDA. However these agreements are the opposite. They cover situations where one party views it as im-

25. For example, a California statute provides a general rule that "every contract by which anyone is restrained from engaging in a lawful profession, trade, or business of any kind is to that extent void." Cal. Bus. and Prof. Code § 16600.

26. Cal. Civ. Code § 1670.5.

27. There is some minimal public control over required assignment of invention rights in some states. E.g. Cal. Lab. Code §§ 2870–2872. The validity of contracts to assign depends on state law, not federal law. Beghin-Say Intern. Inc. v. Ole-Bendy Rasmussen, 733 F. 2d 1568 (Fed. Cir. 1984).

portant to gain information. In that case one bargains for it, and it may be important to spell out what one gets as information. As a reciprocation for providing the information, the provider will usually ask the recipient to agree not to disclose. The obligations to disclose and not to disclose are often wrapped up in one document, which parties may refer to as an NDA. No harm is done, so long as the parties are clear about what the agreement signifies.

- Development agreements. These are agreements that involve one party *developing* a technology or some other valuable thing for another party. One aspect of such agreements involves exchanging information as development proceeds.
- *Licenses* to use technology or a trademark. These are permissions one party grants to another to use a process or technology which is protected by patent, copyright, or trade secret. They are usually set forth in a contract. If the process is a trade secret, then a carefully drawn NDA ought to be included too. Similarly, a trademark owner may decide to license use of the mark.

The key to creating successful contracts lies in being clear. Effective contracts can be long or short. Finally, a truly effective contract is one that never winds up in court. Parties usually create contracts in order to get something done, not to sue each other. To be successful, a contract should reflect the needs of each party. The Open Source movement in software is an example of using contracts. "Open Source" generally refers to cooperative distribution of inventive works. Some developers and manufacturers strongly prefer this approach to one which emphasizes a heavy hand of proprietary control. Sometimes developers need to create compatibly, so that their software will work with other software. At other times, developers wish to modify programs to add new features. The origin of the name comes from the need to gain access to the source code version of software to accomplish these things.[28] Open source licenses grant permission to engage in such activities.

A 2008 decision by the Federal Circuit summarized a number of open source developments:

> Open source licensing has become a widely used method of creative collaboration that serves to advance the arts and sciences in a

---

28. When programs are written they begin with a human readable version, called "source code." They these are translated into other forms of code usable by computers called "object code." Major developers often make only object code available.

manner and at a pace that few could have imagined just a few decades ago. For example, the Massachusetts Institute of Technology ("MIT") uses a Creative Commons public license for an OpenCourseWare project that licenses all 1800 MIT courses. Other public licenses support the GNU/Linux operating system, the Perl programming language, the Apache web server programs, the Firefox web browser, and a collaborative web-based encyclopedia called Wikipedia. Creative Commons notes that, by some estimates, there are close to 100,000,000 works licensed under various Creative Commons licenses. The Wikimedia Foundation, another of the amici curiae, estimates that the Wikipedia website has more than 75,000 active contributors working on some 9,000,000 articles in more than 250 languages.[29]

Antitrust

Financial power or marketplace power can place an individual or an entity in a position that allows it to dictate terms to others or to the public. *Tuttle v. Buck,* discussed earlier, provides one example of this kind of power—an individual using money to put another out of business. In a variety of ways, state and federal lawmakers have attempted to deal with overreaching economic or market power. The field generally takes the name "antitrust" in the United States. State and federal laws curtail the use of monopoly power to control a particular market or to dictate the terms of a contract.

The first section of the federal Sherman Act prohibits "every contract, combination in the form of trust or otherwise, or conspiracy, in restraint of trade or commerce among the several States, or with foreign nations ..."[30] The second section of the Act makes it illegal to "monopolize, or attempt to monopolize, or combine or conspire with any other person or persons, to monopolize any part of the trade or commerce among the several States, or with foreign nations." This law curtails certain uses of monopoly power, but does not prohibit the monopoly itself. A prominent case involving Microsoft illustrates the limits imposed by the Sherman Act. In *United States v. Microsoft,* 253 F.3d 34, 105 (D. C. Cir. 2001), the federal government and several individual states sued Microsoft for antitrust violations. They urged that, among other things, Microsoft used the dominance of its computer operating system to dictate license terms. Determining whether the use of a strong position violates the law requires an exhaustive examination

---

29. Jacobsen v. Katzer, 535 F.3d 1373, 1378 (Fed. Cir. 2008).
30. 15 U.S.C. §1.

of the facts. The Court of Appeals described the general inquiry: "Whether any particular act of a monopolist is exclusionary, rather than merely a form of vigorous competition, can be difficult to discern: the means of illicit exclusion, like the means of legitimate competition, are myriad. The challenge for an antitrust court lies in stating a general rule for distinguishing between exclusionary acts, which reduce social welfare, and competitive acts, which increase it."[31]

The Court sustained a lower court determination that Microsoft had used its dominance of the operating system market to dictate license terms impermissibly. More specifically, Microsoft's Windows Operating System accounted for ninety-five percent of the relevant market in personal computers.[32] It used that power to require licensees to include various features such as Microsoft's website browser, Internet Explorer. The Court of Appeals affirmed the trial court decision that Microsoft had improperly used its power by imposing certain restrictions in its Windows licenses and by building certain forms of incompatibility into the Windows system. Microsoft argued that the copyright of its system gave it a privilege to restrict its licenses and its program compatibility as it saw fit. The Court rejected that argument:

> Microsoft's primary copyright argument borders upon the frivolous. The company claims an absolute and unfettered right to use its intellectual property as it wishes: "[I]f intellectual property rights have been lawfully acquired," it says, then "their subsequent exercise cannot give rise to antitrust liability." That is no more correct than the proposition that use of one's personal property, such as a baseball bat, cannot give rise to tort liability. As the Federal Circuit succinctly stated: "Intellectual property rights do not confer a privilege to violate the antitrust laws."[33]

The Court of Appeals determined that important parts of Microsoft licensing and compatibility practices violated the Sherman Act and sent the case back to the trial court for further proceedings. Those proceedings focused on creating a remedy for the violation.

The case was finally resolved by a consent decree, that is, an agreement of the parties, which is then approved by a court. Before a consent decree is entered, the court must review the proposal and "determine that the entry of such judgment is in the public interest."[34] Among other things, the consent

---

31. 253 F.3d 34, 58.

32. The trial court had found as a matter of fact that the relevant market was "the licensing of all Intel-compatible PC operating systems worldwide." 253 F.3d 34, 52.

33. United States v. Microsoft, 253 F.3d 34, 63 (D. C. Cir. 2001).

34. 15 U.S.C. §16.

decree entered in the case required that Microsoft disclose necessary compatibility information and required that its software "licenses shall be 'reasonable and non-discriminatory' in all regards."[35] The District Court entering the decree noted that the requirements in the decree assured "that Microsoft cannot use its intellectual property rights to undermine the competitive value of its obligations (undertaken in the decree), while at the same time [it] permit[s] Microsoft to take legitimate steps to prevent unauthorized use of its intellectual property."

Antitrust laws offer a check on the bargaining power of powerful entities. However, an antitrust claim is extraordinarily difficult and expensive to pursue.

Remedies

The traditional intellectual property doctrines and the legal theories covered in this chapter provide a range of remedies to try to make an injured party whole.[36] The exact remedies available depend on both the law and the facts in the given case. In general, however, the following remedies are usually available.

Damages

The usual remedy in tort cases, including loss of property, is to award monetary damages to compensate for the loss. In intellectual property cases damages can include lost profits and other contract related financial consequences. Courts also have discretion to award enhanced or punitive damages. Punitive damages usually are awarded only when the defendant willfully disregards another's rights.

The usual remedy in contract cases is also damages, but the scope of the monetary award is more confined. With a contract each side bargains for something. If one side fails to perform, the amount of loss is based on the value of the lost performance, rather than on other harms, such as physical destruction or lost

35. U.S. v. Microsoft, 231 F. Supp. 2d 144, 192 (D.D.C. 2002).

36. Whether one has been truly injured is most often a matter of debate. A legal remedy can not repair serious injuries, such many personal injuries. The National Traffic Safety Administration reports that for decades between 30,000 and 40,000 people have died in vehicle crashes in the United States. In 2007 the number of persona injuries was 1.71 million. FARS Encyclopedia: Crashes, http://www-fars.nhtsa.dot.gov/Crashes/CrashesTime.aspx.

business.[37] For example, if John agrees to sell Bill a used car valued at $1000 on the date of the contract, the loss is $1000, not lost business or inconvenience.

Injunctions and Specific Performance

An injunction is an order to do something or refrain from doing something. They resemble military orders. Injunctions can be enforced by contempt proceedings. One can be sent to jail for refusing to obey an injunction. A failure to pay monetary damages may result in a lien on one's property, but not time in jail. In a lawsuit involving private parties, the full force of government is brought to bear against one party of the controversy when an injunction is granted. In general, such social force ought to be reserved for those instances where the broader public need or good is enforced. Courts ought to be reluctant to exercise power in such a way. Such a strenuous use of power to aid one party in a private controversy ought to be exercised sparingly.[38] Courts should be reluctant to be enlisted by one private party to give orders to another.

Courts usually require a showing of "irreparable harm" before they will grant injunctions. This rule originates in the recognition that certain things like heirlooms or pieces of land are not all the same. In cases like these, there are values that are not compensated by money.

In 2006, the United States Supreme Court applied these basic injunction principles in a patent case. The plaintiff had won a patent suit and received a damages award. However, the trial court denied the plaintiff's motion for a permanent injunction. The plaintiff appealed, and the appellate court reversed the denial of the injunction, relying on a general rule that had developed for patent cases, "that courts will issue permanent injunctions against patent infringement absent exceptional circumstances." The Supreme Court reversed and required that the lower court grant an injunction only if it determined

---

37. This measure of contract damages derives from an English case, Hadley v. Baxendale, 9 Exch. 341, 156 Eng. Rep. 145 (1854).

38. Anglo-American legal doctrine makes a distinction between legal and equitable remedies. Since all of these are imposed by courts, the distinction seems artificial, but is functionally important. "Courts view equitable remedies as more intrusive than legal remedies because they can infringe defendants' autonomy in at least two ways that money judgments do not. First, equitable remedies command personal conduct, rather than merely declare rights and liabilities. Thus, equitable orders can require defendants to engage in affirmative conduct. Second, unlike money judgments, injunctions and other equitable remedies are enforceable by contempt proceedings, which threaten defendants with imprisonment." Rhonda Wasserman, *Equity Transformed: Preliminary Injunctions to Require the Payment of Money*, 70 B. U. L. Rev. 623, 654–55 (1990).

that the harm was "irreparable," that a monetary award would be inadequate, that considering the hardships to each side an order was warranted, and that the public interest would not be harmed.[39]

Specific performance of a contract is similar to an injunction. It orders a party who has broken contract terms to perform them. For instance, a court might order an employee to transfer his rights to an invention to the employer based on the employment contract. Courts are likely to be more reluctant to grant specific performance of contract promises than they are to grant injunctions. Specific performance puts a court into a position of administering the terms of a contract. It can be difficult enough for cooperative contract parties to monitor their own compliance. The difficulties posed for a busy judge would be daunting.

Declaratory Judgments

Sometimes a party may wish to clarify rights. For example, if concerned about another party's patent claims, one might bring a declaratory judgment action to have the patent declared invalid. In some respects, declaratory actions are anticipatory. That is, one party brings a case before a matter boils over into a full controversy with damages. The Federal Circuit explained the purpose of allowing lawsuits in these cases: "In promulgating the Declaratory Judgment Act, Congress intended to prevent avoidable damages from being incurred by a person uncertain of his rights and threatened with damage by delayed adjudication."[40] Declaratory judgments are in some ways the opposite of injunctions. They simply declare, rather than award damages or order a party to do something.

In addition to these remedies, specific statutes may offer others. The Copyright Act, for instance, provides for impounding and destruction of infringing copies of protected works.[41]

Attorney Fees and Court Costs

Any litigation is expensive. Intellectual property litigation is especially so. Thus, recovery of the costs of litigation is an important element. Some statutes pro-

---

39. eBay, Inc., v. MercExchange, LLC, 547 U.S. 388 (2006).

40. Goodyear Tire & Rubber Co. v. Releasomers, Inc., 824 F.2d 953, 956 (Fed. Cir. 1987).

41. 17 U.S.C. §503.

vide that one may recover attorney fees and court costs as part of a judgment of infringement. The copyright and patent statutes, for instance, specifically provide for award of fees. The copyright act provides: "In any civil action under this title, the court in its discretion may allow the recovery of full costs by or against any party other than the United States or an officer thereof. Except as otherwise provided by this title, the court may also award a reasonable attorney's fee to the prevailing party as part of the costs."[42] The general American rule is that each party pays its own attorney fees. That is, only in the exceptional case does the winner collect attorney fees from the other side.[43]

The word "collect" raises another essential point. When one wins a case, one gets a court judgment. Usually people pay their judgments and obey court orders. However, the judgment itself does not automatically get anything done. If the loser does not pay, then the winner must get involved in further legal proceedings. The judgment may be executed by seizing assets, and the seizure of assets also involves proceedings. If there are no assets, then the winner will not get paid. In those cases, the losing defendant is called "judgment proof." Thus, before litigation is commenced, attorneys will ask "can the defendant pay?" It is not quite true that an impecunious defendant is judgment proof, however. A winner can wait until the defendant does get assets, then execute the judgment. There are usually limitations on how long a judgment is valid. However, a judgment is a legal claim, and one may file a new suit to enforce it. That must be done before any relevant time limit or statute of limitations expires.

If the winner is awarded any form of court order, say, an injunction, the order may be enforced against a party failing to obey the order.[44] The process for that is to have a contempt of court hearing. In the hearing, the winner must prove that the other party in fact violated the injunction. The consequences of being in contempt of court include spending time in jail. Since that is the case, the judgment winner is obliged to make a precise showing of exactly who and how the defendant violated the court's order.

The remedies in intellectual property cases are intended to make an injured party whole, but as in the story of Humpty Dumpty, "all the king's horses, and all the king's men, couldn't put Humpty together again." The better course in commercial transactions and intellectual property disputes is often to find an

---

42. 17 U.S.C. §505.

43. By contrast, in England, the winner of the case usually gets an award of attorney fees.

44. An award of damages is not generally accompanied with an order to pay the damages. One who gains an award of award must seek enforcement by seizure of assets, etc., as discussed above.

agreeable middle ground, one that avoids costly, uncertain, and time consuming litigation.

Concluding Observations

Intellectual property practice deals with a range of legal doctrines that concern the use of idea products, trademarks, rights of publicity and privacy, unfair competition, antitrust. It also includes uses of contracts that allocate responsibilities and license intellectual property interests. Often when intellectual property disputes emerge, many legal theories are brought to bear. Often infringements based on two or three, or even five or more legal doctrines are alleged in a single complaint. As a practical matter it is often better for the parties if the attorneys will limit the case to the doctrines and specific claims that truly represent the heart of the controversy.

Chapter Seven

Policy

Introduction

This chapter concerns the reasons for having intellectual property rules. It addresses three related questions: Where did these rules come from? Why do we have them? What are good intellectual property rules? In legal discussions, such inquiries are referred to as "policy questions." See p. 221 for note on References.

Part I. Origins

Pirates!

Computer technologies enable instantaneous transmission of all kinds of data, including music, movies, and photographs. Networked computers and other devices allow people around the world to work, play, and form "virtual" communities on line. Peer-to-peer file sharing (P2P) is a popular example of this phenomenon. A music file sharing case, *A & M Records, Inc. v. Napster, Inc.*, 239 F.3d 1004 (9th Cir. 2001), illustrates P2P and its impact.

In the 1980s, the MP3 music transfer system was developed. The system makes it easy to send music files from one computer to another. MP3 technology takes advantage of decades of information processing innovation. The core of the system is data compression, which converts large data files into smaller ones. The smaller data packets can be more easily transmitted and stored. To the human auditory system, a condensed packet of musical data sounds much the same as the original.

In 1998, Shawn Fanning developed a computer program that helps people swap MP3 music files over the Internet. His program did not make a leap in technology, but it did make it easy for computer users to search for and identify music files they wanted to exchange. In less than two years, Napster, the service he developed, was a success, distributing music to millions of users.

Soon after Napster was launched, nineteen recording companies and a pair of songwriters sued Napster for copyright infringement. The trial court concluded that Napster's activities materially contributed to direct copyright infringement by millions of users. It also determined that the copying was not fair use. The Court enjoined Napster from all further activity. The decision was appealed, and the Ninth Circuit affirmed the essence of the injunction, effectively putting Napster out of business.

The result in the *Napster* case is supported by the law and its application to the facts of the case. However, our present concern is whether that type of outcome actually serves the public interest.

The *Napster* decision did not examine the social value of the copyright law. The Constitution assigns that role to Congress. In the copyright chapter, we explored the privilege to copy copyrighted material, so long as the use is judged to be fair. The *Napster* case, fairness was judged solely on the basis of presentations of only those parties actually before the Court. Furthermore, the injunction was imposed without an actual trial in which testimony would be taken and witnesses cross-examined. The plaintiff record companies owned "valid and subsisting copyrights in and to thousands of musical compositions." Because they owned the copyrights, the record companies controlled the case. They were able to bring a competing distribution system to a halt. Many individuals who had interests in Internet distribution and in music were not represented in the case. A fuller cast of interested parties includes:

- *Songwriters*—without the words and the music, there would be no songs!
- *Performers*—Sometimes the performer is the song writer, but often the performer is someone else.
- *Publishers and distributors*—Parties such as the record companies and Napster, but other types of distributors as well.
- *Creative users*—These include people who use music in creative endeavors, such as school projects.
- *Listeners and the public*—Those who simply enjoy and listen to music.

Music builds on cultural rhythmic patterns, folk tunes, new composition, and a wide range of performances. Composition, distribution and performance of music have evolved over time. For example, in twelfth century Europe, troubadours carried music from village to village, performing tunes and composing variations and new tunes. People in the crowd went away whistling the tunes or played them by ear on guitars or lutes. In the nineteenth century, music reached many middle class foyers by way of two and four hand piano compositions and transpositions. Today, people can enjoy music through traditional instruments and modern means such as, DVDs, CDs, peer-to-peer networks, MP3 players, and Karaoke bars.

Two of the plaintiffs in *Napster* were songwriters, but not all songwriters and artists agreed with the outcome. For example, in 2001, singer Alanis Morissette testified before Congress:

> Though I cannot speak for every artist, my initial resistance to the new services created online was based on the debate having been framed in terms of piracy. Being labeled as such by the record companies, it understandably sent a ripple effect of panic throughout the artistic community. But what I have since come to realize is that for the majority of artists, this so-called "piracy" may have actually been working in their favor.

The CD recording industry won the lawsuit. It nevertheless suffered a major setback. Music CD sales plummeted in the decade after the Napster case, while (authorized and unauthorized) online music sharing thrived. In 2007, media magazine Rolling Stone, asked, "who killed the record industry as we knew it?" Their columnists, BRIAN HIATT and EVAN SERPICK, answered that the industry killed itself.

Controversy over online distribution continues. The Recording Industry Association of America (RIAA) claims that piracy "doesn't even begin to adequately describe the toll that music theft takes on the many artists, songwriters, musicians, record label employees and others whose hard work and great talent make music possible." The Future of Music Coalition, a non-profit organization representing musicians, claims that the recording industry forces musicians to "agree to unfair compensation … or resign themselves to working with indies and a life in the shadows." They see online distribution as a third alternative which "offers musicians a chance to distribute their music with minimal manufacturing and distribution costs."

The practice of file sharing poses broad questions: Should a few parties control public access to music? If so, how much control? The Copyright Act has answered those questions. It grants copyright owners enormous control over access. The Act strictly limited the areas which the Court could examine in *Napster*. The Court was confined to answering these narrow questions: Did Napster assist in unauthorized copying of copyrighted songs and recordings? Was that copying fair use? If copyrights were infringed, what remedies are the plaintiffs entitled to? The recording companies and two songwriters effectively controlled the scope of the inquiry. No parties other than the plaintiffs and defendants could speak to the matter of fair access. As we have seen in the copyright chapter, the remedies available are severe.

That limited inquiry is the one that Congress has chosen. However, copyright law does not have to operate this way. Society can give incentives to innovators without giving copyright owner such rigid control. In this chapter our inquiry shifts from what protection and incentives intellectual property law provides to what protection and incentives it *should* provide. We ask: What are good and useful intellectual property laws?

Policy questions are often posed based on implicit assumptions. A famous trick question exposes the problem of hidden assumptions. During a trial one attorney asks the defendant: "When did you stop beating your wife?" The defendant's attorney is alert and instantly objects. The basis for the objection is that no evidence has been offered that the defendant ever even touched his wife roughly, let alone beat her. One must have evidence that the husband has beaten his wife, before proceeding to inquire into when it stopped!

Law professor Amy Kapczynski gives an interesting example of how a decision may proceed based on unspoken assumptions. The assumptions create a frame of reference for the decision making process. She gives as an example a poor person deciding whether to buy a medicine that costs ten times his daily wage. She says his starting point of reference may be one of these:

- My wages are too low.
- The price is too high.
- God is angry with me, so I don't deserve the medicine.
- The high price is due to research costs.

The frames of reference are wages, price, religious conviction, and research. One might add other starting points for that poor person:

- I need the medicine so I can get back to work.
- My wife is suffering, etc.

The *Napster* case sets the stage for examining policy and hidden assumptions.

Here are some examples of unexplored assumptions that crop up in patent policy discussions:

- Granting patents encourages invention.
- Without patents there would be little or no innovation.
- Patent law is our primary policy tool to promote innovation, encourage the development of new technologies, and increase the fund of human knowledge.

We will examine these assumptions later in the chapter.

"Piracy" is a term that dominates intellectual property discussion. Originally the term referred to attacking ships at sea, seizing them and their goods by force and killing the crews, if necessary. Today, the term "piracy" is used ten times more frequently to refer to activities like file sharing, than it is to the on-going violence of pirates on the high seas. In the "golden age" of piracy there were "good" and "bad" pirates, especially in Anglo-American history. Our story of intellectual property policy begins in a period of time when commerce emerged as the prime force in English, then American, economic and social growth. During that exact period of time, sea pirates were consciously employed by the English and American governments as instruments of national policy. Many pirates became famous, and some, like Sir Walter Raleigh and Sir Francis Drake, were knighted by Queen Elizabeth. To be sure, they were granted the more genteel monicker "privateer," because some of their acts of piracy were commissioned by the Crown.

With regard to copyright and copyright piracy, Barbara Ringer, former Register of the Copyright Office, observed that during most of the nineteenth century, "the United States was exceptionally parochial in copyright matters, not only denying protection to the published works of nonresident foreign authors, but actually appearing to encourage piracy." We turn now to the historical origins of Anglo-American intellectual property policy.

Origins of Intellectual Property

In the eleventh century, European societies were rigidly stratified. At the top was a monarch and a veneer of powerful ducal and royal families and leaders of the church. A second tier comprised nobles, clergy, and petit gentry. The rest were farmers, laborers, craftsmen, tradesmen, merchants, and the desperately poor.

The craftsmen and merchants began to escape from feudal and royal domination by making things, providing services, and engaging in trade. As a class, these groups began to be referred to as the "bourgeoisie," in reference to their origins in towns where industry and trade could develop. Their work became increasingly important to everyone. The value of their work allowed them to accumulate surpluses of wealth or capital. Wealth combined with knowledge gave them power to influence events and purchase property. As they gained sway, the commercial classes naturally sought to have the laws reflect their interests. In England one of their achievements was establishing laws that favored commerce, including the original intellectual property laws of the Anglo-American legal tradition.[1]

---

1. The term "commerce" often refers to production, as well as trade, in the discussion that follows. "Capital" is refers to its standard meaning, "wealth in the form of money or

By the thirteenth century English kings, had consolidated their power. So long as they kept in line with the legitimizing authority of the Church and defeated upstart dukes or invaders, they would retain power. This process of consolidation had proceeded smoothly from William the Conqueror's invasion in 1066 until 1215. In that year, a group of nobles and clergy forced King John to sign the *Magna Carta* at Runnymede on the banks of the Thames River twenty miles west of London.

The *Magna Carta* was revised and reissued several times in its early years. The 1225 revision is celebrated as a milestone in the development of parliamentary power and due process of law in England. Among the promises made by the King was that "no freeman is to be taken or imprisoned or disseised of his free tenement or of his liberties or free customs, or outlawed or exiled or in any way ruined, nor will we go against such a man or send against him save by lawful judgement of his peers or by the law of the land." This provision is viewed as the start of an Anglo-American commitment to rule by laws which bind everyone, including the ruler. Also, from that point onward, English Kings and Queens would be forced to share power with Parliament.

The merchants were not among those who imposed the *Magna Carta* on King John, but several of its provisions recognized their interests. One of these assured common weights and measures. Another recognized freedom for merchants to travel and trade wares throughout the kingdom.

At first, control over economic activity, including commerce, lay in the hands of the Crown, then gradually shifted to a combination of Crown, Parliament, and chartered corporations. From the sixteenth through the seventeenth century, the mechanism of government evolved further. By the late seventeenth century the locus of governmental control in the American colonies had shifted from the Crown and its ministers in London to colonial administrators located in the colonies. Much *de facto* control shifted from the government (wherever located) to dominant commercial interests. We now sketch highlights of that development.

By the sixteenth century, the economic system had evolved to what is called "mercantilism." Professor James Ely describes this system as one in which "government played an active role in regulating commerce and stimulating economic growth. The objective of the mercantile system was to increase national wealth by controlling the economy and securing a favorable balance of trade." Deliberate policies guided the development, but it would be too much to say

---

other assets owned by a person or organization or available or contributed for a particular purpose." *Apple Dictionary*. There are few footnotes in this chapter. Supporting references are noted in the Reference Notes at the end of the chapter.

that mercantilism was a clearly designed ideology. As England developed her North American colonies, it would be important for her to try to impose these policies there. Professor Ely describes the transposition to the American colonies: "A glance at the colonial statutes and ordinances of the seventeenth and early eighteenth centuries demonstrates the pervasive concern of lawmakers with economic regulation and protection of the supply of basic necessities."

During this period, the English Crown developed a system of governing commerce, trade, and production by means of granting privileges called "patents" to certain individuals and entities. The term patent was a broad one at that time. Patents were granted in three general categories:

- permissions for production, such as grinding corn;
- permissions to engage in activities otherwise prohibited (called *non-obstante* patents);
- permissions to engage in regulated trade.

These patents burdened or prohibited activity by merchants and artisans who had not been granted patents. They were, in effect, monopolies.

One such patent brought about litigation and parliamentary action from which the first Anglo-American intellectual property law evolved. Queen Elizabeth had granted an exclusive right to make and import playing cards to a Lord Darcy. The courts eventually overturned Darcy's monopoly. Then Parliament enacted the Statute on Monopolies, which prohibited all monopolies, except for patents of fourteen years or less, granted for "any manner of new manufacture, within this realm, to the true and first inventor and inventors of such manufactures." The statute was a triumph for commercial classes, because it prevented the Crown from interfering with commerce by granting special privileges. It was also an expression of English mercantilism. Dr. Chris Dent observes, that it was "the wealth of the nation as a whole—the '[preservation and] augmentation of the wealth of the Realme' rather than the wealth of individuals that was important."

The Statute on Monopolies was followed by the Statute of Anne, and a succession of statutes which evolved into copyright law. Trademark protection developed independently of patents and copyrights. The practice of marking of goods probably emerged from the need to mark goods, so they would not be stolen or mislaid in the market. The next likely step was to recognize a mark as an identification of a supplier of goods or services. Trademarks appear to have existed *de facto* for a long time. The English courts began to provide legal protection for them in the middle of the eighteenth century.

During these same centuries, England experienced growing political unrest, including two revolutions and the execution of King Charles in 1649. These movements were varied in impetus, but generally involved efforts to gain freedom to choose and practice religion and to build effective democratic institutions. Popular ideas of freedom of speech, of press, and of religion emerged through this activity.

Looking back, one can observe ideas at work that would shape the laws to favor commercial interests. In broad terms, these ideas were: Producing and trading goods and services is worthwhile. Government interference with this productive activity is, by contrast, not good. Encouraging invention is valuable, and so, too, is clear marking of the origin of goods. Political freedoms, such as access to and dissemination of ideas, are valuable to the entire nation. Free flow of information is also of specific value to commerce. Stated more abstractly, one sees four policies at work: freedom to engage in lawful commerce, encouragement of innovation, clear marking of the origin of goods, and freedom to gain and use information.

These policies represented practical approaches to getting things done, rather than expressions of an ideology. Commerce and industry were able to meet community and national needs. Dr. Dent explains the impact of the shift to mercantilism: "Two of the key themes of the mercantilists are relevant to the drafting of the *Statute of Monopolies:* the desire to boost employment, and the benefits of improving the balance of trade. In addition, it may be noted that there was also support amongst the mercantilists for the ideal of patents for invention." Commercial enterprise did a better job of meeting needs and creating national power than did the landed gentry, the church, or the Crown. Mercantilism proved stronger than clumsy monarchial/feudal institutions.

Successive Kings and Queens realized that the government could martial commerce to increase their power at home and abroad. It appears that England was more successful in imperial adventures than her French, Spanish, Dutch, and Portuguese competitors, because she employed mercantilism more skillfully. However, as has been noted, increasingly the Crown was pressed to share power with Parliament and a growing bureaucracy. This shift of power was valuable to the commercial classes, for they could more readily shape the views of legislators and bureaucrats than they could those of nobles and courtiers. Indeed, they could become bureaucrats or Members of Parliament.

The policies of England were carried forth in her American colonies by the Crown's appointed governors and royally chartered corporations. As the colonies assumed more power and independence, their local administrations followed these same general policies. By the time of the Revolution, English laws and policies, including those which governed commerce, had become customary and entrenched. Many scholars find that the thirteen new American states basically adopted English law, "lock, stock, and barrel." The American Revolution severed political ties with England, but continued the same pattern of commercial laws and practices.

Figure 7-1. Playing Cards

The adoption of the Constitution preserved the states as political entities. Thus, their authority remained intact, except where displaced by federal laws. The biggest grant of federal power was to regulate interstate and foreign commerce. The commerce clause powers extend to all manner of commercial activity, so long as that activity has some substantial impact on interstate or foreign commerce. The commerce power includes the power to establish federal trademark laws, as Congress has done in the Lanham Act.

The Constitution contains an explicit provision concerning intellectual property. It grants Congress exclusive power to create copyrights and patents. The theory is: If the innovator enriches society with ideas, then Congress may give that innovator a limited reward. This provision is also the only one in the Constitution that grants the federal government power to create a property right.

The state governments remained free to regulate all other commercial activities, except when Congress acts to the contrary through any of its powers, including its power to regulate interstate commerce.[2] The first ten amendments

2. The states (not the federal government) also were the source of defining or elaborating property rights. For example, eight western states and the state of Louisiana have community property laws. Under that system all property acquired by the labor of either

were added immediately after the ratification of the Constitution. Their purpose was to protect certain freedoms, such as speech, religion, and due process from encroachment by the federal government. The Fourteenth Amendment was added after the Civil War to protect such rights against abridgment by the state governments.

Thus, the traditional intellectual property policies of the United States closely followed the evolution of their English counterparts. The United States diverged in that its Constitution specifically recognized and protected freedom to communicate and gain access to ideas. Also, the Constitution amplified the English tradition by explicitly requiring that patents and copyrights serve a public interest.

The course of intellectual property development has been shaped by two legal institutions, private property rights and business corporations. The term "institution," as used by the legal profession refers to the full range of laws and practices that have legal effect.[3] We turn now to the evolution of those two institutions.

Private Property in England and the United States

In ancient Rome, the *pater familias*, or father of the family, owned even the human beings in his extended family. This pattern of domination persisted in Europe in the forms of feudalism and monarchy. In the seventeenth century, European philosophers began to examine and challenge these heavy-handed notions. They sought a way that people might benefit from rather than be injured by property rights. In Holland, the jurist Hugo Grotius (Huig de Groot, 1583–1645) posited a "natural rights" theory of private property. In England, John Locke took a different position. He posited a conception of private property rights which were earned and justified by productive labor. Locke's ideas have had a profound effect on United States policy concerning private property.

John Locke's young adult life had been a bookish one at Oxford. He had been on a trajectory that would likely have taken him into the clergy. However, in 1667 he became the protégé of Anthony Ashley Cooper, the first Earl of Shaftesbury. Shaftesbury introduced Locke to the world of English politics.

---

spouse during the marriage belongs jointly to the community of the marriage, not to the spouse who worked to acquire the property.

3. This refers to the reality that many factors, in addition to the letter of the law, affect the actual impact of law. These include organizational structure, traditions, philosophy, common practices.

As a result, Locke worked all his life at the hub of government. Under both Charles II and William III, he served on the government ministries dedicated to trade. This work would put him in direct contact with policies related to the expansion of commerce at the time that England was using commerce to consolidate its hold on North America.

Locke developed his concepts about private property and government in the context of ideas and conditions prevalent in his times. There appears to be scholarly consensus that he believed that social institutions must be reconciled with the sovereignty of God, with efforts to secure religious liberty, and with the growing power of commerce. Locke's tenure with the Board of Trade corresponded with the maturing of English commerce, including that nation's entry into the transatlantic African slave trade.

Locke's conclusions were practical. Humans tame and till the land, and to the extent that their labors make something of that effort, they should enjoy property rights in what that labor produced. However, those rights could never come at the expense of the common good. The following passage captures the essence of his views:

> This is certain, that in the beginning, before the desire of having more than man needed had altered the intrinsic value of things, which depends only on their usefulness to the life of man; or had agreed, that a little piece of yellow metal, which would keep without wasting or decay, should be worth a great piece of flesh, or a whole heap of corn; though men had a right to appropriate, by their labour, each one to himself, as much of the things of nature, as he could use: yet this could not be much, nor to the prejudice of others, where the same plenty was still left to those who would use the same industry. To which let me add, that he who appropriates land to himself by his labour, does not lessen, but increase the common stock of mankind: for the provisions serving to the support of human life. *John Locke, Two Treatises on Government, Book II, § 37.*

Locke was concerned to protect people from arbitrary action by the Crown or Parliament. Securing property that one gained by labor against the arbitrary seizure was a strong means to accomplish this end. To Locke, the role of government in this regard was clear: "And so whoever has the legislative or supreme power of any common-wealth, is bound to govern by established standing laws. And all this to be directed to no other end, but the peace, safety, and public good of the people."

Property rights had existed for centuries in England and throughout Europe. These rights allowed owners to control land and personal property, including serfs, and slaves. Ownership, had been concentrated in the hands of the monarch, the nobles, and the church. Locke's theory does not emphasize enhancing property rights, divorced from human need. Instead, it emphasizes assuring that one gains and keeps the benefits of one's labor. Only those fruits are properly labeled property, and they needed protection from the encroachments by the government. As noted, property rights were not insulated from community obligations.

Thomas Jefferson lived a century after John Locke (1743–1826). Much had transpired in that interval, including the American Revolution and the groundwork that would produce the Industrial Revolution. Invention was on the rise. Jefferson himself was an inventor. As part of his duties as Secretary of State under President Washington, he served as the first United States Commissioner of Patents.

In 1813, a few years after his presidency, Jefferson received a letter from a man named Isaac McPherson, who complained about the scope of a patent granted to an inventor named Oliver Evans for a water conveying system. Jefferson's reply to McPherson discussed the patent and the prior art in great detail. He noted that such conveying systems dated back more than a century. He concluded that this history showed "both on reason and the senses that there is nothing new" in Evans' patented system. Jefferson then expressed in some detail his ideas on private property rights, especially with respect to owning inventions. Jefferson stated his understanding that there are some notions of fairness that one might describe as natural rights. These included such things as due process, unbiased judges, and freedom from *ex post facto* laws. But no form of ownership could be considered basic in this way.

> It is agreed by those who have seriously considered the subject, that no individual has, of natural right, a separate property in an acre of land, for instance.... Considering the exclusive right to invention as given not of natural right, but for the benefit of society, I know well the difficulty of drawing a line between the things which are worth to the public the embarrassment of an exclusive patent, and those which are not. *Letter to McPherson, August 13, 1813.*

Jefferson concluded these reflections with a compelling image: "If nature has made any one thing less susceptible than all others of exclusive property, it is the action of the thinking power called an idea.... He who receives an idea from me, receives instruction himself without lessening mine; as he who lights his taper at mine, receives light without darkening me."

The views of Locke and Jefferson have deeply influenced the American legal and social tradition. However, their views ought not be accepted as *a priori* principles, nor would either of them have intended that acceptance. They formulated their views in relation to the realities and knowledge of their times. No doubt they would think through these matters freshly were they alive today.

Property rights cause harm when placed above human rights. Slavery provides an extreme and frightful example. Slavery, the right to "own" other humans, existed in England and the United States throughout the period of time we have been discussing. The contradiction between human slavery and property rights was not resolved by Locke or Jefferson in their lifetimes, nor did either one of them resolve it in their personal lives. Locke had full knowledge of the slave trade, and as a government minister had participated in it. Jefferson owned slaves. United States statutes and the Constitution both affirmed the right to own slaves. After the Civil War, the Constitution was amended to abolish slavery

Property rights vary widely. Much property is public rather than private. For example, parks, roads, and military installations are owned by the people at large through their government. Private ownership can be complex. Eight western states and Louisiana have community property laws. In those states, property acquired by work during a marriage belongs to the community of spouses in equal part. As we have seen, the Copyright Act divides property into six different types. Finally, United States law has never supported the proposition that property rights are absolute. For example, land ownership has always been riddled with conditions. One may not use real property in ways that constitute a nuisance to others, and one must obey zoning laws and building codes.

Corporations

From the twelfth century forward, traders and artisans organized guilds and associations to improve skills and promote common interests. Over time, the English Crown recognized that the guilds were a productive force and a source of revenue. Professor Thomas B. Nachbar observes, that the "development throughout the thirteenth and fourteenth centuries of a middle class of tradesmen and merchants (the burgesses) provided a group of individuals with reputations sufficient to assure the Crown that taxes would be paid." Corporations, as we know them today, evolved from these guilds.

In 1888, American legal scholar Samuel Williston noted that England's trade and imperial ambitions "led to the establishment and incorporation of companies of foreign adventurers, similar in all respects to the earlier guilds, except that their members were foreign instead of domestic traders." Williston noted that corporations allowed "noblemen, gentlemen, shopkeepers, widows, orphans" to get in on the game by a simple investment of money.

Corporations became essential instruments of English policy. The Hudson's Bay Company, Plymouth Bay Company, and the Virginia Company wielded powerful influence in England's North American colonies. Professors Paul D. Halliday and G. Edward White, observe that when "the king chartered trading companies or colonies in various overseas places, he was carving off part of his authority and giving it to others." The corporation was integral to England's construction of its empire, especially during the seventeenth century. Professor A.E. Dick Howard summed the situation up: "Poor by the standards of Spanish and French monarchs, England's Stuart kings were bothered by such nuisances as Parliament's insistence on being consulted about taxes. Thus James I, who came to the throne in 1603, saw the advantage of chartering groups of adventurers who were willing to shoulder the expense of colonization in hopes of profit and reward." Corporations and trading companies constituted the *de facto*, even *de jure* authority that governed many of the American colonies. Above them stood the Lords of Trade and its successor, the Board of Trade. These administrative institutions were for all practical purposes the voice of the monarch. They held sway, yet they could not truly control either the corporations or the growing commercial will of the American colonials.

The use of commerce to advance national interest came to be called "mercantilism" throughout Europe. Mercantilism evolved into capitalism. Professor Herbert Hovenkamp, describes the transition:

> Classical political economy in the United States was dedicated to the principle that the state could best encourage economic development by leaving entrepreneurs alone, free of regulation and subsidy. The classicists believed capital would flow naturally toward investments that promised profit, provided that the channels were clear.

The classical corporation efficiently gathered and protected capital. The investors were attracted, because they could derive income without actually setting up a business. For example, one could make a profit from the manufacture of hammers without being involved in production of hammers. One simply placed an investment in a corporation that produces hammers and received income on the investment depending on the success of the business. One need invest no labor beyond writing a check. The same basic process continues today.

Since the nineteenth century, activities of corporate and private entrepreneurs have controlled working conditions, transportation routes, necessary services, availability of goods, etc. Often these activities have led to harsh work environments, waves of unemployment, denial of adequate health and educational services, and even military actions. These conditions have led to federal and state laws which attempt to regulate the corporation's internal structure and its external responsibilities.

Corporations exist within a fabric of regulation. Business leaders often complain about the regulation, but the fact is that modern business depends completely on regulation. Negotiable paper and banks are established by government action. Contracts depend on courts for enforcement. Corporations must be chartered by a government to become legal entities. Intellectual property rules are yet another an example.

A company's attitude toward a regulation depends on how that regulation affects it. Intellectual property rules allow some competitors to thrive, but deter others. The *Napster* case is a good example. Other external conditions affecting corporate conduct include increasing global trade and vast environmental and cultural concerns.

Professor Hovenkamp claims that "vertical integration" led to evolution of the corporation from a "classical" model into its current form. Vertical integration involves an entity bringing costs of production and distribution into their own operations. Doing this removes those costs from the market, and eventually this can allow a company to dictate a price rather than compete. Professor Hovenkamp summarizes, "Corporations in competition are constantly trying to reduce costs, a goal often accomplished most effectively by internalizing transactions formerly made in the marketplace. As a result of such vertical integration, more and more corporate activity is taken out of the market, where price and offering are more-or-less given, and placed within the corporation itself, where they are subject to considerable discretion." Moving business activities out of the country ("offshoring") further removes corporate activity from domestic regulation and market influences.

Thus, for the past three quarters of a century, what Professor Hovenkamp refers to as the "classical corporation" has been superseded by the multinational corporation under nominal regulation by federal and state governments. Hovenkamp sees the corporation today as subject to multiple layers of regulation, including securities laws, labor regulations, antitrust laws, requirements of "fair competition" administered by the Federal Trade Commission, etc. However, the regulation of corporate conduct is more apparent than real. On the international scene, the multinational corporation enjoys even greater freedom from social accountability. Depending on its resources it can move its facilities here and there. It can use its economic power to influence local governments and international institutions.

Corporations have enjoyed a spectacular rise in recognition, and power. What Professor Williston described as a "fictitious legal person, distinct from the actual persons who compose it," has grown into an entity of superhuman proportions. Since 1868 corporations have enjoyed constitutional rights as if they were living human beings. In that year, the Supreme Court heard a case involving a tax assessment against the Southern Pacific railroad. Without even hearing argument the Supreme Court made the most extraordinary and sweeping pronouncement: "The court does not wish to hear argument on the question whether the provision in the Fourteenth Amendment to the Constitution, which forbids a State to deny to any person within its jurisdiction the equal protection of the laws, applies to these corporations. We are all of opinion that it does." This constitutional protection has continuously expanded since then, but never has the Supreme Court provided the necessary and complete explanation that such a sweeping ruling demands.

Professor Phillip I. Blumburg states,

> Large multinational corporations have come to dominate the national and global economic scene. The scale of their operations is enormous. The largest have grown into enterprises of astonishing magnitude that in their economic dimensions are fully comparable to nation states.

According to one estimate, "twenty-nine to fifty-one of the world's 100 largest economic entities are multinational companies; the remainder are nation states. The gross domestic production of sub-Saharan Africa does not equal the revenues of General Motors and Ford combined." For employees, corporations constitute a *de facto* government. In addition, their economic power allows them to flood the public with advertising and lobby successfully in legislatures, treaty making, and administrative processes around the world.

Property Rights and Civil Obligations

Innovation can be rewarded, trademarks protected, and trade secrets safeguarded by property rights or by general civil obligations. In this section we examine the difference between these two types of legal responsibility. The choice of the type of legal obligation has profound practical and social consequences.

The case of John and Sally will illustrate the differences. They are next door neighbors. John is a good natured and oblivious fellow, while Sally is fastidious and fussy, especially about her garden. One day at the supermarket, John bumps Sally with his shopping cart at the supermarket. John immediately apologizes, "Oh, Sally, I'm so sorry. Please excuse me!" Sally is nonetheless annoyed. John, she thinks, is harmless enough, but generally a nuisance. Later in the day she develops a slight bruise on her arm, apparently where the cart might have banged her. If the bruise turns out to be a serious injury, she may be able to establish that John is liable for the harm to her, but she must prove that the injury really damaged her, that John was the actual cause of the harm, and that he was negligent by an objective standard.

When John gets home, true to form, he sees a bird and wanders off gazing skyward trying to identify it. His wandering take him into Sally's flower garden. Enthralled by the bird, which is building a nest, he sits down on Sally's bench to watch it. Quite comfortable there, John leaves his groceries in his car and dozes off. Sally returns home startled to see a man sitting in her garden. Because John has come into her garden Sally can recover for trespass to real property without proving that John was negligent or harmed her land. If he was conscious as he wandered, he has trespassed.

Lawyers refer to non-property claims as "civil obligations," and property claims as "property rights." Breach of a civil obligation is called a "tort," which is a French word meaning "wrong." Breach of a property right is called a "trespass." Claims of breach of civil obligation inquire into the nature of conduct, while violations of property rights impose nearly automatic liability. Property concepts create a rigid structure of rights, while civil obligations create a flexible one.

Civil obligations focus on behavior. We can see this in many common examples. In cases involving racial discrimination or auto accidents, the complaining party must explain how the defendant's behavior violates an established norm. The complainant bears the burden of showing what conduct was harmful and why it violated the law. In a car crash the plaintiff must show that the other driver was driving negligently. Usually, the law allows a case to go forward only if the plaintiff can point to substantial, as opposed to trivial, damage. Occasionally a statute or rule imposes a more strict form of liability due to the importance of a particular obligation.

Property rights focus on a static condition or status. The primary question is whether the complaining party owns land, a copyright, a patent, etc. A property right claim reverses the obligations of proof. Once the property owner has proved the status of ownership, he or she has a nearly automatic remedy for even trivial interferences with the right. The property owner can win a case without having to prove fault or negligence on the part of the defendant. The owner of a parcel of land, a copyright, patent, or real estate has a rather easy task in proving a case. In addition, property owners can readily obtain a decisive remedy. For example, Napster was put out of business by a preliminary injunction. Such a remedy is granted without a full trial. None of this ease applies when one seeks to enforce a non-property civil obligation.

In a nutshell, one must prove bad behavior and harmful consequences in a civil obligation case. In a property rights case one can usually win if one has proved ownership. An owner need not establish that a defendant behaved in a particular way or that he caused real damage.

Copyright, patent, and trademark law are all cast in terms of property rights. One form of intellectual property, trade secrets, uses civil liability rules, rather than property rights to resolve competing claims. A plaintiff claiming that another appropriated a secret must prove that the defendant had a particular obligation with respect to it, and that the defendant violated that obligation.

Part II. Selected Policy Problems

Copyrights

English printing laws began to evolve soon after John Gutenberg's printing technology arrived. At first they were in the form of privileges granted by the Crown. Professor Tomás Gómez-Arostegui states that this practice "stemmed from the Crown's belief that it had the absolute right to control and dispose of certain classes of books, much as it could other property." In 1557, Philip and Mary I granted a printing monopoly to the Company of Stationers. The company had evolved from a guild of copyists and illuminators before the arrival of the printing press. Professor Adrian Johns describes their headquarters a short distance from St. Paul's Cathedral in London:

> [A] building of indeterminate age with a stone façade. You pass along a brief, twisting entranceway and into an elegant antechamber. But then the passage suddenly and dramatically opens out, leading into a vast, formal hall. It is richly decorated with 17th-century panelling and arrayed flags, all illuminated by stained-glass windows portraying Caxton, Shakespeare, Cranmer and Tyndale. You are in Stationers' Hall, the centre of London's old book trade.

The company's duties included acting as censor to assure that seditious or heretical writings were not published by it or its licensees.

In 1707, the Statute of Anne was enacted, which granted authors and their assignees a "copyright," an exclusive right to print their works for a period of fourteen years. At around the same time, English courts were beginning to articulate a common law copyright. Scholars have disputed the scope of this right, but a number of English cases observed that the common law right was a "perpetual" right of authors to publish their work. Both the rights under the Statute of Anne and the common law copyright had been enforced by damage awards and by injunctions.

Thus, by the time of the Constitution, various policies or reasons had existed for copyrights—government control, commercial enterprise, and reward for authorship. The fact that powerful remedies, including injunctions, could be awarded for infringements gave copyrights a forcefulness that applies to property rights, but which is rarely present with regard to civil (or non-property) obligations. The United States Constitution insisted that federal copyrights must be for limited times and only in order to pursue a public interest, "to promote the Progress of Science and useful Arts."

Congress has power to create copyright laws and to define the nature of that right. It has chosen to establish a property right, rather than a civil obligation. As we have seen, property rights are rigid and take little account of behavior or circumstance. By contrast, civil obligations examine the nature of the conduct of all relevant parties. Property rights start with the assumption that "the owner is always right." Civil obligations start with an inquiry, "what are the relative responsibilities in this case?" Our concern is whether Congress made a good choice by making copyright a property right rather than a civil obligation?

As we saw in Chapter Three, the copyright property right vests initial ownership in the author, or in some instances an employer or one who has commissioned a work. That owner may readily transfer ownership of the copyright. Transferability of rights is an essential feature of property rights. Copyright as a property right thus offers advantages to those engaged in commerce: ease of transfer, relative ease of evaluation, and strong enforcement. Disadvantages include control over communication, imbalance of bargaining power, and lack of assurance of a reward for creative effort

Authors, performers, and other creative people often operate from a weak bargaining position. Their services and works can be viewed as "optional." Musicians, for example, survive on gigs, recording contracts, or working at some other job. Most musicians will not be offered recording contracts at all. The Future of Music Coalition describes the results for those who do get contracts:

> When artists sign contracts with major labels, they typically transfer the copyright ownership of their recordings over to the record label. The label usually agrees to pay for recording, manufacturing and promoting the record, and sometimes gives the artist an "advance." The label basically acts like a bank: it provides a loan to the performer to cover costs, as well as the advance, and then "recoups" those expenses by deducting the loaned amount from any royalty payments owed to the artist. Sadly, the overwhelming majority of recordings never recoup, which means most artists never receive any money from the sales of their recordings.

The Copyright Act does not assure that an author or performer will receive either the copyright reward or any other compensation.

The *Napster* case showed the power of enforcing a property right by use of an injunction. In addition to suing commercial distributors like Napster, record companies have sued thousands of individuals who have uploaded or downloaded music files. In one such case, decided in 2010, four major record companies sued Joel Tenenbaum, who had illegally downloaded and shared thousands of songs when he was a student. The jury trial focussed on thirty of those songs. Since Tenenbaum admitted infringement, the only question for the jury was how much he should pay in damages. Willful infringement entitles a copyright owner to $750 to $150,000 damages per infringement even when no loss has been proved. The jury found that Tenenbaum's conduct was willful and awarded $22,500 per song for a total verdict of $675,000.

Tenenbaum's attorneys asked the judge, Nancy Gertner, to grant a "*remittitur*," which is an order which reduces the amount of the award, when it is "grossly excessive, inordinate, shocking to the conscience of the court." The plaintiffs would then have had the option of accepting the award or demanding a new trial. Judge Gertner noted that the plaintiffs "made it abundantly clear that they were "going for broke," and would not accept a *remittitur*. Since she was likely to have the same issue come up after another trial, she ruled on Mr. Tenenbaum's objection that the award violated constitutional due process.

The Supreme Court has ruled that enhanced damages called "punitive damages" violate due process if they can be categorized as arbitrary. The Court has not, however, ruled directly on statutory damages under the Copyright Act. Judge Gertner applied the Supreme Court rules on punitive damages to the statutory damages verdict. She noted that "Tenenbaum was an ordinary young adult engaging in noncommercial file-sharing, not a wealthy railroad bilking customers for its own profit." She concluded that the award was unconstitutional because it bore "no rational relationship to the government's interests in compensating copyright owners and deterring infringement." She reduced the award to $2,250 for each of the thirty infringed works, which she judged to be unquestionably severe and adequate to compensate the record companies and deter unlawful copying.

Judge Gertner's ruling may be persuasive to other courts, but they will not be bound to follow it. Even if the First Circuit were to affirm the ruling, only District Courts within that circuit would be bound by the ruling. A Supreme Court decision would cover the entire United States, but it would be likely limited to the finding that the award in Tenenbaum's case was unconstitutional. Other awards might be reasonable. Thus, the basic policy question would remain: Should a party that is not an author or performer be entitled to huge copyright damages without showing actual harm?

Congress has many choices other than to continue the present system. It can modify the rigidity of the property rights model or replace it with a civil obligation. It can reduce the size of statutory damages or abolish them. It can make it easier for a larger range of parties to present evidence on fair use. It can tailor the length of the copyright term so that it is limited to realistic compensation to authors. The Constitution requires that copyrights serve the public interest and be limited in duration.

Patents

As we have seen, Anglo-American patent law originated as a limited exception to a prohibition of monopolies enacted by Parliament early in the seventeen century. A patent might be allowed for limited years for those who perfect "any manner of new manufacture, within this realm." Below the surface lies the concept of a reward for inventions that are useful to the public at large. Usefulness to the public remains the prime justification for patents today. The Constitution requires that an innovation must "promote science and useful arts," if it is to receive a patent.

Humans by nature seek easy, efficient solutions to problems. In addition, many people like to tinker, whether it be with a rusty gate or a Sudoko puzzle. Some people are curious and always want to know more. These propensities have caused humanity to expand its store of knowledge and invent things. Cooperation and transmission of knowledge play major roles in science and its applications. Isaac Newton, another seventeenth century luminary, stated, "If I have seen a little further it is by standing on the shoulders of Giants." The development of the first antibiotic, penicillin, illustrates this social dimension of science and innovation. Alexander Fleming pinpointed the active antibiotic ingredient, penicillin, in the 1920s, yet this discovery was based on knowledge which had built up over centuries of practical work and experimentation with bacteria and fungi.

Today, scientific and technological advances often require huge investments of time and money. The Large Hadron Collider (LHC), the world's largest supercollider, probes the frontiers of our knowledge of matter. That collider is seventeen miles in circumference buried hundreds of feet below the surface of the earth, and it is crammed with expensive components. It has cost of billions of dollars to construct that machine, and it will take billions more to use and maintain it. Knowledge of the brain has exploded exponentially in the last two decades. Cancer research has also accelerated in that period. Brain and cancer research do not always require a huge physical plant like the LHC, but they do require sophisticated laboratories, equipment, and lots of time, thought and dedicated effort.

The scale of required investment for the innovative infrastructure cannot be supported by patents. A company driven by short term profit will not invest on the chance that it will be the first to get to the patent office. Nothing in the Patent Act requires that any return on the patent be invested in research. Patents are likely to encourage searches for specific solutions, rather than general knowledge. Private research tends to be secretive and competitive, rather than collaborative. Competition may encourage effort, but secrecy inhibits the exchange of ideas.

In sum, modern technical advances require an accumulation of capital, which requires public commitment, usually provided in the form of government investment, creation of institutions, approval of cartels, provision of infrastructure, etc. A fair patent system can give a boost to this infrastructure, but cannot create or support it.

In 2003, Robert Hahn reviewed the extensive economic literature on the effectiveness of the patent system. He concluded that "the empirical literature is inconclusive on the question of whether stronger patents increase *or* decrease innovation." A 2009 Yale study indicated that a 25.5 billion dollar loss is caused by the issuance of patents that do "not promote economic welfare because they do not reward true innovations."

The equivocal value of patents is partly due to the fact that patents deter innovation, as well as encourage it, especially in advanced technological environments. The development of integrated circuits (ICs) provides an example. ICs are used in computer processes from thermostats to supercomputers. Each IC is itself a complex assembly of parts. ICs can contain any of the components one finds in a 1930s radio—amplifiers, capacitors, resisters, etc. In ICs, these components have been reduced to tiny dimensions and packed by the hundreds or hundreds of thousands into semiconductor chips. Both the design of the chips and their manufacturing processes can vary. Since the Patent Act allows patents for even minuscule innovations, hundreds of thousands of patents have been issued covering chip devices or manufacturing processes.

The huge number of patents creates the following problem: Suppose an innovator discovers a revolutionary method to process data in ICs. The invention might use a new form of logic, or it might allow ICs to run a hundred times faster, but use less power. The invention has the capacity to improve every single computer process on the market. However, the dense web of existing patents may force a producer of the invention to design around many existing patents or get licenses to them before it can produce an IC that incorporates the technology. A company with a large portfolio of minor patents can deter or even block the innovation from getting to market.

Another social cost of the patent system is the allocation of legal resources to patent disputes and litigation. Patent litigation diverts resources from serving other legal and administrative needs. Patent lawsuits are so expensive that it is prohibitive for most individuals and small companies to defend themselves against patent claims, even weak ones.

Congress might consider a range of features in a redesign of the patent system. These include: tailoring patent rights to fit different fields of inventive activity; requiring a percentage of royalties to be invested in research and development; establishing reasonable licensing requirements, such as restrictions of selective licensing and compulsory licenses; beefing up the utility requirement to weed out undeserving patents. Congress might also consider a more fundamental change, recasting the patent privilege in terms of a civil obligation, rather than a property right.

Assessing the utility of the patent system involves the following questions: How much incentive is needed or justified? What actual benefit does a given class of patents confer on the public? Does that benefit vary among different fields of research and development? For example, should the incentives for medical technologies be different than incentives for technologies that require less research investment? How does the cost of a class of patents compare with the benefits it confers? What should be the scope and conditions of the patent right? What licensing rights and conditions should be provided? Many of these questions can be answered in part by a cost benefit analysis. The effectiveness of incentives and patent requirements should be assessed at the time that Congress sets up the patent laws. This way, appropriate rewards, terms, and conditions of the patent grant can be established. Businesses are accustomed to such calculations in their planning.

The Patent Reform Act of 2009 proposed a cost benefit analysis be applied at the damages stage of a patent case. Damages should be limited "to the portion of the economic value of the infringing product or process properly attributable to the claimed invention's specific contribution over the prior art." The proposed damage limits would assess costs and benefits after the fact of infringement. However, Congress needs to apply that approach up front when designing the structure and details of the patent law.

Dozens of law journal articles have been devoted to patent law reform in the past three years. Many of those emphasize some form of cost/benefit analysis. Here is a sample:

Flexible rights or "pliability rules." Professors Bell and Parchomovsky note that an optimal patent term would balance the utility of the invention against "the monopoly-induced deadweight loss." Calculating an optimal term would be difficult, so they propose that patents should be constructed in accordance with "pliability rules." That is, the patent reward ought to combine features of property rights with features of civil liability rules. "Pliable rules are contingent rules that provide an entitlement owner with property rule or liability rule protection as long as some specified condition obtains." They suggest that there be two terms for patents. In the first term, the patent owner would have the current property right, with its strict liability features. The second term would create civil rights and duties. For example there could be a first term of perhaps ten years, during which the patentee would enjoy the same exclusive rights a patent enjoys today. That would be followed by a second twenty year term which would provide for remedies based on showing some wrongful conduct by an interfering party. Also, during the second period, the patent would be subject to a compulsory license.

A spectrum of alternative patent policies. In 2006 Professor Robert Weissman analyzed the intellectual property treaty called "TRIPS." A major focus of his analysis was the need for effective drugs in developing countries. "The primary concerns of a rational drug policy for Third World nations should be disseminating useful drugs as widely and cheaply as possible, and encouraging research and development of products to address local illnesses."

Weissman observes that nations adopt patent laws to serve national interests or dominant economic interests within their borders. Developing nations often start with weak patent protection or none, then switch. "Virtually every industrialized country adopted strong patent laws after developing their technological infrastructure, in significant part through copying strategies." This is not surprising. If a community observes a better or more effective way of building a bridge, treating disease, or waging war, it is likely to adopt it. With regard to drugs, a number nations have chosen to build a strong generic domestic drug industry coupled with public investment or selective partnering. "If a Third World country is going to rely on the private sector—rather than government entities—to market and perhaps do final stage development of the drugs, then it is likely to need a built-up domestic industry with which it can enter into formal or informal partnership."

Weissman sketches a broad spectrum of patent policies. At the most restrictive end is the current United States patent system, which grants a hard edged property right with no compulsory licensing. At the other end is no patent protection. Between these poles lie many options:

- Allow patents for either processes of products, but not both. "Until recently, India's patent scheme was process-only for pharmaceuticals. A drug inventor could patent the process by which he produced a pharmaceutical, but not the drug itself."

- Vary the term of patent protection. He says, "there is no inherent reason why the protection could not be afforded for only ten years—or thirty years, for that matter."
- Require patentees to "grant non-exclusive licenses to competitors, or any entity that wants to use the patent, in exchange for a reasonable licensing fee." Until recently Canada had such a system for pharmaceuticals.
- "Use it or lose it." Require the patentee to work the patent within a reasonable time or forfeit it.

Professor Weissman suggests taxation systems in order to pass economic benefits back to the community. "Taxes can be levied on the sale of patented goods, with the proceeds allocated to purposes such as domestic research." In addition, a nation ought to consider price controls, since medicines can be so precious to life and health. "Price controls on pharmaceuticals are common throughout the industrialized world."

Proposed United States patent reforms. Since 2005, Congress has considered various patent reforms. None have yet been adopted. A proposed "Patent Reform Act of 2010" would preserve the current Patent Act with very minor modifications. These include: 1) In a patent lawsuit a court may "consider whether one or more of a party's damages contentions lacks a legally sufficient evidentiary basis." 2) To recover enhanced damages for willful infringement a part must specify a reason and show "objectively reckless" conduct. 3) Reduce the public's ability to obtain damages for falsely marking goods as patented. 4) Assure that patent cases will be tried "in the most convenient" location. 5) Reduce or eliminate the ability to invalidate a patent which fails to disclose the best mode of using the invention. 6) Grant a patent to the first to file for a patent, rather than the first to invent. 7) Allow third parties to comment on prior art before a patent application is approved. The 2010 proposal has been described as offering "the first major reforms to the U.S. patent system in more than 50 years," but it does not propose any review of basic patent policies.

Economics

The discussion of patents has brought economics to the fore. We turn now to the role that economic analysis plays in intellectual property law and policy.

Intellectual property laws have traditionally been premised on propositions such as "the purpose of copyrights and patents is to serve the people at large." Legal scholars call such approaches "normative," meaning that the rules are derived from paramount principles.[4] Normative reasoning is common in discussions and daily decisions: "I send my child to a private school, because that is best for her." "I send mine to a public school, so he will be well rounded." "You shouldn't tax advertising leaflets, because that violates free speech."

A problem with normative reasoning in law-making is that starting premises may be hidden from view or ill-examined. Another objection is that normative reasoning fails to take into account realities, such as attitudes of judges. Some critics urge that normative approaches are self serving or old fashioned, because true public good is achieved by economic efficiency. In short, normative approaches are viewed as moralistic, rather than realistic. Put another way, law needs to achieve practical results, not impose views.

Such objections have led to the evolution of two influential schools of jurisprudence. The earlier of these, American Legal Realism, had a strong influence in the first half of the twentieth century. Professor Brian Z. Tamanaha describes legal realism as "an awareness that judges must sometimes make choices, that they can manipulate legal rules and precedents, and that they can be influenced by their political and moral views and by their personal biases."

The second school is referred to as Economic Analysis of Law (or Law and Economics). It places great emphasis on the influence of economic factors, and it has influenced academics and some policy makers since the 1970s. Professor Jody Kraus urges that "the superior determinacy of the economic analysis, explains why judges would be intuitively attracted to reasoning that is best reconstructed in economic terms, notwithstanding the superior normative force of ... moral theory." Professor Kraus acknowledges vulnerabilities of economic analysis, "especially the postulate of individual rationality," yet he concludes that for the past twenty five years economic analysis of law has "reigned unchallenged as the predominant theoretical mode of analysis in private law scholarship and pedagogy."

Economic analysis focusses on comparing the costs and benefits of a course of action, stating the relevant factors in terms numbers, statistics, and dollars. People routinely engage in such cost-benefit analysis in decisions that range from buying a new winter coat to framing laws. One asks: What do I need or want? Will this do the trick? How much will it cost? Might it turn out to do more harm than good? The approach is captured by the aphorism that asks, "is the

---

4. "Normative—establishing, relating to, or deriving from a standard or norm, esp. of behavior: *negative sanctions to enforce normative behavior.*" Apple Dictionary.

game worth the candle?" Professors Bell, Parchomovsky, and Weissman employed such practical analyses in their proposals discussed above.

Cost-benefit analysis is necessary and appropriate in intellectual property policy making. For example, a proposal that patent infringement be made a crime would prompt such inquiries as: What do we want to accomplish? Will a criminal penalty encourage innovation? Will it make innovators reticent? Is this the type of conduct that deserves jail time? Will it be easy or cumbersome to enforce? What are the costs of enforcement? Will legal resources be diverted from other tasks? These questions assess ends and means. They ask how important is the law, and what are the actual costs and benefits? The inquiry into costs and benefits lends itself to statistics and numbers.

Professors Russell B. Korobkin and Thomas S. Ulen describe this practical use of economics:

> First, the law can serve as a powerful tool to encourage socially desirable conduct and discourage undesirable conduct. In the hands of skillful policymakers, the law can be used to subsidize some behaviors and to tax others. Second, the law has efficiency consequences as well as distributive consequences. Intentionally or unintentionally, legal rules can encourage or discourage the production of social resources and the efficient allocation of those resources.

Some law and economics writings go beyond the practical assessment of costs and benefits just described. They emphasize numbers and mathematical analysis to the near exclusion of assessment of other factors. It is this latter emphasis which is most often referred to as the "law and economics" school of thought. Professor Lawrence B. Solum describes this approach:

> Legal economics, like economics generally, has a descriptive (or positive) and a prescriptive (or normative) branch. Descriptive economics seeks to predict and explain economic behavior, and descriptive legal economics typically seeks to predict and explain economic behavior as it is affected by legal rules. Normative economics is concerned with the evaluation of economic behaviors and government policies, while normative law and economics is concerned with the evaluation of legal rules.

Professor Richard Markovits comments on this approach: "Many, if not most, economists and law-and-economics scholars write and speak as if the analysis of economic efficiency ... is an algorithm for the determination of the right answer to all prescriptive moral questions. Rather than confining themselves to the claim that their analyses reveal which policy would be most economically efficient, these scholars typically assert that their analyses reveal the 'optimal' policy or the policy that would secure 'the social optimum.'"

Markovits believes that when economic analysis is appropriate, it ought to be applied in a sufficiently precise and discriminating manner. For example, he urges that one should note that development of new products differs from development of new production processes. "The premise that we devote too few resources from the perspective of allocative efficiency to investment in general and R&D in particular is too broad-sweeping in that it fails to distinguish between (1) product R&D and investments in product quality and variety on the one hand and (2) investments in production-process R&D on the other."

Cost-benefit analysis can help in designing a patent system, since the objective of such a system is delivery of useful processes and products. However, patent rules are part of the larger legal system. To serve people well, a legal system must address social needs that cannot be reduced to numbers: health, education, wisdom, satisfaction and cooperation. Designing a useful patent system requires policy makers to determine, as best they can, what rules best serve the entire society. Numbers help assess, but standing alone, they cannot answer that question.

Intellectual Property as Capital

In recent decades intellectual property rights have been treated increasingly as a form of capital. That is, their power of control is recognized as a competitive advantage that can be given a capital or dollar value and carried on the books. The phenomenon is not entirely new, but it diverges sharply from the traditional intellectual property policies which we surveyed at the beginning of this chapter. The capital value of intellectual property does not reward invention, does not identify goods, and does not enhance free entry into commerce for all comers. In most every instance, it concentrates power and allows some entities to overcome competitors and to influence legislation and international relations.

Throughout this chapter, "capital" has referred to a standard meaning, wealth or resources that can be devoted to a productive purpose. However, the term can be misleading. It is used in two ways that resemble each other, yet are highly contradictory:

1) *Capital as useable resource.* Capital refers to some form of usable resource. Perhaps this is the core concept people struggle to express

when employing the term. For example water flowing in a stream is a valuable resource. We may call it a "capital" resource. Ownership of water rights cannot increase the flow in the stream. A skilled and ready workforce is another form of capital. Management of such a workforce can make it more or less effective in accomplishing a task. Management may aid the work force by providing education and better tools, but a mere change of identity of managers will not in alter the productivity of the workforce.

2) *Capital as market value and power.* Capital is also used to refer to ownership, rather than a productive resource. As a mechanism to control others, intellectual property rights are valuable capital. They can command a high price in a capital market. The brand name "Coca Cola" can be valued in billions of dollars. Increasing the strength of an intellectual property right increases its capital value in this sense.

It is apparent that enhancing the dollar value or marketability of an intellectual property right increases the price it can command in a market. On the other hand, neither market value nor ownership of a patent can alter the functions of an invention. Transfer of ownership of a water purifying patent will not alter the effectiveness of the process. On the other hand, increasing the term of its patent will give the patent a higher market value. Making the trademark "Coca Cola" a "famous brand" will increase the value of its trademark, but will not change the contents of the bottled drink.

Several interrelated phenomena are at work in the discussion that follows:

1) Enhancing the scope and force of intellectual property rights.
2) Treating those rights as a form of capital.
3) Using those rights as a means of advancing "national competitiveness."
4) The role of corporations in determining intellectual property policy.

The first two depart from traditional policies which were intended only to reward innovation and prevent fraud. The third, enhancing "national competitiveness," is a modern descendent of seventeenth century mercantilism. The fourth, corporate power, threatens public accountability, public control, and democracy.

The Federal Circuit

The 1980s saw a strong shift toward strengthening the intellectual property rights of American owned businesses. One aspect of this effort was to strengthen patent rights domestically by creating the Federal Circuit, which we have seen functions as the court of appeals in patent cases.

Judge Pauline Newman, of the Federal Circuit, summarized the history and activities of her Court as follows:

> Twenty-three years ago the United States embarked on a juridical experiment, the only major change in federal court structure in a hundred years. This new structure, the formation of a circuit court of national jurisdiction in assigned areas of law, was not directed at changing the law; it was focused and targeted, and the target was the nation's economic future. The purpose was to reinvigorate the nation's industrial strength and technologic leadership, with the assistance of a revived and effective patent system.

Prior to becoming a judge, Pauline Newman had been active in promoting the competitiveness approach. In 1979, she served on a committee to conduct a Domestic Policy Review of Industrial Innovation convened by President Carter. The committee's goal "was to aid recovery of the economy through stimulus of technological industry, an area of commerce in which the United States had national strength and international leadership." The committee viewed a patent not as "a payment or reward by government, but the perfection of a property right.... The patent right may pragmatically be viewed as a form of economic self-help, whereby commercial opportunity is enhanced for a limited time for those who create, disclose, and invest in new things that meet the legal criteria of patentable invention." Patents were viewed largely as a source of capital. As investments, patents were subject to the uncertainties of lawsuits. To make patents more secure as a form of investment, the committee recommended "the formation of a national court for patent appeals." Congress established such a court, the Federal Circuit, in 1982.

The Federal Circuit is now twenty-five years old. Its decisions are often viewed by commentators as favoring the patent claimant and diminishing the defenses of those who resist the claim. Professor Robert Merges (1995) observes that "just under the surface ... the creation of the Federal Circuit had a clear substantive agenda: to strengthen patents." Merges finds that intellectual property has become "corporatized," and that there has been a decided increase in intellectual property legislation in recent decades due to the "growing economic importance of the underlying assets, and increasing strength of the property rights that attach to them, largely at the hands of the courts." Merges concludes that intellectual property rights have aided economic growth, and have increased "wealth."

However, increasing the value of an existing patent does not create new resources, it merely enriches the patent owner. The enhanced value does not provide an incentive for the innovation, for that incentive was already awarded by the original terms of the patent. The owner who has acquired a patent by purchase or transfer has not been the innovator. Even though much research and development now must be done in expensive facilities and by employees, granting an owner a high capital value to its intellectual property does nothing to assure that one penny will be invested in further innovative activity. That capital value may be spent on advertising, lobbying, dilution of stock values, stock options, "golden parachutes," etc.

Super and Special 301

In the 1980s, federal legislation helped intellectual property right holders to extend the force of their rights beyond the borders of the United States. A combination of provisions called "Super 301" and "Special 301" (references to statutory provisions) enabled them to bring the force of the United States government to bear in enforcing their claims to protection internationally. Under these provisions, federal administrative power is available to block entry of allegedly offending goods and to influence foreign governments directly. Pressure on foreign governments is achieved by way of the office of the United States Trade Representative (USTR). The statute requires the USTR to identify countries that "deny adequate and effective protection of intellectual property rights, or deny fair and equitable market access to United States persons that rely upon intellectual property protection." The USTR cooperates closely with industries to identify nations that fail to provide the desired levels of protection. The USTR possesses a broad range of administrative and negotiating power which can be brought to bear on an offending nation.

International Intellectual Property

Since the mid-nineteenth century, nations have considered and adopted treaties that establish multinational obligations regarding intellectual property rights. The earliest of these are the Paris Convention (1883) which protects trademarks and "industrial property" or patents and the Berne Convention (1886) which protects copyrights. These treaties do not provide directly enforceable legal rights, but oblige treaty members to respect each others' grants of intellectual property rights. In general, these treaties obligate the signatories to give similar protection to foreign intellectual property right as they do to rights created under their own laws.

Protection of intellectual property rights has also become part of the international regulation of trade. In 1947, a group of twenty three nations formed the General Agreement on Tariffs and Trade (GATT) in order to reduce trade barriers. In succeeding rounds of negotiations, the number of nations grew and created reciprocal tariff reductions among the signatory nations. In 1995, GATT matured into the World Trade Organization (WTO) which was granted power to adjudicate trade disputes among the member nations. The WTO now comprises 153 nations. In effect, membership in the WTO has become a necessity for any nation which wishes to participate in global trade. The WTO obliges all its member to establish and enforce intellectual property rights in accordance with principles and rules set forth in the treaty.

The creation of the WTO in 1995 reaffirmed the obligations of the Paris and Berne Conventions, but went far beyond them. The Agreement on Trade-related Aspects of Intellectual Property Rights (TRIPS) is a mandatory part of the WTO system. TRIPS reaffirms the principle that a nation must provide the same degree of protection of intellectual property for foreigners as it does for its own nationals. TRIPS establishes minimum mandatory definitions of intellectual property rights and mandatory means of enforcing them. This mandatory minimum dictates the substance of domestic law.

International protection of intellectual property affects the allocation of resources. For example, nations are required to devote resources to litigation of intellectual property disputes. In so doing, they may be pressed to forgo using legal resources to resolve family disputes, administer criminal laws, or protect human rights. Some communities can afford to allocate these resources to the expensive intellectual property rights litigation. Others cannot do so without sacrificing other important legal and governmental processes.

A small number of multinational corporations apparently succeeded in controlling the agenda and engineering adoption of TRIPS. Professor Weissman concludes that the treaty was in large part a product of lobbying by pharmaceutical companies, seeking "to force all nations to adopt restrictive patent laws on the model of the United States." Professor Susan K. Sell agrees: "If it had not been for the twelve American-based transnational corporations of the Intellectual Property Committee (IPC), there would be no Agreement on Trade Related Aspects of Intellectual Property Rights (TRIPS) today." Even if these observations overstate the situation, they correctly identify a major defect: A group of private corporations wielded power in a way that allowed them to circumvent study and planning by accountable public institutions.

Concluding Thoughts

Intellectual property policy inquiries should be deep and probing. Those who advocate intellectual property rights should be obliged to demonstrate a public benefit. This approach accords with the traditional policy that favors freedom to engage in legitimate commerce and industry. Most intellectual property rules emerged as limited exceptions to that tradition.

Intellectual property rules should advance an articulated public, rather than private interest. Once the public need is identified, the rights should be tailored to meet those needs. The assessment should include the relative economic costs and benefits of those rights. The world's peoples are more interdependent than ever, thus, intellectual property rules need to take into account the needs of other nations and global needs, as well as those of the United States.

If Congress and state legislatures are to serve their constituents, they need to begin the process of review of existing intellectual property rules. The inquiry should include such matters as:

- Identification of the need for each form of intellectual property.
- Whether property rights or civil obligations better serve the public.
- Standing to raise public interest matters in intellectual property cases.
- Appropriate length of copyright protection.
- Enhancing the utility requirement for patents.
- Whether criminal penalties are appropriate in intellectual property matters.
- Appropriate scope of trademark protection.

Policy References

In place of numerous footnotes, selected major references for Chapter Seven, organized by subject, are provided in this section. Within each subject, references are organized by type of reference and within each type of reference, references are organized alphabetically.

Piracy

Case

A & M Records, Inc. v. Napster, Inc., 239 F.3d 1004 (9th Cir.2001).

Legal Articles

Douglas R. Burgess, *Hostis Humani Generi, Piracy, Terrorism and A New International Law,* 13 U. Miami Int'l. & Comp. L. Rev. 293 (2006).

Barry Hart Dubner, *Human Rights ... International Law of Sea Piracy,* 23 Syracuse J. Int'l. L. & Com. 1 (1997).

Other References

Douglas R. Burgess, The Pirates' Pact: The Secret Alliances Between History's Most Notorious Buccaneers and Colonial America (McGraw-Hill Education, 2008).

E. Keble Chatterton, The Romance of Piracy: The Story of the Adventures, Fights & Deeds of Daring of Pirates, Filibusters & Buccaneers from the Earliest Times to the Present Day (Seeley, Service & Co., 1914).

David Mitchell, Pirates (Delacorte Press, 1976).

Patrick Pringle, Jolly Roger: The Story of the Great Age of Piracy (Dover Publications, 2001).

Public Policy

Law

Magna Carta Paras. 25 and 30.

The Statute on Monopolies (21, James I Ch. 3, 1623) (the first patent statute).

The Statute of Anne (8 Anne Ch. 19, 1710) (the first copyright statute).

U.S. Const. Art. I § 8, cl. 8 (the patent and copyright clause).

Case

Graham v. John Deere Co. of Kansas City, 383 U.S. 1 (1966).

Legal Articles

Abraham Bell & Gideon, *A Theory of Property,* 90 Cornell L. Rev. 531 (2005).

R.H. Helmholz, *Magna Carta and the Ius Commune,* 66 U. Chi. L. Rev. 297 (1999).

Amy Kapczynski, *The Access to Knowledge Mobilization and the New Politics of Intellectual Property,* 117 Yale L.J. 804 (2008).

Private Property

Case

Dred Scott v. Sandford, 19 How. 393, 15 L.Ed. 691 (1857).

Legal Articles

Edward S. Corwin, *The 'Higher Law' Background of American Constitutional Law*, 42 Harv. L. Rev. 149 (1928).

Daniel J. Hulsebosch, *Imperia in Imperio: The Multiple Constitutions of Empire in New York, 1750–1777*, 16 Law & Hist. Rev. 319 (1998).

Claire Priest, *Creating an American Property Law: Alienability and Its Limits in American History*, 120 Harv. L. Rev. 385 (2006).

Glen O. Robinson, *Personal Property Servitudes*, 71 U. Chi. L. Rev. 1449 (2004).

Other References

HANS AARSLEFF, *Locke's Influence* in THE CAMBRIDGE COMPANION TO LOCKE (Vere Chappell, ed.) (1994).

JOHN DUNN, LOCKE: A VERY SHORT INTRODUCTION (Oxford University Press, 1984).

Letter from Thomas Jefferson to Isaac McPherson (Monticello, August 13, 1813) (available online at http://www.temple.edu/lawschool/dPost/mcphersonletter.html).

JOHN LOCKE, TWO TREATISES ON GOVERNMENT, Book II, §37.

Patents and Copyrights

Cases

Capitol Records v. Thomas-Rasset, 93 U.S.P.Q.2d 1989 (D. Minn. 2010).

Warner Bros. Entm't v. RDR Books, 575 F. Supp. 2d 513, 539–40 (S.D.N.Y. 2008).

White v. Samsung Elecs. Am., Inc., 989 F.2d 1512 (9th Cir. 1993) (Kozinski, J., dissenting).

Legal Articles

Annemarie Bridy, *Why Pirates (Still) Won't Behave: Regulating P2P in the Decade After Napster*, 40 Rutgers L.J. 565 (2009).

Dan L. Burk & Mark A. Lemley, *Policy Levers in Patent Law*, 89 Va. L. Rev. 1575 (2003).

Chris Dent, *'Generally Inconvenient': The 1624 Statute of Monopolies as Political Compromise*, 33 Melb. U. L. Rev. 415 (2009).

Ben Depoorter, *The Several Lives of Mickey Mouse: The Expanding Boundaries of Intellectual Property Law*, 9 Va. J.L. & Tech. 4, 30 (2004).

Sharon E. Foster, *Invitation to a Discourse Regarding the History, Philosophy and Social Psychology of a Property Right in Copyright*, 21 Fla. J. Int'l L. 171 (2009).

Mark A. Lemley, *Property, Intellectual Property and Free Riding*, 83 Tex. L. Rev. 1031 (2005).

Mark A. Lemley & Philip J. Weiser, *Should Property or Liability Rules Govern Information?* 85 Tex. L. Rev. 783 (2007).

Robert P. Merges, *The Economic Impact of Intellectual Property Rights: An Overview and Guide*, 19 J. Cultural Econ. 103 (1995).

Robert P. Merges, *The Concept of Property in the Digital Era*, 45 Hous. L. Rev. 1239 (2008).

Barbara Ringer, *The Role of the United States in International Copyright—Past, Present, and Future*, 56 Georgetown L.J. 1050 (1993).

Sabrina Safrin, *Chain Reaction: How Property Begets Property*, 82 Notre Dame L. Rev. 1917 (2007).

Economic Analysis of the Law/Law and Economics

Legal Articles

Douglas G. Baird et al., *The Future of Law and Economics: Looking Forward*, 64 U. Chi. L. Rev. 1129 (1997).

Sean M. Coughlin, *Is the Patent Paradox a Result of a Large Firm Perspective?—Differential Value of Small Firm Patents Over Time Explains the Patent Paradox*, 23 Santa Clara Computer & High Tech. L.J. 371 (2007).

Richard A. Epstein, *Law and Economics: Its Glorious Past and Cloudy Future*, 64 U. Chi. L. Rev. 1167 (1997).

Russell B. Korobkin & Thomas S. Ulen, *Law and Behavioral Science: Removing the Rationality Assumption from Law and Economics*, 88 Cal. L. Rev. 1051 (2000).

Jody S. Kraus, *Transparency and Determinacy in Common Law Adjudication: A Philosophical Defense of Explanatory Economic Analysis*, 93 Va. L. Rev. 287 (2007).

Richard S. Markovits, *On the Relevance of Economic Efficiency Conclusions*, 29 Fla. St. U. L. Rev. 1 (2001).

Pauline Newman, *The Federal Circuit in Perspective*, 54 Am. U. L. Rev. 821 (2005).

Pauline Newman, *The Federal Circuit—A Reminiscence*, 14 Geo. Mason U. L. Rev. 513 (1992).

Rex R. Perschbacher & Debra Lyn Bassett, *The End of Law,* 84 B.U. L. Rev. 1 (2004).

Brian Z. Tamanaha, *Understanding Legal Realism,* 87 Tex. L. Rev. 731 (2009).

Corporations

Cases

Santa Clara County v. Southern Pac. R. Co., 118 U.S. 394 (1886). (Treating corporations as "persons" under the Fourteen Amendment.)

Citizens United v. Federal Election Commission, 130 S.Ct. 876, 899–900 (2010). Extending corporate constitutional rights to political expenditures.

Legal Articles

Phillip Blumberg, *Accountability of Multinational Corporations: The Barriers Present by Concepts of the Corporate Juridical Entity,* 24 Hastings Int'l & Comp. L. Rev. 297 (2001).

Richard S. Gruner, *General Counsel in an Era of Compliance Programs and Corporate Self-Policing,* 46 Emory L.J. 1113 (1997).

Paul D. Halliday & G. Edward White, *The Suspension Clause: English Text, Imperial Contexts, and American Implications,* 94 Va. L. Rev. 575 (2008).

Herbert Hovenkamp, *The Classical Corporation in American Legal Thought,* 76 Geo. L.J. 1593 (1988).

A.E. Dick Howard, *The Bridge at Jamestown: The Virginia Charter of 1606 and Constitutionalism in the Modern World,* 42 U. Rich. L. Rev. 9 (2007).

Janet McLean, *The Transnational Corporation in History: Lessons for Today?,* 79 Ind. L.J. 363 (2004).

Thomas B. Nachbar, *Monopoly, Mercantilism, and the Politics of Regulation,* 91 Va. L. Rev. 1313 (2005).

Susan K. Sell, *Industry Strategies for Intellectual Property and Trade: The Quest for TRIPS, and Post-TRIPS Strategies,*10 Cardozo J. Int'l & Comp. L. 79 (2002).

Samuel Williston, *History of the Law of Business Corporations Before 1800,* 2 Harv. L. Rev. 105 (1888).

Treaties

Law

Agreement on Trade-related Aspects of Intellectual Property Rights (TRIPS), reprinted in 1869 UNTS 299, 33 ILM 1197 (1994), and available at http://www.wto.org/english/tratop_e/trips_e/t_agm0_e.htm.

Legal Articles

Howard C. Anawalt, *International Intellectual Property, Progress, and the Rule of Law,* 19 Santa Clara Computer & High Tech. L.J. 383 (2003).

Dennis S. Karjala, *Biotech Patents and Indigenous Peoples,* 7 Minn. J. L. Sci. & Tech. 483 (2006).

A. Samuel Oddi, *TRIPS—Natural Rights and a "Polite Form of Economic Imperialism,"* 29 Vand. J. Transnat'l L. 415 (1996).

Susan K. Sell, *TRIPS and the Access to Medicines Campaign,* 20 Wis. Int'l L.J. 481 (2002).

Robert Weissman, *A Long Strange TRIPS: The Pharmaceutical Industry Drive To Harmonize Global Intellectual Property Rules, and the Remaining WTO Legal Alternatives Available to Third World Countries,* 25 U. Pa. J. Int'l Econ. L. 1079 (2004).

Peter K. Yu, *Currents and Crosscurrents in the International Intellectual Property Regime,* 38 Loy. L.A. L. Rev. 323 (2004).

Appendix

An Internet Case Study—
Perfect 10 v. Google

Introduction

The Internet and its use provide an excellent framework for examining intellectual property and its practices and policies. In this case study we look at excerpts from original documents from an Internet case, Perfect 10 v. Google. *Looking at these primary materials helps one to understand how a court approaches decision making.*

While legal procedures sometimes seem puzzling, their primary purposes are practical. Administrative processes such as applying for a patent or registering a copyright are intended to obtain the necessary information to make a decision or give notice to the public. Trial procedures are intended to notify parties of matters at issue, to provide an opportunity to present evidence, and to have the case decided in accordance with law by an unbiased judge.

Written legal arguments and court decisions are often wordy. The published decisions of the trial court and the appellate court in the Perfect 10 *case, run more 100 pages. The legal arguments and documents filed with the courts number in the thousands of pages. One really gets a feel by slogging through the actual cases and record. Attorneys do that kind of work on a daily basis. The selected documents in this appendix have been edited down to around twenty pages. Most citations to cases referred to in the court opinions have been omitted. Ellipses indicate places where the text has been edited down.*

Document 1—
Perfect 10 v. Google, Amended Complaint

The case begins with the plaintiff's statement of what the case is about. Pleadings and motions like this are public, but one usually has to go to the Court to see them or subscribe to a service which provides them. The full

Amended Complaint is thirty nine pages long. This first page is reproduced below, followed by an edited version of the rest of the complaint. As noted, ellipses indicate omitted text.

Figure A-1. Amended Complaint

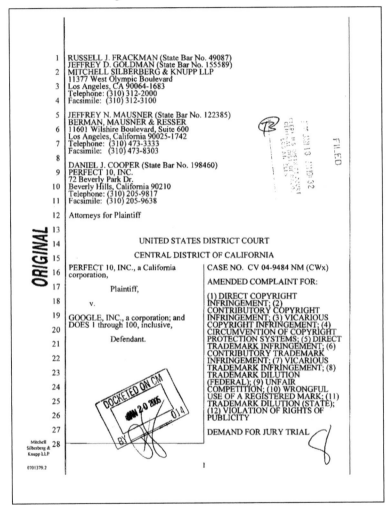

United States District Court, C.D. California.
PERFECT 10, INC., a California corporation, Plaintiff,

v.

GOOGLE, INC., a corporation; and Does 1 through 100, inclusive,
Defendant.
Case No. CV 04-9484 NM (CWx).[1]
January 14, 2005.

Amended Complaint for: (1) Direct Copyright Infringement; (2) Contributory Copyright Infringement; (3) Vicarious Copyright Infringement (4) Circumvention of Copyright Protection Systems; (5) Direct Trademark Infringement (6) Contributory Trademark Infringement; (7) Vicarious Trademark Infringement; (8) Trademark Dilution (Federal); (9) Unfair Competition; (10) Wrongful Use of a Registered Mark; (11) Trademark Dilution (state); (12) Violation of Rights of Publicity Demand for Jury Trial

Plaintiff Perfect 10, Inc. ("Perfect 10") avers:

JURISDICTION AND VENUE

1. *Jurisdiction.* This action arises under the Copyright Act, 17 U.S.C. § 101 *et seq.*, and the Lanham Act, 15 U.S.C. § 1051 *et seq.* This Court has jurisdiction over the subject matter of this action pursuant to 28 U.S.C. §§ 1331, 1338(a) and (b) and principles of supplemental jurisdiction....

3. *Personal Jurisdiction.* Personal jurisdiction is proper over the Defendants because they either reside in California or the wrongful activity at issue concerns Defendants' operation of commercial businesses through which Defendants knowingly transact business and enter into contracts with individuals in California ...

THE PARTIES

4. Plaintiff Perfect 10 is a California corporation with its principal place of business in Beverly Hills, California. Plaintiff publishes the popular magazine PERFECT 10 and owns and operates the internet website located at *perfect10.com*, which domain name Perfect 10 owns.

5. Defendant Google, Inc. ("Google") is a California corporation which owns and operates the internet website located at *google.com*....

THE BUSINESS OF PERFECT 10

8. The business of Perfect 10 consists of the design, creation, production, marketing, promotion, and sale of copyrighted adult entertainment products, including photographs, magazines, video productions, and other media.

---

1. Author's note. "Does" are unknown persons. They are added to the complaint, so the plaintiff can amend later and include them, if and when they are identified.

9. Perfect 10 is the publisher of the well-known magazine PERFECT 10.

11. Perfect 10 owns and operates the internet website *perfect 10.com.* The Perfect 10 website receives approximately 100,000 unique visitors per month. Consumers are provided access to content owned by Perfect 10 and made available on the *perfect10.com* website through an individual password and in return for the payment of a membership fee of $25.50 per month....

THE BUSINESS OF GOOGLE

18. Google operates the internet website *google.com.* Consumers visit Google's website to locate text, images, and other material, including adult images. Google earns its revenue primarily by attracting consumers, whose presence allows it to attract and charge fees to advertisers. Google offers two distinct search functions. The standard search function is called "Web Search," which allows the consumer to specify certain search terms. When the search terms are input into a box on Google's website, computer programs created by Google generate a list of links to websites purportedly related to the search terms. This list appears on *google.com* along with a short description of the content in each such website. In response to a search request, Google also often provides a link to Google servers that contain copies of one or more pages that purportedly represent an archived "snapshot" of the identified websites as they appeared several days to many months earlier. These archived pages are stored on Google's servers, at times for ten months or longer, and are made available to consumers for viewing, printing, copying, downloading, distributing to others, e-mailing, and otherwise manipulating. Included among the archived pages on Google's servers are many full-sized images of the Perfect 10 Copyrighted Works.

21. Much of the adult content provided by Google comes from websites (the "Stolen Content Websites") that infringe the Perfect 10 Copyrighted Works, the Perfect 10 Marks, and the Perfect 10 Rights of Publicity, as well as the rights of other owners of intellectual property, including by reproducing, distributing, adapting, and publicly displaying the Perfect 10 Copyrighted Works, by improperly using the Perfect 10 Marks in commerce, and by infringing the Perfect 10 Rights of Publicity....

FIRST CLAIM FOR RELIEF

(Copyright Infringement — 17 U.S.C. § 101 *et seq.*)

37. Each of the Perfect 10 Copyrighted Works consists of material original with Perfect 10 and each is copyrightable subject matter.

38. Google has copied, reproduced, distributed, adapted, and/or publicly displayed the Perfect 10 Copyrighted Works without the consent or authority of Perfect 10, thereby directly infringing Perfect 10's copyrights....

FOURTH CLAIM FOR RELIEF

(Circumvention of Copyright Protection Systems — 17 U.S.C. § 1201(a))

65. By knowingly publishing *perfect10.com* passwords on Google.com and/or linking consumers to Stolen Content Websites which contain otherwise un-available passwords to provide access to *perfect10.com,* Google has circum-vented technological measures that effectively control access to works protected by the Copyright Act, and that protect Perfect 10's rights in the Perfect 10 Copyrighted Works, and/or have aided and abetted such circumvention....

WHEREFORE, plaintiff Perfect 10 prays for judgment against Google, and each of the Doe Defendants, as follows:

1. That Google, and each of the Doe Defendants, and their officers, agents, servants, employees, representatives, successors, and assigns, and all persons in active concert or participation with them, be enjoined from:

a. copying, reproducing, distributing, adapting, or publicly displaying the Perfect 10 Copyrighted Works; ...

2. That Google be ordered to destroy all photographs, documents, and other items, electronic or otherwise, in its possession, custody, or control, that in-fringe the copyrights, trademarks, or rights of publicity of Perfect 10.

3. That Google be ordered to remove all links between its website and all Stolen Content Websites, and be prohibited from performing advertising and link-ing functions for such Stolen Content Websites.

4. For restitution in the amount of the benefit to Google by reason of their unlawful conduct.

5. For Perfect 10's actual damages.

6. For an full accounting under supervision of this Court of all profits, in-come, receipts, or other benefits derived by Google as a result of its unlawful conduct.

7. For statutory damages under the Copyright Act.

8. For treble damages under the Lanham Act.

9. For statutory damages under California Civil Code Section 3344.

10. For punitive damages.

11. For attorneys' fees and full costs.

12. For such other and further relief as this Court deems just and appropriate.

Document 2—
Perfect 10 v. Google, District Court Decision on Preliminary Injunction

Perfect 10 won at this stage. A District Court, which is a trial court, may grant an injunction based on summary evidence (affidavits, etc.) without having a full trial.[2] The general rule is that the trial court needs to be convinced that there will be enough proof at trial that the party will win the case when it is tried, and that there will be "irreparable injury" to that party if an injunction is not granted. The preliminary injunction is such a powerful remedy that when a plaintiff obtains one, the plaintiff will win without ever going to trial. A preliminary injunction was granted in its favor. The case is reported at Perfect 10 v. Google, Inc., 416 F. Supp. 2d 828 (C.D.Cal. Feb 17, 2006) (NO. CV 04-9484AHM).[3]

A decision on a preliminary injunction is made before final trial. It is made on the basis of affidavits submitted to the court. The purpose of a preliminary injunction is to give temporary relief or preserve the status quo pending a final trial. Because of the expense of trial, the length of time proceeding to trial, and the immediate impact of a preliminary injunction, the preliminary injunction is often the most important result in a case like this. In many instances, the ruling ends the matter. The following is edited down from the opinion granting the preliminary injunction which runs seventy pages. As a consequence many of the issues the Court examination are omitted or truncated.

United States District Court, C.D. California.
PERFECT 10, Plaintiff,

v.

GOOGLE, INC., et al., Defendants.
No. CV 04-9484AHM
Feb. 17, 2006.

ORDER GRANTING IN PART AND DENYING IN PART PERFECT 10'S MOTION FOR PRELIMINARY INJUNCTION AGAINST GOOGLE

MATZ, District Judge.

I. *INTRODUCTION*

The principal two-part issue in this case arises out of the increasingly recurring conflict between intellectual property rights on the one hand and the dazzling capacity of internet technology to assemble, organize, store, access, and display intellectual property "content" on the other hand. That issue, in a nutshell, is: does a search engine infringe copyrighted images when it displays them on an "image search" function in the form of "thumbnails" but not in-

---

2. Author's note. Perfect 10 had sued Google and Amazon.com, Inc. The suits were consolidated into one. The suit against Amazon was addressed in a separate order.

3. Author's note. "AHM" designates the initials of the judge to whom the case has been assigned, A. Howard Matz.

fringe when, through in-line linking, it displays copyrighted images served by another website?

Plaintiff Perfect 10, Inc. ("P10") filed separate suits against Google, Inc. and against Amazon.com, Inc. and its subsidiary, A9.com, Inc. (collectively, "Amazon"), alleging copyright and trademark infringement and various related claims. The suits were consolidated. P10 moves now for a preliminary injunction against both Defendants, solely on the basis of its copyright claims. P10 seeks to prevent Defendants' image search engines from displaying "thumbnail" copies of P10's copyrighted images and also from linking to third-party websites which host and serve infringing full-size images....

The Court conducted a hearing on November 7, 2005. The Court now concludes that Google's creation and public display of "thumbnails" likely do directly infringe P10's copyrights. The Court also concludes, however, that P10 is not likely to succeed on its vicarious and contributory liability theories.

This Order will address P10's motion for preliminary injunctive relief against Google. Amazon licenses from Google much of the technology whose use by Amazon P10 challenges. A separate order will address P10's motion against Amazon.

II. *BACKGROUND*

A. *The Parties*

1. Perfect 10

P10 publishes the adult magazine "PERFECT 10" and operates the subscription website, "perfect10.com," both of which feature high-quality, nude photographs of "natural" models.... During the last nine years, P10 has invested $36 million to develop its brand in its magazine and its website. This investment includes approximately $12 million spent to photograph over 800 models and create 2,700 high quality images that have appeared in its magazine, along with an additional approximately 3,300 images that have appeared on perfect10.com. P10 has obtained registered copyrights for its photographs from the United States Copyright Office.

P10 generates virtually all of its revenue from the sale of copyrighted works: (1) it sells magazines at newsstands ($7.99 per issue) and via subscription; (2) it sells website subscriptions to perfect10.com for $25.50 per month, which allow subscribers to view P10 images in the exclusive "members' area" of the site; and (3) since early 2005, when P10 entered into a licensing agreement with Fonestarz Media Limited, a United Kingdom company, for the worldwide sale and distribution of P10 reduced-size copyrighted images for download and use on cell phones, it has sold, on average, approximately 6,000 images per month in the United Kingdom.... Aside from the licensing agreement with

Fonestarz Media Limited, P10 has not authorized any third-party individual or website to copy, display, or distribute any of the copyrighted images which P10 has created…. *[The screen shot of the Perfect 10 website has been added and is not part of the Court's opinion.]*

Figure A-2. Perfect 10

Source: Screen shot of Perfect 10's website, April 2011.

2. Google

Google describes itself as a "software, technology, Internet, advertising, and media company all rolled into one." … Google is one of the most highly frequented websites on the internet…. Google operates a search engine located at the domain name "google.com." Google's search engine indexes websites on the internet via a web "crawler," *i.e.,* software that automatically scans and stores the content of each website into an easily-searchable catalog…. Websites that do not wish to be indexed, or that wish to have only certain content indexed, can do so by signaling to Google's web crawler those parts that are "off limits." Google's web crawler honors those signals.

Google operates different search engines for various types of web content. All search queries are text-based, *i.e.,* users input text search strings representing their query, but results can be in the form of text, images, or even video…. Thus, for example, Google's basic web search, called Google Web Search, located at http://www.google.com, receives a text search string and returns a list of *textual* results relevant to that query. Google Image search, on the other hand, receives a text search string and returns a number of reduced-sized, or "thumbnail" images organized into a grid.[4]

Google stores content scanned by its web crawler in Google's "cache." For Google Web Search, because its "web page index is based entirely on the textual part of web pages and not the images, [its] web page cache contains only the text pages, and not the images that those pages include when displayed." ... For Google Image Search, too, the results depend solely on the text surrounding an image.[5] But for Image Search, Google also stores thumbnails in its cache, in order to present the results of the user's query.... A user of Google Image Search can quickly scan the grid of returned thumbnails to determine whether any of the images responds to his search query. He "can then choose to click on the image thumbnail and show more information about the image and cause the user's browser ... to open a 'window' on the screen that will display the underlying Web page in a process called 'framing.'" ...

"Framing" is a method of "combin[ing] multiple pages in a single window so that different content can be viewed simultaneously, typically so that one 'frame' can be used to annotate the other content or to maintain a link with an earlier web page." In other words, when a user clicks on a thumbnail returned as the result of a Google Image Search, his computer pulls up a page comprised of two distinct frames, one hosted by Google and a second hosted by the underlying website that originally hosted the full-size image. The two frames are divided by a gray horizontal line a few pixels high. The upper frame is the Google frame. It contains the thumbnail, retrieved from Google's cache, and information about the larger image, including the original resolution of the image and the specific URL associated with that image.[6] The Google frame

4. A "thumbnail" is a lower-resolution (and hence, smaller) version of a full-size image. Thumbnails enable users to quickly process and locate visual information. For example, users of Google Image Search are presented with a set of thumbnails that are *potentially* responsive to their search queries. Because thumbnails are smaller in size, more of them can be displayed at the same time on a single page or screen. Users can quickly scan the entire set of thumbnails to locate the particular full-size image for which they were looking. [Footnote by Court.]

5. Google Image Search does *not* have the ability to accept an *image* as a search query and return similar images. Only text-based search queries can be input. Google Image Search returns those images on the internet whose *surrounding text* was deemed responsive to the user's textual search string. [Footnote by Court.]

6. Since URLs may often be extremely long, Google displays the domain name of the third-party website and the file name of the image, but the middle portion of the URL frequently contains an ellipsis indicating that the full URL has been truncated. Attached hereto as Exhibit A is an example of the two-frame structure just described, containing in the

also states that the thumbnail *"may be scaled down and subject to copyright"* and makes clear that the upper frame is not the original context in which the full-size image was found, stating, "Below is the image in its original context on the page: http://<URL>." The lower frame contains, or shows, the original web page on which the original image was found. Google neither stores nor serves any of the content (either text or images) displayed in the lower frame; rather, the underlying third party website stores and serves that content. However, because it is Google's webpage that composites the two frames, the URL displayed in the browser's address bar displays "images.google.com."

Google generates much of its revenue through two advertising programs: Ad-Words, for advertisers, and AdSense, for web publishers.... Through AdWords, advertisers purchase advertising placement on *Google's* pages, including on search results pages and Google's Gmail web-based email service. Google's Ad-Sense program allows pages on *third party sites* "to carry Google-sponsored advertising and share [with Google the] revenue that flows from the advertising displays and click-throughs." ... "To participate [in AdSense], a website publisher places code on its site that asks Google's server to algorithmically select relevant advertisements" based on the content of that site....

---

upper frame one of the thumbnail images that appeared on the display of thumbnails retrieved by an image search for "Vibe Sorenson," a P10 model. [Footnote by Court.]

Figure A-3. Exhibit A, Google Images

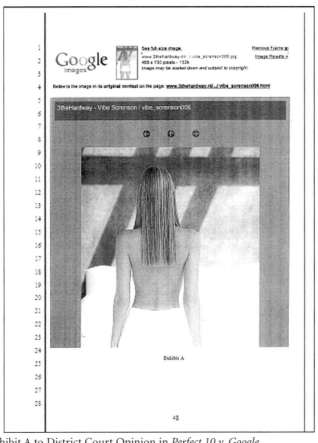

Source: Exhibit A to District Court Opinion in *Perfect 10 v. Google.*

B. *Procedural History (Omitted)* ...
III. *DISCUSSION*
A. *Legal Standard for Preliminary Injunction*
1. General Principles

"A preliminary injunction should be granted if a plaintiff can show either: (1) a combination of probable success on the merits and the possibility of irreparable harm; or (2) that serious questions are raised and the balance of hardships tilt in the plaintiff's favor." ... In any preliminary injunction analysis, courts also look to "whether the public interest will be advanced by granting preliminary relief." ...

2. Affirmative Defenses

Google does not contest that photographs are copyrightable subject matter or that P10's certificates of copyright registration have sufficiently established its ownership. Google does, however, dispute P10's contention that its copyright interests have been directly infringed. Although Google admits creating and storing thumbnail copies of P10's full-size images (found on third-party websites), as well as displaying those thumbnails as search results on Google Image Search, it argues that such use is protected under the fair use doctrine, as codified by 17 U.S.C. § 107.

"The plaintiff's burden of showing a likelihood of success on the merits includes the burden of showing a likelihood that it would prevail against any affirmative defenses raised by the defendant." ... ("Even though fair use is an affirmative defense [,] plaintiffs, as the parties moving for a preliminary injunction, have the burden of proving a likelihood of success on their infringement claim, including the fair use defense.") ...

Accordingly, ... P10, on its motion for preliminary injunction against Google, carries the burden of overcoming Google's fair use defense....

B. *Likelihood of Success*

P10 asserts that Google is both directly and secondarily liable for copyright infringement. P10 alleges that Google's image search engine directly infringes by copying, distributing, and displaying thumbnails and full-size images of P10's copyrighted photographs. P10 alleges that Google is secondarily liable for the actions of third-party websites that host infringing images and unauthorized perfect10.com username/password combinations to which Google's search engine links, as well for the actions of individuals who are led by Google Image Search to infringing images and subsequently download infringing copies themselves....

1. Direct Infringement

To establish direct copyright infringement, a plaintiff must prove two elements: (1) ownership of a valid copyright, and (2) violation of one of the exclusive rights granted under copyright.

a. What Actions by Google Allegedly Constitute Direct Infringement?

... Google concedes that it creates and displays thumbnails; it denies that it "displays," creates, or distributes what is depicted in the lower frame; and it challenges P10's argument that any of its activities can be the basis for direct infringement.... *[An extensive discussion of prior precedents is omitted.]* ... These cases, however, are distinguishable because in none of them did defendant actually *display* anything ... In contrast, Google's in-line linking causes the appearance of copyrighted content on Google's webpage, even though that content may have been stored on and served by third-party websites....

The Court concludes that in determining whether Google's lower frames are a "display" of infringing material, the most appropriate test is also the most straightforward: the website on which content is stored and by which it is served directly to a user, not the website that in-line links to it, is the website that "displays" the content....

Applying the server test, the Court concludes that for the purposes of direct copyright infringement, Google's use of frames and in-line links does not constitute a "display" of the full-size images stored on and served by infringing third-party websites. Thus, P10's claim of direct infringement with respect to these actions will likely fail.

c. "Display" for Purposes of Thumbnails

Applying the server test to Google's use of thumbnails the Court finds that Google does "display" thumbnails of P10's copyrighted images. Google acknowledges that it creates and stores those thumbnails on its own servers—and that upon receiving search queries, it responds by displaying a grid of those thumbnails.

[Author's comment. The District Court distinguished the way Google handled the **full** *sized images from the way it handled the reduced resolution, "thumbnails." In the discussion above, the Court determined it was unlikely that proof at trial would show that Google did not infringe the full sized images directly. In other part of the opinion which are omitted, the District Court determined that it was unlikely that Perfect 10 would succeed n proving that Google's activity indirectly infringed the ful sized photos. The Court noted that unlike cases like* Napster *(discussed in Chapter Sevem) "Google has not actively encouraged users to visit infringing third-party websites." The Court also determined it was unlikely that Perfect 10 would be able to establish that Google should be held "vicariously liable" for a direct financial benefit from an activity that it might have supervised. In sum, the injunction focused on the use of the thumbnails.]*

d. What Constitutes a "Public Distribution"?

The foregoing considerations also inform whether Google directly infringes P10's distribution right. With respect to P10's full-size images, Google does not. A distribution of a copyrighted work requires an "actual dissemination" of copies.... In the internet context, an actual dissemination means the transfer of a file from one computer to another. Although Google frames and in-line links to third-party infringing websites, it is *those* websites, not Google, that transfer the full-size images to users' computers. Because Google is not involved in the transfer, Google has not actually disseminated—and hence, and has not distributed—the infringing content....

Accordingly, the Court concludes that by merely framing and in-line linking to third-party websites, Google has not "distributed" infringing copies of
P10's copyrighted full-size photographs....

2. Fair Use

Having found that the thumbnails directly infringe P10's copyrights, the
Court turns to Google's affirmative defense of fair use. Google argues that its
creation and display of thumbnails is fair under 17 U.S.C. § 107. "From the
infancy of copyright protection, some opportunity for fair use of copyrighted
materials has been thought necessary to fulfill copyright's very purpose, '[t]o
promote the Progress of Science and useful Arts ...' ...."

But unlike *Arriba* [referring to a case cited by the Court], Google offers and
derives commercial benefit from its AdSense program. AdSense allows third
party websites "to carry Google-sponsored advertising and share revenue that
flows from the advertising displays and click-throughs." ... If third-party websites that contain infringing copies of P10 photographs are also AdSense partners, Google will serve advertisements on those sites and split the revenue
generated from users who click on the Google-served advertisements. Google
counters that its AdSense Program Policies prohibit a website from registering
as an AdSense partner if the site's webpages contain images that appear in
Google Image Search results: "In order to avoid associations with copyright
claims, website publishers may not display Google ads on web pages with ...
Image Results." ... However, Google has not presented any information regarding the extent to which this purported policy is enforced. Nor has it provided examples of AdSense partners who were terminated because of violations
of this policy. In contrast, P10 has submitted numerous screenshots of third-
party websites that serve infringing content and also appear to be receiving
and displaying AdSense ads from Google.

... Google has a strong incentive to link to as many third-party websites as
possible—including those that host AdSense advertisements....

That a use is commercial does not preclude a defendant from tipping the balance back to a finding of fair use by showing that its use is "transformative,"
as opposed to "consumptive." A consumptive use is one in which defendant's
"use of the images merely supersede[s] the object of the originals ... instead
[of] add[ing] a further purpose or different character." ...

It is by now a truism that search engines such as Google Image Search provide great value to the public. Indeed, given the exponentially increasing
amounts of data on the web, search engines have become essential sources of
vital information for individuals, governments, non-profits, and businesses
who seek to locate information. As such, Google's use of thumbnails to sim-
plify and expedite access to information is transformative of P10's use of re-

duced-size images to entertain. But that does not end the analysis, because Google's use is simultaneously consumptive as well. In early 2005, after it filed suit against Google, P10 entered into a licensing agreement with Fonestarz Media Limited for the sale and distribution of P10 reduced-size images for download to and use on cell phones. Google's use of thumbnails does supersede this use of P10's images, because mobile users can download and save the thumbnails displayed by Google Image Search onto their phones. Google's thumbnail images are essentially the same size and of the same quality as the reduced-size images that P10 licenses to Fonestarz. Hence, to the extent that users may choose to download free images to their phone rather than purchase P10's reduced-size images, Google's use supersedes P10's....

e. Conclusion Regarding Fair Use and Direct Infringement

The Court concludes that Google's creation of thumbnails of P10's copyrighted full-size images, and the subsequent display of those thumbnails as Google Image Search results, likely do not fall within the fair use exception. The Court reaches this conclusion despite the enormous public benefit that search engines such as Google provide. Although the Court is reluctant to issue a ruling that might impede the advance of internet technology, and although it is appropriate for courts to consider the immense value to the public of such technologies, existing judicial precedents do not allow such considerations to trump a reasoned analysis of the four fair use factors.[7]

To summarize, then: (1) at this stage P10 has not established that it is likely to prove that Google's framing of and in-line linking to infringing (full-size) copies of P10's images constitutes a public display or distribution rendering Google liable for *direct* infringement; but (2) P10 has established a likelihood of proving that Google's creation and public display of thumbnails does directly infringe P10's copyrights....

3. Secondary Copyright Liability-Contributory and Vicarious Infringement

P10 contends that Google is likely to be held secondarily liable under the doctrines of contributory and vicarious infringement. "One infringes contributorily by intentionally inducing or encouraging direct infringement ... and

---

7. Author's note. The Court refers to the Copyright Act statement of the fair use privilege. "In determining whether the use made of a work in any particular case is a fair use the factors to be considered shall include—(1) the purpose and character of the use, including whether such use is of a commercial nature or is for nonprofit educational purposes; (2) the nature of the copyrighted work; (3) the amount and substantiality of the portion used in relation to the copyrighted work as a whole; and (4) the effect of the use upon the potential market for or value of the copyrighted work." 17 U.S.C. §107. The District Court and the Court of Appeals will refer to these factors a number of times in their discussions.

infringes vicariously by profiting from direct infringement while declining to exercise a right to stop or limit it...." ...

P10 argues that parties other than Google directly infringe its copyrights in two ways: (1) third-party websites directly infringe by reproducing, displaying, and distributing unauthorized copies of P10's copyrighted photographs and (2) users of Google directly infringe by downloading such images, thereby making infringing reproductions. Google does not contest that numerous third-party websites directly infringe by serving P10's copyrighted images. However, Google does argue that P10 has presented no evidence indicating that individual users of Google engage in direct infringement upon finding copyrighted P10 photos on the web. Google contends that "[t]here are countless ways Google searchers can 'use' Google's search results, including fair uses, and Perfect 10's evidence is missing on this point." On this point, the Court agrees with Google. P10 has not submitted evidence showing that individual users of Google themselves infringe P10's copyrights. P10 has demonstrated only that users of Google search are *capable* of directly infringing by downloading the underlying webpage or image. It is not unlikely that many users do just that, but on this preliminary injunction motion there is no evidence in the record proving so. In contrast, in the *Napster* and *Grokster* cases, there was overwhelming evidence that on a massive scale file-sharers were using those defendants' software (essentially, peer-to-peer music search engines) to download, and thereby directly infringe, copyrighted works. See, e.g., *A & M Records, Inc. v. Napster, Inc.,* 239 F.3d 1004, 1013–14 (9th Cir. 2001); *Grokster,* 125 S.Ct. at 2772. Furthermore, in those cases the file-sharers actually had to download songs in order to enjoy the music, thereby making infringing reproductions. In contrast, to view P10's photos, users of Google's search engine need only visit the third-party website that hosts and serves the infringing adult content....

P10's arguments that Google is secondarily liable therefore must be assessed in light of the only direct infringement (other than as to thumbnails) for which there is evidence: that of third-party websites that reproduce and display unauthorized copies of P10's photographs. As to these websites' actions, P10 argues that Google is aware of, materially contributes to, profits from, and declines to supervise such direct infringement by (1) providing infringing websites an "audience" (by helping users locate them) and (2) providing a revenue stream to infringing websites via AdSense.

a. Contributory Infringement

To substantiate its claim of contributory infringement, P10 must show (1) that Google had knowledge of the infringing activity and (2) that Google induced, caused, or materially contributed to that activity.... *[An extensive analy-*

sis of whether Google assisted others in infringing or knowingly profited from their infringements is omitted.] ...

4. Conclusion Regarding Likelihood of Success

P10 is likely to succeed in proving that Google directly infringes by creating and displaying thumbnail copies of its photographs. P10 is unlikely to succeed in proving that Google can be held secondarily liable.

C. *Irreparable Harm*

In copyright cases, irreparable harm is presumed once a sufficient likelihood of success is raised.[8] ... Google argues that P10 first sent notices of infringement in May 2001 and then "waited three and a half years before filing this lawsuit [and] another nine months to seek a preliminary injunction." Google contends that this constitutes "unreasonable delay" and rebuts any presumption of immediate or irreparable harm. Although P10 did begin sending notices of infringement as early as May 2001, those notices concerned solely Google Web Search. P10 was not aware until May 2004 that Google displayed thumbnails of P10's copyrighted images on Google *Image* Search. Shortly thereafter, P10 began sending notices of infringement. Although P10 did wait six months to file suit and another nine months to seek a preliminary injunction, P10 did so justifiably; it was engaged in settlement discussions with Google and was evaluating whether Google would remove the infringing thumbnail images from its index. P10 has satisfied the "irreparable harm" element.

D. *Public Interest*

... Google argues that the "value of facilitating and improving access to information on the Internet ... counsels against an injunction here." This point has some merit. However, the public interest is also served when the rights of copyright holders are protected against acts likely constituting infringement. Furthermore, in this case a preliminary injunction can be carefully tailored to balance the competing interests described in the first paragraph of this Order: those of intellectual property rights on the one hand and those promoting access to information on the other. The Court ORDERS P10 and Google to propose jointly the language of such an injunction, and to lodge their proposal by not later than March 8, 2006.

IV. *CONCLUSION*

... For the reasons discussed above, the Court GRANTS IN PART and DENIES IN PART P10's motion for a preliminary injunction against Google.

---

8. Author's note. This presumption is most likely no longer valid. See *eBay, Inc., v. MercExchange, LLC*, 547 U.S. 388 (2006), discussed in Chapter Six. Plaintiffs will likely have to show the irreparable injury, not have it presumed.

Document 3—
Perfect 10, Inc. v. Amazon.com, Inc.,
508 F.3d 1146 (9th Cir. (Cal.) 2007)

[The appeal in the Google case.][9]

United States Court of Appeals, Ninth Circuit.
PERFECT 10, INC., a California corporation, Plaintiff-Appellant,
v.
AMAZON.COM, INC., a corporation; A9.Com Inc., a corporation,
Defendants-Appellees.
Perfect 10, Inc., a California corporation, Plaintiff-Appellant,
v.
Google Inc., a corporation, Defendant-Appellee.
Perfect 10, Inc., a California corporation, Plaintiff-Appellee,
Argued and Submitted Nov. 15, 2006.
Filed May 16, 2007.
Amended Dec. 3, 2007.

IKUTA, Circuit Judge:

In this appeal, we consider a copyright owner's efforts to stop an Internet search engine from facilitating access to infringing images. Perfect 10, Inc. sued Google Inc., for infringing Perfect 10's copyrighted photographs of nude models, among other claims. Perfect 10 brought a similar action against Amazon.com and its subsidiary A9.com (collectively, "Amazon.com"). The district court preliminarily enjoined Google from creating and publicly displaying thumbnail versions of Perfect 10's images, *Perfect 10 v. Google, Inc.*, 416 F. Supp. 2d 828 (C.D. Cal. 2006), but did not enjoin Google from linking to third-party websites that display infringing full-size versions of Perfect 10's images. Nor did the district court preliminarily enjoin Amazon.com from giving users access to information provided by Google. Perfect 10 and Google both appeal the district court's order. We have jurisdiction pursuant to 28 U.S.C. § 1292(a)(1)....

---

9. Author's footnote. As noted before, there were two cases, one against Google, the other against Amazon. The main case was really against Google. As the District Court noted: "Amazon licenses from Google much of the technology whose use by Amazon P10 challenges." Perfect 10, Inc. v. Google, Inc., 416 F. Supp. 2d 828, 831 (C.D. Cal. 2006).

The district court handled this complex case in a particularly thoughtful and skillful manner. Nonetheless, the district court erred on certain issues, as we will further explain below. We affirm in part, reverse in part, and remand.

I
Background

Google's computers, along with millions of others, are connected to networks known collectively as the "Internet." "The Internet is a world-wide network of networks ... all sharing a common communications technology." ... Computer owners can provide information stored on their computers to other users connected to the Internet through a medium called a webpage. A webpage consists of text interspersed with instructions written in Hypertext Markup Language ("HTML") that is stored in a computer. No images are stored on a webpage; rather, the HTML instructions on the webpage provide an address for where the images are stored, whether in the webpage publisher's computer or some other computer. In general, webpages are publicly available and can be accessed by computers connected to the Internet through the use of a web browser.

Google operates a search engine, a software program that automatically accesses thousands of websites (collections of webpages) and indexes them within a database stored on Google's computers. When a Google user accesses the Google website and types in a search query, Google's software searches its database for websites responsive to that search query. Google then sends relevant information from its index of websites to the user's computer. Google's search engines can provide results in the form of text, images, or videos.

The Google search engine that provides responses in the form of images is called "Google Image Search." In response to a search query, Google Image Search identifies text in its database responsive to the query and then communicates to users the images associated with the relevant text. Google's software cannot recognize and index the images themselves. Google Image Search provides search results as a webpage of small images called "thumbnails," which are stored in Google's servers. The thumbnail images are reduced, lower-resolution versions of full-sized images stored on third-party computers.

When a user clicks on a thumbnail image, the user's browser program interprets HTML instructions on Google's webpage. These HTML instructions direct the user's browser to cause a rectangular area (a "window") to appear on the user's computer screen. The window has two separate areas of information. The browser fills the top section of the screen with information from the Google webpage, including the thumbnail image and text. The HTML instructions also give the user's browser the address of the website publisher's computer that stores the full-size version of the thumbnail. By following the

HTML instructions to access the third-party webpage, the user's browser connects to the website publisher's computer, downloads the full-size image, and makes the image appear at the bottom of the window on the user's screen. Google does not store the images that fill this lower part of the window and does not communicate the images to the user; Google simply provides HTML instructions directing a user's browser to access a third-party website. However, the top part of the window (containing the information from the Google webpage) appears to frame and comment on the bottom part of the window. Thus, the user's window appears to be filled with a single integrated presentation of the full-size image, but it is actually an image from a third-party website framed by information from Google's website. The process by which the webpage directs a user's browser to incorporate content from different computers into a single window is referred to as "in-line linking." *Kelly v. Arriba Soft Corp.*, 336 F.3d 811, 816 (9th Cir. 2003). The term "framing" refers to the process by which information from one computer appears to frame and annotate the in-line linked content from another computer. *Perfect 10*, 416 F. Supp. 2d at 833–34....

II
Standard of Review

We review the district court's grant or denial of a preliminary injunction for an abuse of discretion.... The district court must support a preliminary injunction with findings of fact, which we review for clear error.... We review the district court's conclusions of law de novo....

Section 502(a) of the Copyright Act authorizes a court to grant injunctive relief "on such terms as it may deem reasonable to prevent or restrain infringement of a copyright." 17 U.S.C. § 502(a). "Preliminary injunctive relief is available to a party who demonstrates either: (1) a combination of probable success on the merits and the possibility of irreparable harm; or (2) that serious questions are raised and the balance of hardships tips in its favor. These two formulations represent two points on a sliding scale in which the required degree of irreparable harm increases as the probability of success decreases."...

Because Perfect 10 has the burden of showing a likelihood of success on the merits, the district court held that Perfect 10 also had the burden of demonstrating a likelihood of overcoming Google's fair use defense under 17 U.S.C. § 107. *Perfect 10*, 416 F. Supp. 2d at 836–37. This ruling was erroneous. At trial, the defendant in an infringement action bears the burden of proving fair use.... Because "the burdens at the preliminary injunction stage track the burdens at trial," once the moving party has carried its burden of showing a likelihood of success on the merits, the burden shifts to the non-moving party to show a likelihood that its affirmative defense will succeed.... Accordingly, once Perfect 10 has shown a likelihood of success on the merits, the burden shifts to Google to show a likelihood that its affirmative defenses will succeed.

In addition to its fair use defense, Google also raises an affirmative defense under title II of the Digital Millennium Copyright Act ("DMCA"), 17 U.S.C. §512. Congress enacted title II of the DMCA "to provide greater certainty to service providers concerning their legal exposure for infringements that may occur in the course of their activities." ... Sections 512(a) through (d) limit liability for (respectively): "(1) transitory digital network communications; (2) system caching; (3) information residing on systems or networks at the direction of users; and (4) information location tools." *Id.* at 1077. A service provider that qualifies for such protection is not liable for monetary relief and may be subject only to the narrow injunctive relief set forth in section 512(j). 17 U.S.C. §512(a). If Perfect 10 demonstrates a likelihood of success on the merits, Google must show a likelihood of succeeding in its claim that it qualifies for protection under title II of the DMCA....

III
Direct Infringement

Perfect 10 claims that Google's search engine program directly infringes two exclusive rights granted to copyright holders: its display rights and its distribution rights. "Plaintiffs must satisfy two requirements to present a prima facie case of direct infringement: (1) they must show ownership of the allegedly infringed material and (2) they must demonstrate that the alleged infringers violate at least one exclusive right granted to copyright holders under 17 U.S.C. §106." ... Even if a plaintiff satisfies these two requirements and makes a prima facie case of direct infringement, the defendant may avoid liability if it can establish that its use of the images is a "fair use" as set forth in 17 U.S.C. §107. See *Kelly*, 336 F.3d at 817....

The district court held that Perfect 10 was likely to prevail in its claim that Google violated Perfect 10's display right with respect to the infringing thumbnails. *Id.* at 844. However, the district court concluded that Perfect 10 was not likely to prevail on its claim that Google violated either Perfect 10's display or distribution right with respect to its full-size infringing images. *Id.* at 844–45. We review these rulings for an abuse of discretion....

A. Display Right

In considering whether Perfect 10 made a prima facie case of violation of its display right, the district court reasoned that a computer owner that stores an image as electronic information and serves that electronic information directly to the user ("i.e., physically sending ones and zeroes over the [I]nternet to the user's browser," *Perfect 10*, 416 F. Supp. 2d at 839) is displaying the electronic information in violation of a copyright holder's exclusive display right. *Id.* at 843–45; see 17 U.S.C. §106(5). Conversely, the owner of a computer that does not store and serve the electronic information to a user is not displaying that information, even if such owner in-line links to or frames the electronic information. *Perfect 10*, 416 F. Supp. 2d at 843–45. The district court referred to this test as the "server test." *Id.* at 838–39.

Applying the server test, the district court concluded that Perfect 10 was likely to succeed in its claim that Google's thumbnails constituted direct infringement but was unlikely to succeed in its claim that Google's in-line linking to full-size infringing images constituted a direct infringement. *Id.* at 843–45. As explained below, because this analysis comports with the language of the Copyright Act, we agree with the district court's resolution of both these issues.

We have not previously addressed the question when a computer displays a copyrighted work for purposes of section 106(5). Section 106(5) states that a copyright owner has the exclusive right "to display the copyrighted work publicly." The Copyright Act explains that "display" means "to show a copy of it, either directly or by means of a film, slide, television image, or any other device or process...."17 U.S.C. §101. Section 101 defines "copies" as "material objects, other than phonorecords, in which a work is fixed by any method now known or later developed, and from which the work can be perceived, reproduced, or otherwise communicated, either directly or with the aid of a machine or device." *Id.* Finally, the Copyright Act provides that "[a] work is 'fixed' in a tangible medium of expression when its embodiment in a copy or phonorecord, by or under the authority of the author, is sufficiently permanent or stable to permit it to be perceived, reproduced, or otherwise communicated for a period of more than transitory duration." *Id.*

We must now apply these definitions to the facts of this case. A photographic image is a work that is " 'fixed' in a tangible medium of expression," for purposes of the Copyright Act, when embodied (i.e., stored) in a computer's server (or hard disk, or other storage device). The image stored in the computer is the "copy" of the work for purposes of copyright law. See *MAI Sys. Corp. v. Peak Computer, Inc.*, 991 F.2d 511, 517–18 (9th Cir. 1993) (a computer makes a "copy" of a software program when it transfers the program from a third party's computer (or other storage device) into its own memory, because the copy of the program recorded in the computer is "fixed" in a manner that is "sufficiently permanent or stable to permit it to be perceived, reproduced, or otherwise communicated for a period of more than transitory duration" (quoting 17 U.S.C. §101)). The computer owner shows a copy "by means of a ... device or process" when the owner uses the computer to fill the computer screen with the photographic image stored on that computer, or by communicating the stored image electronically to another person's computer. 17 U.S.C. § 101. In sum, based on the plain language of the statute, a person displays a photographic image by using a computer to fill a computer screen with a copy of the photographic image fixed in the computer's memory. There is no dispute that Google's computers store thumbnail versions of Perfect 10's copyrighted images and communicate copies of those thumbnails to Google's users.[10] Therefore, Perfect 10 has made a prima facie case that Google's communication of its stored thumbnail images directly infringes Perfect 10's display right.

Google does not, however, display a copy of full-size infringing photographic images for purposes of the Copyright Act when Google frames in-line linked images that appear on a user's computer screen. Because Google's computers do not store the photographic images, Google does not have a copy of the images for purposes of the Copyright Act. In other words, Google does not have any "material objects … in which a work is fixed … and from which the work can be perceived, reproduced, or otherwise communicated" and thus cannot communicate a copy. 17 U.S.C. § 101.

Instead of communicating a copy of the image, Google provides HTML instructions that direct a user's browser to a website publisher's computer that stores the full-size photographic image. Providing these HTML instructions is not equivalent to showing a copy. First, the HTML instructions are lines of text, not a photographic image. Second, HTML instructions do not themselves cause infringing images to appear on the user's computer screen. The HTML merely gives the address of the image to the user's browser. The browser then interacts with the computer that stores the infringing image. It is this interaction that causes an infringing image to appear on the user's computer screen. Google may facilitate the user's access to infringing images. However, such assistance raises only contributory liability issues, … and does not constitute direct infringement of the copyright owner's display rights.

Perfect 10 argues that Google displays a copy of the full-size images by framing the full-size images, which gives the impression that Google is showing the image within a single Google webpage. While in-line linking and framing may

---

10. Because Google initiates and controls the storage and communication of these thumbnail images, we do not address whether an entity that merely passively owns and manages an Internet bulletin board or similar system violates a copyright owner's display and distribution rights when the users of the bulletin board or similar system post infringing works. *Cf. CoStar Group, Inc. v. LoopNet, Inc.,* 373 F.3d 544 (4th Cir. 2004). [Footnote by the Court.]

cause some computer users to believe they are viewing a single Google webpage, the Copyright Act, unlike the Trademark Act, does not protect a copyright holder against acts that cause consumer confusion. *Cf.* 15 U.S.C. § 1114(1) (providing that a person who uses a trademark in a manner likely to cause confusion shall be liable in a civil action to the trademark registrant).

Nor does our ruling that a computer owner does not display a copy of an image when it communicates only the HTML address of the copy erroneously collapse the display right in section 106(5) into the reproduction right set forth in section 106(1). Nothing in the Copyright Act prevents the various rights protected in section 106 from overlapping. Indeed, under some circumstances, more than one right must be infringed in order for an infringement claim to arise. For example, a "Game Genie" device that allowed a player to alter features of a Nintendo computer game did not infringe Nintendo's right to prepare derivative works because the Game Genie did not incorporate any portion of the game itself. See *Lewis Galoob Toys, Inc. v. Nintendo of Am., Inc.*, 964 F.2d 965, 967 (9th Cir.1992). We held that a copyright holder's right to create derivative works is not infringed unless the alleged derivative work "incorporate[s] a protected work in some concrete or permanent 'form.'" *Id.* In other words, in some contexts, the claimant must be able to claim infringement of its reproduction right in order to claim infringement of its right to prepare derivative works.

Because Google's cache merely stores the text of webpages, our analysis of whether Google's search engine program potentially infringes Perfect 10's display and distribution rights is equally applicable to Google's cache. Perfect 10 is not likely to succeed in showing that a cached webpage that in-line links to full-size infringing images violates such rights. For purposes of this analysis, it is irrelevant whether cache copies direct a user's browser to third-party images that are no longer available on the third party's website, because it is the website publisher's computer, rather than Google's computer, that stores and displays the infringing image.

B. Distribution Right

The district court also concluded that Perfect 10 would not likely prevail on its claim that Google directly infringed Perfect 10's right to distribute its full-size images. *Perfect 10,* 416 F. Supp. 2d at 844–45.... Though Google indexes these images, it does not have a collection of stored full-size images it makes available to the public. Google therefore cannot be deemed to distribute copies of these images....

... Accordingly, the district court correctly concluded that Perfect 10 does not have a likelihood of success in proving that Google violates Perfect 10's distribution rights with respect to full-size images.

C. Fair Use Defense

Because Perfect 10 has succeeded in showing it would prevail in its prima facie case that Google's thumbnail images infringe Perfect 10's display rights, the burden shifts to Google to show that it will likely succeed in establishing an affirmative defense. Google contends that its use of thumbnails is a fair use of the images and therefore does not constitute an infringement of Perfect 10's copyright. See 17 U.S.C. § 107.

The fair use defense permits the use of copyrighted works without the copyright owner's consent under certain situations. The defense encourages and allows the development of new ideas that build on earlier ones, thus providing a necessary counterbalance to the copyright law's goal of protecting creators' work product. "From the infancy of copyright protection, some opportunity for fair use of copyrighted materials has been thought necessary to fulfill copyright's very purpose…." *Campbell*, 510 U.S. at 575, 114 S.Ct. 1164. "The fair use doctrine thus 'permits [and requires] courts to avoid rigid application of the copyright statute when, on occasion, it would stifle the very creativity which that law is designed to foster.'" *Id.* at 577, 114 S.Ct. 1164 …

We must be flexible in applying a fair use analysis; it "is not to be simplified with bright-line rules, for the statute, like the doctrine it recognizes, calls for case-by-case analysis…. Nor may the four statutory factors be treated in isolation, one from another. All are to be explored, and the results weighed together, in light of the purposes of copyright." *Campbell*, 510 U.S. at 577–78, 114 S.Ct. 1164; see also *Kelly*, 336 F.3d at 817–18. The purpose of copyright law is "[t]o promote the Progress of Science and useful Arts," U.S. CONST. art. I, § 8, cl. 8, and to serve "'the welfare of the public.'" *Sony Corp. of Am. v. Universal City Studios, Inc.*, 464 U.S. 417, 429 n. 10, …[11]

In applying the fair use analysis in this case, we are guided by *Kelly v. Arriba Soft Corp.*, which considered substantially the same use of copyrighted photographic images as is at issue here. See 336 F.3d 811. In *Kelly*, a photographer brought a direct infringement claim against Arriba, the operator of an Internet search engine. The search engine provided thumbnail versions of the photographer's images in response to search queries. *Id.* at 815–16. We held that Arriba's use of thumbnail images was a fair use primarily based on the transformative nature of a search engine and its benefit to the public. *Id.* at 818–22. We also concluded that Arriba's use of the thumbnail images did not harm the photographer's market for his image. *Id.* at 821–22.

---

11. Author's note. Previously, most case citations have been omitted. At this point, many of them have been retained. This shows how decisions usually appear, peppered with case and statutory references. The cases cited here may also be of interest to the reader.

In this case, the district court determined that Google's use of thumbnails was not a fair use and distinguished *Kelly*. *Perfect 10*, 416 F. Supp. 2d at 845–51. We consider these distinctions in the context of the four-factor fair use analysis.

The fact that Google incorporates the entire Perfect 10 image into the search engine results does not diminish the transformative nature of Google's use. As the district court correctly noted, *Perfect 10*, 416 F. Supp. 2d at 848–49, we determined in *Kelly* that even making an exact copy of a work may be transformative so long as the copy serves a different function than the original work, *Kelly*, 336 F.3d at 818–19. For example, the First Circuit has held that the republication of photos taken for a modeling portfolio in a newspaper was transformative because the photos served to inform, as well as entertain. See *Nunez v. Caribbean Int'l News Corp.*, 235 F.3d 18, 22–23 (1st Cir. 2000). In contrast, duplicating a church's religious book for use by a different church was not transformative. See *Worldwide Church of God v. Phila. Church of God, Inc.*, 227 F.3d 1110, 1117 (9th Cir.2000). Nor was a broadcaster's simple retransmission of a radio broadcast over telephone lines transformative, where the original radio shows were given no "new expression, meaning, or message." *Infinity Broad. Corp. v. Kirkwood*, 150 F.3d 104, 108 (2d Cir.1998). Here, Google uses Perfect 10's images in a new context to serve a different purpose.

The district court nevertheless determined that Google's use of thumbnail images was less transformative than Arriba's use of thumbnails in *Kelly* because Google's use of thumbnails superseded Perfect 10's right to sell its reduced-size images for use on cell phones. See *Perfect 10*, 416 F. Supp. 2d at 849. The district court stated that "mobile users can download and save the thumbnails displayed by Google Image Search onto their phones," and concluded "to the extent that users may choose to download free images to their phone rather than purchase [Perfect 10's] reduced-size images, Google's use supersedes [Perfect 10's]." *Id.*

Additionally, the district court determined that the commercial nature of Google's use weighed against its transformative nature. *Id.* Although *Kelly* held that the commercial use of the photographer's images by Arriba's search engine was less exploitative than typical commercial use, and thus weighed only slightly against a finding of fair use, *Kelly*, 336 F.3d at 818–20, the district court here distinguished *Kelly* on the ground that some website owners in the AdSense program had infringing Perfect 10 images on their websites, *Perfect 10*, 416 F. Supp. 2d at 846–47. The district court held that because Google's thumbnails "lead users to sites that directly benefit Google's bottom line," the AdSense program increased the commercial nature of Google's use of Perfect 10's images. *Id.* at 847.

In conducting our case-specific analysis of fair use in light of the purposes of copyright, *Campbell*, 510 U.S. at 581, 114 S.Ct. 1164, we must weigh Google's superseding and commercial uses of thumbnail images against Google's significant transformative use, as well as the extent to which Google's search engine promotes the purposes of copyright and serves the interests of the public. Although the district court acknowledged the "truism that search engines such as Google Image Search provide great value to the public," *Perfect 10*, 416 F. Supp. 2d at 848–49, the district court did not expressly consider whether this value outweighed the significance of Google's superseding use or the commercial nature of Google's use. *Id.* at 849. The Supreme Court, however, has directed us to be mindful of the extent to which a use promotes the purposes of copyright and serves the interests of the public. See *Campbell*, 510 U.S. at 579, 114 S.Ct. 1164....

We note that the superseding use in this case is not significant at present: the district court did not find that any downloads for mobile phone use had taken place. See *Perfect 10*, 416 F. Supp. 2d at 849. Moreover, while Google's use of thumbnails to direct users to AdSense partners containing infringing content adds a commercial dimension that did not exist in *Kelly*, the district court did not determine that this commercial element was significant. See *Id.* at 848–49. The district court stated that Google's AdSense programs as a whole contributed "$630 million, or 46% of total revenues" to Google's bottom line, but noted that this figure did not "break down the much smaller amount attributable to websites that contain infringing content." *Id.* at 847 & n. 12 (internal quotation omitted).

We conclude that the significantly transformative nature of Google's search engine, particularly in light of its public benefit, outweighs Google's superseding and commercial uses of the thumbnails in this case. In reaching this conclusion, we note the importance of analyzing fair use flexibly in light of new circumstances. *Sony*, 464 U.S. at 431–32, 104 S.Ct. 774; *Id.* at 448 n. 31, 104 S.Ct. 774 ("'[Section 107] endorses the purpose and general scope of the judicial doctrine of fair use, but there is no disposition to freeze the doctrine in the statute, especially during a period of rapid technological change.'"... We are also mindful of the Supreme Court's direction that "the more transformative the new work, the less will be the significance of other factors, like commercialism, that may weigh against a finding of fair use." *Campbell*, 510 U.S. at 579, 114 S.Ct. 1164.

Accordingly, we disagree with the district court's conclusion that because Google's use of the thumbnails could supersede Perfect 10's cell phone download use and because the use was more commercial than Arriba's, this fair use factor weighed "slightly" in favor of Perfect 10. *Perfect 10*, 416 F. Supp. 2d at 849. Instead, we conclude that the transformative nature of Google's use is more significant than any incidental superseding use or the minor commercial aspects of Google's search engine and website. Therefore, this factor weighs heavily in favor of Google....

Having undertaken a case-specific analysis of all four factors, we now weigh these factors together "in light of the purposes of copyright." *Campbell*, 510 U.S. at 578, 114 S.Ct. 1164; see also *Kelly*, 336 F.3d at 818 ("We must balance [the section 107] factors in light of the objectives of copyright law, rather than view them as definitive or determinative tests."). In this case, Google has put Perfect 10's thumbnail images (along with millions of other thumbnail images) to a use fundamentally different than the use intended by Perfect 10. In doing so, Google has provided a significant benefit to the public. Weighing this significant transformative use against the unproven use of Google's thumbnails for cell phone downloads, and considering the other fair use factors, all in light of the purpose of copyright, we conclude that Google's use of Perfect 10's thumbnails is a fair use. Because the district court here "found facts sufficient to evaluate each of the statutory factors ... [we] need not remand for further factfinding." *Harper & Row,* 471 U.S. at 560, 105 S.Ct. 2218 (internal quotation omitted). We conclude that Google is likely to succeed in proving its fair use defense and, accordingly, we vacate the preliminary injunction regarding Google's use of thumbnail images....

[The discussions of contributory and vicarious infringement are omitted and Google's claim of limitation of liability under Digital Millennium Copyright (17 U.S.C. §512) Act are omitted.]

VI

We conclude that Google's fair use defense is likely to succeed at trial, and therefore we reverse the district court's determination that Google's thumbnail versions of Perfect 10's images likely constituted a direct infringement. The district court also erred in its secondary liability analysis because it failed to consider whether Google and Amazon.com knew of infringing activities yet failed to take reasonable and feasible steps to refrain from providing access to infringing images. Therefore we must also reverse the district court's holding that Perfect 10 was unlikely to succeed on the merits of its secondary liability claims. Due to this error, the district court did not consider whether Google and Amazon.com are entitled to the limitations on liability set forth in title II of the DMCA. The question whether Google and Amazon.com are secondarily liable, and whether they can limit that liability pursuant to title II of the DMCA, raise fact-intensive inquiries, potentially requiring further fact finding, and thus can best be resolved by the district court on remand. We therefore remand this matter to the district court for further proceedings consistent with this decision.

Because the district court will need to reconsider the appropriate scope of injunctive relief after addressing these secondary liability issues, we do not address the parties' arguments regarding the scope of the injunction issued by the district court. For the same reason, we do not address the parties' dispute over whether the district court abused its discretion in determining that Perfect 10 satisfied the irreparable harm element of a preliminary injunction.

Therefore, we reverse the district court's ruling and vacate the preliminary injunction regarding Google's use of thumbnail versions of Perfect 10's images.[12] We reverse the district court's rejection of the claims that Google and Amazon.com are secondarily liable for infringement of Perfect 10's full-size images. We otherwise affirm the rulings of the district court. We remand this matter for further proceedings consistent with this opinion. Each party shall bear its own costs on appeal....

AFFIRMED IN PART; REVERSED IN PART; REMANDED.

[Author's comment. The Court of Appeals' emphasis on the "significantly transformative nature of Google's search engine, particularly in light of its public benefit," invites some further discussion and inquiry as to exactly what that benefit is. One can imagine judges in another circuit (or two sets of Supreme Court Justices) disputing as follows:

A. One group of judges urges that fair use has been demonstrated. They emphasize the search function. The search engine functions as a modern equivalent of old methods of locating information, such as a card catalog in a library. Such a catalog consists of filing cabinets whose drawers contain book and author information on three by five cards in alphabetical order. They were in common use throughout the nation until a few decades ago.

B. A second group agrees about the importance of searching, but they urge that it can be done with descriptive words that involve no reproduction of any of the images. For example, they point out that card catalogs simply listed authors, titles, Dewey decimal location numbers, and brief descriptive data. Those catalogs did not reproduce any form of expression. This can be done online as well. Therefore, there is no need to intrude on copyrighted material at all. In particular, Google does not need to reproduce a photo of any resolution.

The Court of Appeals concluded its opinion with an order: "We remand this matter for further proceedings consistent with this opinion." As of 2010 those proceedings were going ahead in the District Court. They included an amended complaint concerning further copyright allegations and "violation of rights of publicity under Cal. Civ. Code §3344 and the common law," a type of legal action discussed in Chapter Six. The case may proceed to trial, but it should be borne in mind that often they are settled. The Perfect 10 case also illustrates the time and expense that either party can demand of its opponent.[13]]

---

12. Because we vacate the injunction, Google's motion for stay of the injunction is moot. [Footnote by Court.]

13. See Perfect 10, Inc. v. Google, Inc., No. CV04-9484, 2008 WL 4217837,(C. D. Cal. 2008). This is an "unreported case," indicating it has little legal authority to it. The full docket number (court identification number) and date is No. CV 04-9484 AHM (SHx).

Figure A-4. Card Catalog

July 16, 2008. That information is useful in seeking further information about the current status of a case. Some of that investigation can be done online. The website for the Central District of California is http://www.cacd.uscourts.gov. Generally, the final outcome of a cases is not known from reading formal published opinions, such as the ones in this Appendix and referred to in this book, because they usually settle only issues of law. Often the cases have further proceedings. Furthermore, a case can be usually be settled even after an appeal is over.

* * *

Concluding Comments

These opinions show that attorneys and judges must become familiar with technologies, public uses, and business practices. They do this through hard work and competent evidence, including consulting experts in fields that require special knowledge, such as programming. Sometimes it has been argued that technology cases ought not be handled by non-professional decision makers, such as average judges and juries.[14] However, attorneys and judges must cover complicated technical issues in cases involving building construction, medical injury, securities fraud, engineering failures, failures of materials, and many others. Traditional disputes such as those that crop up in a neighborhood or car accident may present such issues today. If the judicial system were to cordon off some portion of intellectual property disputes because of technical issues, then one ought to explain why this would not be done with other types of cases as well. This copyright case is replete with the need to understand how a technology works. Neither the trial judge, nor the author of the Circuit Court opinion appears to have had a particular technical training in software of any other form of engineering. Judge Matz received a BA as an undergraduate, and Judge Ikuta was a journalism major.

Internet search technologies also present patent opportunities. For example, here is the abstract for a patent covering linking technology:

> United States Patent   6,285,999
> Page   September 4, 2001
> Method for node ranking in a linked database
> *Abstract*
>   A method assigns importance ranks to nodes in a linked database, such as any database of documents containing citations, the world wide web or any other hypermedia database. The rank assigned to a document is calculated from the ranks of documents citing it. In addition, the rank of a document is calculated from a constant representing the probability that a browser through the database will randomly jump to the document. The method is particularly useful

---

14. This argument has often been presented regarding patent litigation. See, for example, Kimberly A. Moore, "Are District Court Judges Equipped to Resolve Patent Cases?", 15 *Harv. J.L. & Tech.* 1, 8–12 (2001).

in enhancing the performance of search engine results for hyperme-
dia databases, such as the world wide web, whose documents have a
large variation in quality.

Inventors: Page; Lawrence (Stanford, CA)

Assignee: The Board of Trustees of the Leland Stanford Junior University (Stanford, CA)

The patentee, Lawrence Page, is one of the co-founders of Google. The Perfect 10 case is also discussed in Chapter Three, and Internet patents are discussed
in Chapter Two.

About the Author

Howard C. Anawalt has practiced, taught, and written about law since the 1960s. His law practice has included labor litigation, civil rights claims, criminal defense, draft cases, courts martial and intellectual property cases. For the past several decades his writing, practice, and teaching have focussed on intellectual property. He taught for many years at Santa Clara University Law School, where he is now Professor Emeritus. He was active in establishing that school's intellectual property program. He has been a visiting scholar at Boalt Hall (University of California, Berkeley), Stanford, and the University of Washington. In 2000 he was Visiting Researcher at the Institute of Intellectual Property of Japan (IIP). He has made intellectual property presentations in Japan, Austria, Denmark, England, Sweden, and Italy. He is the author of an intensive guide for attorneys, *IP Strategy: Complete Intellectual Property Planning, Access, and Protection* (West Group—1996 through 2011 eds.).

He lives with his wife, Susan, in Northern California. He likes to write and enjoys the subject matter of this book, with all of its human adventure and content. He has two sons, Bradley and Paul, who live on the West Coast with their families.

Index